HANDING OVER THE
◇ GOODS ◇

HANDING OVER THE ◇ GOODS ◇

—

DETERMINED TO PROCLAIM NOTHING BUT CHRIST JESUS & HIM CRUCIFIED

—

ESSAYS IN HONOR OF JAMES ARNE NESTINGEN

EDITED BY

STEVEN D. PAULSON & SCOTT L. KEITH

FIFTEEN-SEVENTEEN PUBLISHING · 1517.

Published by:
1517 Publishing
PO Box 54032
Irvine, CA 92619-4032

Publisher's Cataloging-In-Publication Data
(Prepared by The Donohue Group, Inc.)

Names: Keith, Scott Leonard, editor. | Paulson, Steven D., editor. | Nestingen, James Arne, honoree.
Title: Handing over the goods : determined to proclaim nothing but Christ Jesus and Him crucified : (a festschrift in honor of Dr. James A. Nestingen) / edited by Scott Keith & Steven Paulson.
Description: Irvine, CA : 1517 Publishing, [2018]
Identifiers: ISBN 9781945978111 (hardcover) | ISBN 9781945978135 (softcover) | ISBN 9781945978098 (ebook)
Subjects: LCSH: Lutheran Church. | Luther, Martin, 1483–1546—Criticism and interpretation. | LCGFT: Essays.
Classification: LCC BX8065.3 .H36 2018 (print) | LCC BX8065.3 (ebook) | DDC 230.41—dc23

Cover design by Brenton Clarke Little

1517 Publishing is a boutique publishing house focused on producing high-quality, theological resources to fuel a new Reformation. We promote the defense of the Christian faith, the distinction between law and gospel, vocation and civil courage, and the proclamation of Christ crucified for you.

Printed in the United States of America

Contents

Introductory Note

The festschrift is the academic tradition, popular in Europe, in which the retirement of a noted scholar is celebrated by other scholars who contribute original works to a bound volume dedicated to the honoree—in this case, Dr. James A. Nestingen. Jim retired some time ago, and the production of this festschrift is long overdue. It has been the attempt of the editors of this volume to bring together a group of Jim's friends, colleagues, and students to honor the impact that he has had on their lives. Much of that impact is in earthly terms immeasurable and ineffable, but we have all done our best to reflect what Jim has meant and means to us.

Many festschrifts are meant to simply highlight the academic accomplishments of the honored recipient and his or her students. But Jim is much more than an academic. Jim's life and career have involved his calling into multiple vocations. He is a dedicated husband and father, acclaimed academic, beloved teacher, preacher of Christ Jesus, and distinguished author, as well as a friend and much-loved mentor to many of us. In some cases, he even serves as a surrogate father figure.

The title of this work is *Handing Over the Goods: Determined to Proclaim Nothing but Christ Jesus and Him Crucified*. The title was not chosen haphazardly or accidentally. In 2006 at the Word Alone conference, Jim gave a lecture—an intimate talk, really—later titled "Handing Over the Goods." In this talk, Jim highlights what is important to us all. This is the reality—that faith always comes to us on the lips of another sinner. The Word of Christ Jesus flows from the lips of one sinner to the ears of another and, by the power of the Holy Spirit, into the heart, thus turning our hearts of stone into hearts of flesh. Handing over the goods means handing over the gospel of Christ Jesus' forgiveness of sins recklessly and with great abandon.

By handing over the goods himself, Jim has influenced many people from a variety of cultural, theological, synodical, and denominational backgrounds. Those who have contributed to this volume represent the diversity of opinions that characterizes Jim's openness, kindness, and willingness to stretch himself while stretching others. As such, the authors have expressed in their various essays a plethora of theological opinions and ideas. A festschrift is meant to exhibit the influence the honoree has had on other people's lives and careers. It is not intended to set forward any synodical point of view.

Accordingly, this work is investigational in character. The ideas presented are probing and questioning in nature while at the same time expositional and proclamatory. The editors do not necessarily agree with every idea presented here and at times were highly critical of the authors regarding their points of view. But we are confident that the essays in this volume were written to honor Jim and the influence he has had on people's lives. Please read this brief work with that gracious attitude in mind.

Lastly, thank you, Jim, for all that you have done for us. We love you and announce the grace of God unto you because of our Lord and Savior Jesus Christ.

Kindly,

Scott L. Keith and Steven D. Paulson
July 1, 2018

The End of the Law and the Antinomians

Steven D. Paulson

The red thread that runs throughout James Nestingen's scholarship is the place of the law in the theological system. More to the point, he has documented the surprising fact that there is actually an end to the law. Luther discovered this alarming fact from hard experience. Over the course of time, theologians have expended considerable effort to hide the truth for the obvious reason that it overthrows history as sinners are bound to tell it and so, in brief, kills them. Who wants to tell the story of our lives with anything but success and glory as the inevitable ending? So from his master's thesis, "The Antinomian Controversy," through his doctoral thesis, "Christ the End of the Law," to his masterful work on repentance and Luther's catechisms that are organized simply as law followed by gospel (full stop), Nestingen has made the central matter of theology his repeated refrain: Christ is the end of the law.

The end of the law is a very upsetting proposition and indeed is precisely outside the boundaries of the rules of history as a scientific discipline, which has made Nestingen an unusual historian, to say the least. How does one use a logical, and so by definition a legal, method for telling the tale of the church and the world that sets a clear boundary on what is possible, real, and true, when one already finds himself beyond this limit as a free Christian? The answer is that you do history ironically and—especially—offensively at just the right place. The laws of history are followed right up to the giving of the gospel itself, when they are suddenly trounced in such befuddling things as resurrection, the death of death, and a Christ who operates with the law behind Him.

Consequently, the most contested matter theologically regarding Law and Gospel, especially among those who consider themselves followers of Luther, is the divine law's end (Rom. 10:4). Can the law actually end if it is the very will of God (Nominalists), or the mind of God itself (Calvinists), or at least the natural structure set up by God from the beginning for human flourishing that we call "being" or "ontology" (Old School)? Is the law not in fact eternal, and once sin is conquered, is the law not in fact pleasant just as God Himself is? If not, is Christian freedom not simply chaos, anarchy, unrest, and hell itself?

The Second Antinomians

For this reason, Nestingen recognized that the most interesting aspect of the ongoing antinomian controversies among Lutherans is not in the first but rather the second antinomian dispute that culminated in the Eisenach Synod of 1556. That synod came to be known by its latter-day victors pejoratively as the extermination of "second" antinomians—Luther having got rid of the first bunch. Thus the last ember of antinomians was understood to die at Eisenach once old-man Luther was no longer there to do it himself. But just as the church was reduced to three people after Nicaea (the chief being the old survivor and redoubtable Athanasius), so the true church following Luther's death was reduced to a mere handful of German pastors (Poach, Neander, Otho, and Musculus) who refused all the offered Lutheran options at the time—Philippist and Gnesio alike. Their banner thesis was simple but upsetting twice over: *the New Man is totally free from the law; the Old Man is totally under the law.* This watchword was like the New Hampshire military declaring, "Live free or die," except that the dogged pastors who professed it were already dead. With this, the last of the Lutherans finally replaced the old Augustinian slogan that had ruled the West for a thousand years that said the gospel was the "new law" in the form of the *power of grace to fulfill the law.* No more for these true preachers! Instead, they knew that the law is actually ended by Christ. No more pastors herding sheep into the fold of the law. But they insisted, then, that the baptized must be distinguished as two, the old and new, and each total—each having the opposite relation to the law. They learned that a preacher was not leading his flock from the dark terror and threat of the law into the bright light of the mystical, joyful obedience of the law like the pied piper. The New Man is not guided or exonerated by law but is already beyond it so that law is not yet to be done but already done and eternally left behind. After all, the scripture never did say exactly who was to fulfill the law, and of course it was a shock to everything we hold as sacred to have Christ announce one day that He had already fulfilled the law for our sakes, and in such a way that it was never to be done again—could never and would never be fulfilled by any other. Subsequently, these pastors learned that an absolution from Christ was not the beginning of a new spiritual experience of the exonerating and blessing law but was the absolute silence and emptiness of the law altogether. What, then, was left for a preacher or a Christian to do once the absolution was laid down? Nothing. Nothing at all.

This second antinomian controversy and the Synod of Eisenach revealed a systematic problem that the second generation of Lutherans invariably had with both Luther and scripture. On the one hand, they knew the law had to end, as they put it, *practically* because—after all—Paul had said it. Paul must be right, in some sense, that Christ is the end of the law. On the other hand, this truth threw them into a moral and logical conundrum. Reason and will, as any historian can tell you, require that God's way of thinking and choosing is rational. Working with this assumption, then, Logos is rational, and therefore, history can be recorded by using the rules of that rational law. Word and law must finally be found to be a single truth that is none other than the essence of God Himself. Otherwise, so the thinking goes, what kind of God would possibly have given a law that did nothing to make us righteous and, in fact, hindered us? The law could not possibly be without some positive purpose for justifying the ungodly. God could not possibly have given a law without a rationale that has something to do with justice, could He? Consequently, the victorious Lutherans at Eisenach limited the end of the law to psychology. They figured Paul must be referring only to the law's effect on the human psyche as an accusation and the feeling of guilt.

They divided the man into a feeling and a being. That is what they meant by "practically" ending the law. Logically, then, the problem with the law is attitudinal, and justification must then be a transformation from fear and terror of the law to love and respect of the same. What Christ was unable to accomplish in ending the law, psychology did in an instant.

Yet by history's lengthy standard, it did not take long for a whole generation to opine: But what if we don't feel guilty anymore? Of what use is the gospel to us? One day the world woke up and did not feel guilty anymore! They were now modern rather than medieval—and the dividing line had something, it appeared, to do with Luther, but no one could quite put a finger on what that was. Perhaps it was that Luther refused to accept Roman tradition and demanded Protestant reason instead? Perhaps Luther refused the imposition from without of an external law—heteronomy—and instead stood up for himself as an individual: Here I stand, autonomous! Perhaps Luther discovered that God was love rather than hate and so ushered in the new embrace of the divine for the whole world? Ever since, no one has been able to be sure of what created the Reformation, but we seem to know one thing definitely—the trick in dealing with the law is not to feel its sting. The law must cease attacking and become a friend, a guide, or even a mystical participation in the being of the divine in the utter bliss of silence. Overcoming guilt and shame became its own cottage industry.

Suddenly the whole notion of the gospel had the wind sucked from its sails, and preachers found themselves with a relic no one needed. What did pastors concern themselves with, then, once the law was presented as a friend and a blessing rather than a judge? Cheap grace! Consequently, the gospel itself was perceived to be the basic problem of life. At Eisenach, the victorious pastors then made a lamentable distinction: while the law ended *practically*, it must continue *theoretically/abstractly* forever. If the law were not theoretically eternal, it would imply an end to God Himself.[1] What is this monster

---

[1] Nestingen made use of the old Finns early on, especially L. Haikola, *Usus Legis* (1958), and its argument is carried on presently by Nicholas Hopman in two essays: Steven D. Paulson and Nicholas Hopman, "Christ, the Hated God,"

they called "theoretical" law? They figured that theoretical, eternal law had no direct revelation but instead had to be inferred from the stories of scripture's two most famous trees: Adam's and Christ's. In the garden, law must have been presented to Adam in order to provide an opportunity for humans to move from temporal animals to eternal divinities. Unfortunately, we shall never know for certain of this possibility because of the unexpected turn of events that accrued once Adam made his monumentally stupid choice. Thus this first tree along with its dream of the law is precisely hypothetical—inferred, assumed according to another, external requirement. It simply must be the case, so the thinking goes, that law was presented as an opportunity and possibility of bliss, or the law would really have been given by God for nothing more than a threat and terror: "You shall die!" What kind of God would give a law that would always and forever accuse?

Then, subsequently, one could secure this speculation about Adam's tree and the law by measuring the effect on Christ of the law and the second tree. Christ's merit on the cross is sufficient payment, as scripture and Luther often said, implying that the operating assumption of the crucifixion is God finding a clever way of maintaining justice by means of the law despite the universal fall of Adam. It is this implication of Christ's tree that secures the theory floated about Adam's tree. The law that was first an opportunity for Adam had to become so again by using Christ's tree. Accordingly, these erstwhile pastors who intended to remove second antinomians forever speculated that the law must once have carried the water of salvation—theoretically—before sin entered with the first tree. If Adam had completed his simple task and received the reward of the law, the act would have led directly to eternal life. But once sin entered, the second tree—the cross—was needed to bring God's fractured attributes of mercy and justice, grace and law, into one simple union again. That is, the law must be saved from being an accusing agent—a nasty tool—if it is to be God's own mind and heart

Lutheran Quarterly 30, no. 1 (2016): 1–27; and Nicholas Hopman, "Luther's Antinomian Disputations and Lex Aeterna," *Lutheran Quarterly* 30, no. 2 (2016): 152–80.

and become our future hope. Once Adam unexpectedly sinned, God needed the cross to unite Himself and reestablish the real benefit of the law as a guide for Christian living in order to keep the law as His will. Christ had to be crucified to save the eternal law and so God's own being.

Thus God's gospel was made (by sincere Lutherans!) to fit within the universal, eternal, infinite, objective, rational order of the divine law—since God's theoretical essence must be law. Whether we speak of Flacius Illyricus's distinction between God's *essential* righteousness and the *function* of the law among us, or Chemnitz's distinction between the divine and human performance of Christ in the cross, or the attempts of Melanchthon's other students to find a third use of the law that does not accuse Christians qua Christian, the pattern was set from the agreement of Eisenach onward for the subsequent century of Lutheranism to become an orthodoxy whose first principle was the eternal, hypothetical, abstract law of God—that law that does not accuse but rather exonerates. Thus Lutheranism opted for a theory of eternal law over the gospel itself and has never recovered.

The most notable thing about the history of the church, and in a special way of Lutheranism itself, is the strange mixing of Law and Gospel into a simple, unsavory soup. For example, Aquinas could never differentiate between justice and God, since the law is imposed on everyone. However, the dumb ox figured God must be the one on whom it is not imposed because it *is* Him eternally, at least it is His practice.[2] Even when Nominalists, like those who taught Luther, are blamed for destroying the church's received tradition merely by implying that Law and Gospel are "essentially different,"[3] and who therefore stripped Augustine's "new Law" (gospel) of its legal character, we should be reminded of what Gabriel Biel actually did with the distinction. He simply accepted the whole tradition from Origen up to his own day—including Aquinas and Ockham—that assumed the distinction of Law and Gospel found in Paul or Augustine was

---

[2] Thomas Aquinas, *Summa Theologiae* 1a IIae q. 91 a.1.

[3] See Georg Ott's argument in Heiko Oberman, *The Harvest of Medieval Theology: Gabriel Biel and Late Modern Nominalism* (Cambridge: Harvard University Press, 1963), 117 n. 90.

a minor event theologically and not worth mentioning. It is not what makes the two words *different* but what makes them the *same* that really mattered to Biel and every theologian prior to him (with some exceptions applied to Augustine). It was this, however, that Luther utterly rejected.

The First Antinomian

So we must return to the question of what an antinomian really is and why this phenomenon keeps appearing (though only in speculation, not in actual history) as an issue for Lutherans whenever the gospel is unleashed as the law's one and only end. Luther saw through this from the beginning. Antinomians are staging a play with no one in the audience. They are posing a dream, a hypothesis, of what must eternally be so without any sense of what Christ's absolution actually does to a person in the present and, indeed, what that absolution does with the entire future—the *eschaton*. The hidden secret of an antinomian is not, as the name implies, someone who opposes the law itself but rather someone who thinks that for the gospel to work, the law must actually arrive in a palatable and even sanctifying form. An antinomian is a nomian of a higher—that is, speculative and theoretical—sort. Such a cobbler then peddles a product that assures its practitioners that the law, applied properly, will not accuse. He is a psychologist offering self-help. An antinomian stands against the accusation of the law and poses as a friend of the law itself—but only hypothetically. When he helped name his former student and friend, Agricola, an antinomian, Luther had in mind the true, biblical use of the law as something that accuses—essentially, always, and forever. But even though Agricola was not yet very refined in the first antinomian controversy, he really did feel misunderstood, since he knew he was a great advocate of the law—a pronomian, or nomiophile, in its purified, Christianized sense as seeking the nonaccusatory form and eternal order of love itself. Luther appeared to Agricola as vacating his own teaching by insisting that the law really comes to an end.

As a high school athlete, I learned how to sing the eschatological anthem *In Heaven There Is No Beer* on long bus rides. As a Lutheran, I recognized there was something profound about this elegy but also something terribly wrong. Of course, there is beer in heaven (where nothing from the outside can defile us), likely brewed by Katie Luther. So the urgency to drink it here on Earth is not because of its lack up yonder. But the ditty was grasping for some more profound truth that had to do with the central theological matter of the place of the law in the theological system. The law limits beer's use to adults who are not driving and warns of its ill effects in excess, especially in the image of a squandered, dissipate life terminated in a dark alley where people say of you, "He squandered a life that could have amounted to something." What the song was reaching for was an honest confession of the experiential truth that the law always accuses. Sooner or later you will pay, and for that reason, it appears as if everything desirable on Earth, including the body or beer itself, must finally be removed for holiness' sake.

That monastic path of humble denial and detachment is apparently the only way for the law's accusation to end. No earthly song can imagine that there is anything else but the law in heaven. Yet that logic then requires objects of earthly desire to be removed, leaving nothing but pure spirit—with no bodily things to tempt it. Such is the poverty of eschatology not only among high school boys but also as exercised by almost every theologian on the planet—including the great Albert Schweitzer and his (temporary) ruination of the quest for the historical Jesus by the discovery that Jesus was thoroughly future oriented. But surely, he assumed, this is the kind of Christ who would sacrifice Himself and His desires for the greater good of the law—and so Christ goes to Jerusalem to end His quixotic quest in failure.

Yet this is where the whole disparate song goes wrong. It is not that in heaven there is no beer but rather that in heaven there are no nomians—that is why we have to exercise the law here. Only antinomians (of the second sort) actually populate heaven, and so we have to enjoy our law here on Earth while it lasts. Indeed, we even love it, as the Psalmist keeps pining, although even his hope is actually not in the beloved law but in the Christ who is to come. Consequently, we say things on Earth like, "We are a nation of laws!" Indeed, we can thank God for order amid our chaos. Let us sing a paean to the law for a moment. Without the law, we would lack our most precious earthly possessions—a limit to evil and a positive help for fostering and preserving life. The law gives us an order and plan to defend us against chaos and death at the hands of others in a world that is nasty, brutish, and short. However, we do not take this law with us to heaven. The leviathan is beheaded. The eschatological *absence* of our greatest good on Earth (or as Luther refined his teaching in the first several phases of the antinomian controversies, the law's *quiescence*) is why most Christians do not want to go across the River Styx at all when they die—they do not want to go to heaven and live without the constant voice of the friendly law. To be precise, the future eternal (and so eschatological) is not so much antinomian as postnomian. The law in heaven is eternally behind us—*done*, not *to be done*—over and finished, not yet to be finished. For this reason, the law's present accusation (drinking beer) will never transform into a heavenly blessing by which the law becomes a joyful obedience where we finally see the joy of not drinking beer and living without bodies. Instead, the law in its proper function *and* essence goes silent; it is emptied and thus truly comes to an end.

It is not just teenage boys who have a difficult time with this silence of the law, but theologians have made a practice of saying the very opposite of this good news as a way of protecting the good, true, and beautiful law. They assume that they are heroically protecting God Himself from ignominy and blasphemy by doing this. But nowhere is this problem of the end of the law clearer than in the subsequent, confused teaching of Christ, the Son, and specifically His crucifixion regarding the "second tree" of the Bible. The law must be fulfilled, that is true, but it does not say by whom. Moreover, the law can rightly be said to be eternal, but not as the mind, heart, or essence of God. Rather, the law remains eternally in heaven as an empty office or unused tool that not only ceases to utter its condemnation of sinners but also stops speaking altogether—it goes mute once it has nothing more to accuse. The law, following Christ's taking of the sin of the world, has nothing more to say. Its office is vacated, even though the old building remains unused. Passersby will say of it, "Look at that old institution; we are glad to be free of it once and for all. Let us return to kneel at the throne of Christ and see what he has to say instead."

For this reason, the Lutheran theology is really done from this point—that the law has ended—outward. This displaces the usual, pedestrian theology that emerged among the second generation of Lutherans at Eisenach. That theology begins with the assumption of the eternal law as God's true mind and unfailing pact with His humans even before sin. It then produces its misguided advice that swills Epicurus and drowns in Lucian: we better drink our beer here, for this delight will be removed from us in glory. There and then we will supposedly delight only in the law by participating in it as in God's very own being and ultimately leave behind such earthly things and temptations.

But as powerful as this fake theology is, it did not quite squelch the last remaining Lutheran pastors. After all, the Holy Spirit has promised the church will remain forever, and so three or four members were preserved. A true theologian is not only one who parses Law and Gospel but also one who recognizes that the law actually comes to an end—and precisely where this happens. That person is the one who distinguishes properly, all the way to the root, and so is aptly called a radical Lutheran. I learned this in large part from James Nestingen, first as a student and then as a colleague in teaching. Yet not only recognizing but actually enacting the end of the law is a perilous thing; who dares to do it? All sorts of things could go wrong—theoretically. People may get the wrong idea, as Erasmus expressed this very fear to Luther, and then run around like farm animals set free from fences—snorting, rooting up, creating chaos, and generally living like pigs while calling this their "Christian freedom." What of cheap grace? What happens to God's law in the meantime? Better not tell the herd the whole truth of the gospel, lest they get the wrong idea and equate faith with licentiousness.

The perils of the gospel end up appearing much greater than any accusation of law. Pastors in particular begin imagining all the potential problems that would come from having the whole collection of forgiven sinners acting freely without a script. People may figure that they already live in heaven, as the fanatics do, and so prove their faith by sacrificing their bodies—not to the neighbor but to their own lusts. Paul faced that herd in Corinth and anticipated the same at Rome. Let us sin the more, that grace may abound! Then again, people may decide once they hear the gospel, as they did in Galatia, that freedom *from* the law is at the same time freedom *for* the law—thus one may freely acquiesce to one little thing, a circumcision, not as a good work but as a sign of God's grace. These folks suppose that the real matter of grace is to learn to love the law, to become friends with the law, and so to enter into the mystical world of a joyous obedience that finds the law not onerous but rather the paramount gift of blessing from almighty God. There are all kinds of things that could go wrong once the law's end is discovered—taking leave of the law too quickly or attempting to leave it altogether. What disasters could result?

Nestingen, of course, was not going to take this on sideways. He did as he normally does and plowed ahead directly and so went from Luther Seminary to Toronto to work on a thesis concerning the most controversial word on this matter: "Christ is the end of the law" (Rom. 10:4). And of course, he was determined to show the history of exegesis on this particular matter to the foremost Roman Catholic theologian who challenged Luther on this very matter. Harry J. McSorely had written the definitive ecumenical text that supported Luther in every possible way (as a Paulist Father would—but for the heart of the matter), when Luther, as McSorely says, "asked a question which cannot be fully answered. . . . 'How I ask you, will these two positions agree: Judas can will not to betray, and Judas must necessarily will to betray?'"[4] Luther, McSorely sadly announces, went too far down an otherwise decent road. Luther became an extreme necessitarian who believed so much in God's freedom, and likewise so much in human freedom, that he went beyond the law for each. Responsibility without free will yields faith without rationality—so Luther's tail feathers must be clipped. Then we would have an ecumenical master. It is not without irony that McSorely notes how few Lutherans followed Luther on the main matter, either in the Formula of Concord or in the twentieth century. Why shouldn't Vatican theologians follow suit and reject Luther on this one matter along with the Lutherans?

Since I have recently taken up matters of Luther's *Bondage of the Will* elsewhere, I will follow Nestingen's lead for where Luther's

---

[4] Harry J. McSorely, *Luther: Right or Wrong? An Ecumenical-Theological Study of Luther's Major Word, The Bondage of the Will, By a Roman Catholic Scholar* (New York: Newman Press, 1969), 321.

argument went concerning the law. In brief, beside Luther's great lectures on Galatians and Genesis, it led to the astounding Antinomian Disputations from 1537 to 1540, in which Luther took up details of the matter of the end of the law that were forced upon him by Johann Agricola's new preaching proposal that the law not be preached in church. Agricola had some reason to propose this once he saw what the first church Visitation Articles looked like. At the same time, Luther had to deal with Melanchthon's harsh response to this antinomianism, since Melanchthon recognized that the developing system of evangelical theology was indeed under attack and was intent upon preserving it.

The name "antinomian," however, has become a broad brush that easily loses its point, even though the proposal was really only attempted by one man, fitfully, and then squelched so thoroughly among Lutherans that one wonders why it keeps rearing its head as the beast that will not die—unless you see what lies underneath it all. Since the Latin term has been Anglicized, *antinomian* means anyone and anything that stands against the law. Specifically, this seems to be applicable to anyone who thinks that the law ends or, better yet, that Christ is the end of the law. It would be hard to say that Christ Himself was an antinomian, since He not only upheld every iota of the law, but the law also came through Him, just as everything created has come through Christ. Still, Christ did not treat the law kindly in the end. No wonder Agricola began to muse about both Christ's relation to the law—which does seem oppositional at times, such as "for the law was given through Moses; grace and truth came through Jesus Christ" (John 1:17)—and His own relation to the law as a public preacher of the gospel. If the gospel justifies (while the law does not), what exactly is a preacher doing uttering the law?

More to the point, since Agricola's answer to his own queries were indeed not only a strange preaching hypothesis but also the death knell to preaching itself, we must ask, What exactly is an antinomian if Christ is, as Paul says, the end of the law? For example, the anti-Christ is the direct opponent of Christ. It was shocking to find the pope as the chief anti-Christ, but so it is, and Luther was not afraid (eventually) to say it. Likewise, an antinomian would seem to be the direct opponent of the law, which a preacher clearly cannot be—even though he is responsible for bringing about the end of the law in people's actual lives. Yet while law is not the gospel, and more-over law is not the thing that saves and furthermore is not even the proper work of the preacher, still the law is a necessary, alien work of the preacher himself. How does one speak of the end of the law, then? What name would one give it? It is not metanomian or über-nomian, rising above the law as a divinity. Perhaps even God could not say that about Himself—who knows? It is not antenomian, as if even Adam and Eve in the garden lived before the law and its accu-sation went into effect; they were told directly that they would die if they ate. We could possibly name the person a postnomian, living beyond the law, though the fanatic attempt in Corinth of thinking that one was already raised in the new body outside Christ's promise and without the old Adam hanging about the neck is an example of the problem with such a name.

It is true as well that a theologian, like any teacher, philosopher, or politician, never gets to name himself but rather limps with the names given him by his enemies—including names like Lutheran or evangelical. So rather than attempt to name ourselves, let us stick to the limited, but essential, work of figuring out what Luther meant by an "anti-nomian" and specifically how it was that Agricola—despite myriad agreements with Luther—posed such a problem that we must attend today to the peculiar evils of an antinomian as much as a nomian.

What, or Who, Is an Antinomian?

What is an antinomian, and how shall we be rid of such? This cannot be answered in the abstract, as systematic theologians would prefer, with a category or type of human being. It must be answered his-torically and in relation to Johann Agricola—since no one before or since has ever dared do what he did (until very recent days, it would appear). But at least Agricola said what he thought *wittingly*—he actually knew what he was attempting and why he attempted remov-ing law from the pulpit (unlike modern antinomians, who are unwit-ting). Agricola himself was not possible, as was antinomianism impossible until there was Luther. An antinomian is not the same thing as a libertine (or as Luther calls them, pigs). There have always been pigs who ignore the law and take whatever they want. Nor is an antinomian a person who is weak on the theoretical attempt to teach a "third" use of the law, though even that seemed to require Luther to distinguish "uses" of law along with specific users of law. This is the typical misnomer used presently among Lutherans—anyone who does not accept the fact of a third use and a Christian as its user ends up an antinomian—that is, a person who denies the preacher is giving guidance to the baptized from the law in a way that will not accuse but rather excuse them from the law's full implementation since they are not fully saint, but on the way.

Antinomianism was only possible once Luther broke into scholasticism with the categorical distinction between Law and Gospel. These, however, are precisely not two steps toward salvation, nor are Law and Gospel coordinated (originally one) or eschatologically united (eventually the same)—they are rather separated from each other as far as the east is from the west. Furthermore, the two words are both divine and both to be uttered by a preacher—with the first always being the law. These words go right to the heart of the matter of what happens to the hearers when they are uttered—specifically, if the law actually kills or only wounds, and if the gospel actually rises from the dead or only perfects what has begun. In short, Luther taught something brand new about repentance—new at least since the onset of scholastic teaching that had combined Law and Gospel into one. Moreover, the words of Law and Gospel tell us what Jesus Christ's cross is, and what it did, so that it has become a preachable "word of the cross" to the ungodly. The cross did something to the law, and vice versa. The gospel then speaks to people caught up in the accusation of the cross. But what it says is not the same thing as the law. In fact, the gospel says something in opposition to that law that leads us to say strange things like God ends up opposing Himself.

This is where an erstwhile student of Luther's like Agricola, who wanted to preach the gospel in its fullness, actually got caught up in a problem like a cat chasing its own tail. As a preacher, Agricola tried to manufacture the gospel by manipulating the psychology of his hearers. He made a basic error that has been commonly repeated ever since—he took Law and Gospel to be two psychological descriptions of the effect these words have on their hearers. Then one thinks like a psychiatrist in terms of how to produce true repentance—not a mere declaration but an actual physical, psychological, human change. Luther can and did speak this way occasionally, defining law especially as whatever terrorizes us. It is this kind of description, which is true in and of itself but not only by itself, that led Agricola to sign onto Luther's Smalcald Articles and then immediately turn around and preach the first known antinomian sermon attempting to remove the law, in which he said that true repentance was not going to happen by a law that frightened (the hearer of that only runs or buttons up) but rather would arise only through *sympathy with Christ's suffering* on the cross. In this way he proposed to put the cross of Christ where the law belonged. That attempt to remove the law failed, however, as it always does.

With this first antinomian sermon ever given in Christendom, the preacher was now going to attempt to turn a person toward Christ by using a carrot rather than a stick. Even Pelagius didn't try that. But Agricola figured that if the preacher only evoked fear, the hearer would run rather than repent. But if the preacher, instead, attracted the hearers' sorrow and remorse through sympathy with Christ's suffering, then the poor hearers would truly turn and pursue Christ rather than their own works. Two things were born from this antinomian experiment concerning repentance and preaching. One was the manipulation of the psyche as the work of the preacher, the other was to turn Christ, and so God, into the suffering deity who evokes our deepest desire of sympathy and pathos. Christ's suffering is God's suffering. God's suffering evokes my own suffering—not in the form of fear so that I run from God but now presumably in the form of like liking like in an attraction to suffering rather than revulsion to the thing. Christ's cross makes me desire suffering rather than run from it. And with this, the modern era is born. The suffering God becomes the mark of true preaching, and sympathy is what such preachers are after. They actually believe they can make Christ's awful cross into something desirable, in direct opposition to Isaiah's sermon: "he had no form or majesty . . . that we should desire him" (Isa. 53:2).

Of course Agricola's new preaching experiment affects all doctrines, but most especially it wants to say, "Repentance is to be taught, not from the Decalogue, or any law of Moses, but from doing

violence to the Son through the Gospel." This principle became the
banner thesis of the anonymous *Certain Positions* that Luther was
forced to respond to, as he says, lest his silence be taken as approval.
Thus the formal Antinomian Disputations commenced in reply. It
did not take long to reveal Agricola as the author of these *Certain
Positions* and to make him defend himself publicly for preaching into
the process of "stimulating people to love" rather than killing and
raising them—or as Agricola derisively says, "harping on the law."[5]
So here is the call of Agricola's actual antinomianism: preachers, stop
harping on the law and begin stimulating people to love. In Luther's
day, no one tried this foolhardy formula but for Agricola. Recently,
however, it has become the whole hog of modern preaching in the
century of new love.

But while this new preaching proposal came to be known by
Luther as antinomianism, it is not so opposed to the law as the name
seems to indicate. Love, after all, is the fulfillment of the law. Agricola
was attempting not to remove law as God's divine will but to get rid
of what he calls "old law" that he thought he heard in Luther's lectures to him. Quoting Luther on Psalm 19, "the heavens declare,"
meaning "he simultaneously abrogates the old law that" produces
either despair (for not doing it) or pride (for having done it)—that is
the old Augustinian distinction of the two kinds of sin.[6] The problem
with this old law is presumably that it did not produce the one thing
necessary for salvation, which was love. Love is never evoked by the
old law, but only the new kind of love that Christ Himself exempli-
fies once someone forgoes following Christ fearfully and begins to
follow Him sympathetically—out of compassion for what Christ has
done for us in His suffering. But this is the stickler. The compassion
for Christ's cross that Agricola was seeking is the futile attempt to
discover a human way to love that cross—and this love of the cross

---

[5] Martin Luther, *Solus Decalogus Est Aeternus: Martin Luther's Complete
Antinomian Theses and Disputations*, ed. Holger Sonntag, trans. by Holger
Sonntag (Minneapolis: Cygnus Press, 2008), 23 and 27, which are the first of
Agricola's "positions" and the second of his "purities."

[6] Ibid., 27, the fourth of Agricola's purities—that is, Luther when he has not
lapsed back into the old law!

must be not only heard but also felt in the heart. How can we love the cross?

For this reason, Agricola goes after his main nemesis, Melanchthon, in the Saxon Visitation Articles for thinking that church reform would come through "harping on the law." Of course, Agricola has a point, and this is not lost on Luther in the Disputations. But Agricola also went after Luther's greater Galatians commentary—specifically, where Luther says the law troubles the conscience *so that* it recognizes Christ. That is, Agricola refused Luther's assertion of the law's office in preaching—the law troubles the conscience *so that . . .* The law's work is to reveal sin—to make it great. But anyone can tell you, Agricola mused, that only love is able to recognize Christ. Yet the real thorn in Agricola's side was precisely what happens to Christ on the cross—He is cursed and so not loved, as Luther makes clear from Galatians 3. That means these two words of Law and Gospel actually come into direct conflict in an amazing duel within God Himself. What really bothered Agricola was not the preaching of the old law—that is bad enough when Melanchthon thinks this will change the dissipate churches by positively affecting the human psyche—but that Luther himself fails to preach the *new law of love*. It is quite true, as Agricola claims, "as soon as you think, thus and thus things should be in Christendom, there should be decent honorable, holy, chaste people, you have already missed the Gospel, Luke 6."[7] That observation about church reform, of course, is the downfall of the church, not its reformation. But what Agricola puts in the place of good works and "living according to the law" (which belongs in the town hall, not the pulpit) is hearing the word of the gospel, which is "an experience of the heart"—that is, love.[8]

No wonder Agricola spent his later days making ecumenical agreements with the papal party and imposing them on the hapless Lutheran church, to which he had wittingly or unwittingly returned in the form of *the gospel is love*. This in turn, Agricola determined, is precisely not the end of the law but the law's fulfillment. That fulfillment is made possible not by the law's *threats* but by Christ's *suffering*.

---

[7] Ibid., 31, the eighth of the summative theses.

[8] Ibid., the sixth of the summative theses.

Love seems to be opposite the law, which always accuses. But of course love is really the epitome of the law, only as fulfilled through the attraction of the heart. That is, love fulfills the law through sympathy to Christ's self-giving—the law is never fulfilled by scolding. Indeed, after one has been a preacher for a time, who does not want to escape from scolding and become an empathetic motivator—not of the will and good works but of the heart and what it truly loves? Should the preacher not in fact be leading his troop to the love of Christ's cross? Is that not what the gospel is?

Luther's approach to this problem is to take up the proper *distinction*. He takes up the true doctrine of law first, and then afterward he takes up the doctrine of the gospel, all the while knowing that these are not scholastic categories but rather preaching offices: "There is no better way of teaching and preserving the pure doctrine than that we follow this method, namely, that we divide Christian doctrine into two parts, Law and Gospel; as there are also two things which are set before us in God's word, namely, either wrath or grace, sin or righteousness, death or life, hell or heaven."[9] This is the same as Luther's earlier splitting of theology into the two categories of *confessions* (rather than objects): "I, the sinner" and "God the justifier" as in his commentary on Psalm 51. It is also precisely the way of an evangelical catechism, unlike any before or since, that is organized simply by law first, whose full and only job is accusing sin—revealing sin for what it is, wherever it is found. Indeed, the law kills. Then comes the gospel, with the Father's giving of Himself wholly and completely, withholding nothing in the things of creation, the Son's giving Himself wholly and completely, withholding nothing in the cross—but a cross in which Christ is killed by lawless men and accused by the very law given by His Father—and the Holy Spirit, who gives Himself wholly and completely, withholding nothing in the mouth of the preacher saying "I absolve you" while you are yet ungodly under the law's accusation, fully and completely.

But the primary matter of the law ends up at the cross, which is precisely impossible to love. Gospel is where, when, and how the law is ended—silenced, emptied—not so that the law can now bless where

---

[9] Ibid., 42–43.

before it only cursed but because Christ is not the law and what He says to His chosen sinners is not legal in any way—the pure opposition to the law itself in the form of the absolution: I forgive you. You did not love Christ on the cross and never will. An antinomian might well feel that this is exactly what he teaches, but in fact, as with Agricola (and even the second generation of Lutherans at Eisenach), they do not want the absolution to have the final word. They all want the final word to be that of the happy law that Christians befriend and that exonerates them by becoming a joyful obedience, a happy participation in the order and mind of God as it was, is, and always will be in the form of the one simple, perfect law.

But as Nestingen has shown, the gospel is not the law, and neither is God the law. The law never was given from the beginning, with the "first tree," as a nonaccusatory blessing, but was from the first a threat: "You shall die." Law then proceeds to do nothing but accuse—even finally accusing Christ, the sinless one, who for our sakes has become sin. The cross is able to elicit not your sympathy but only your ignominy. But once the Holy Spirit has given His preacher and bestowed the election in the words of the absolution, the law is eternally behind us, silent and empty— then and only then will the postnomians populating heaven hear one and only one voice, that of Christ, who does not say, "Now let us enjoy the law as it was meant to be enjoyed" but who says instead, "Arise, I choose you, you are mine, and this one word is yours forever: I forgive you."

With that declaration, the law is evacuated, silent—not having anything further to say, including guidance or blessing or the promise of an order into which we find our own life in participating or playing our part in God's overall schema. Wherever Christ is speaking, the law is dumb, and never the twain shall meet. With this, the second antinomians finally have their say—apart from later Lutheran, scholastic, or Reformed theories of a hypothetical, nonaccusatory law. Then we can find that the church that had shrunk to three or four pastors in the whirlpool of pronomians, as it had in Athanasius's day among the Arians or Elijah's day among the syncretists, is populated by more than we had anticipated, even though it was and will always be for eternity a remnant of the free Christians who are not only freed from sin, death, and the devil but also freed, as Paul and all of scripture make clear, from the law of God. But such people are not antinomians—they are free Christians, and they know very well how to preach the law in all its awful power.

Steve Paulson
Easter, 2018

Luther's Transformation of Scholastic Terms

Dr. Robert Kolb

Luther and Language

Martin Luther's love affair with human language—words, grammar, syntax, genre, sound, and above all, the content it conveyed—entangled him in the biblical text in ways that led him to translate its message in a manner that spoke to the heart of his hearers and readers. His own personality, his background in the Ockhamist philosophy of his instructors, his use of the tools for linguistic and textual study of the so-called biblical humanists, and his engagement with the biblical text first as an Augustinian friar (with obligations to preach in parish churches as well as in the cloister) and then as a university professor of Bible, all combined to enable him to expose biblical writers to his sixteenth-century hearers and readers in new and fresh ways.

Johannes von Lüpke observed that Luther's "way of using language forms a connecting thread running through the variety of tasks which he undertook as exegete, translator, preacher, pastor, theological teacher, poet, and author." Von Lüpke asserts that "his thinking was based in language and took its specific form linguistically. His theology is therefore certainly also linguistic *theory*; it contains insights into the significance of language from both theological and anthropological points of view."[1]

An important aspect of this engagement with language was Luther's ability to transform definitions and usage of traditional theological terms to conform to what he regarded as the native biblical usage. As his own command of Hebrew and Greek grew stronger in the early 1510s through the use of the tools provided by the biblical humanists, especially Johannes Reuchlin, Desiderius Erasmus, and Jacques Lefèvre d'Étaples, his sensitivity to the significance of key terms sharpened. Without abandoning certain terms, he altered their meaning to reverse the loss of their original significance in the ancient languages, which had been forfeited under the influence of Aristotle as earlier generations integrated an Aristotelian framework for thinking into the presentation of biblical concepts.

Luther's reading of scripture led him to conclude that God's speaking constitutes the origin and foundation of reality. Luther comments on Genesis 1 in his lecture course in 1535 that "all created things are produced and governed by God's Word. He spoke, and it happened."[2] "By speaking God created all things and worked through his Word. All his works are words of God, created by the uncreated Word."[3] "God speaks a mere Word, and immediately the birds are brought forth from the water. If the Word is spoken, all things are possible."[4] In lecturing on Psalm 2, Luther had explained exegetically "what the Hebrews always knew," that God's Word constitutes all things: דבר (davar, the Hebrew word for both word and thing). "The words of God are not empty air but things very great and wonderful,

---

[1] Johannes von Lüpke, "Luther's Use of Language," in The Oxford Handbook of Martin Luther's Theology, ed. Robert Kolb, Irene Dingel, and Lubomir Batka (Oxford: Oxford University Press, 2014), 143.

[2] WA 42,23,5–13, LW 1:30; cf. his lecture on Psalm 2, 1532, WA 40,2:230,20–32, LW 12:32.

[3] WA 42,35,38–40, LW 1:47.

[4] WA 42,37,4–6, LW 1:49.

which we see with our eyes and feel with our hands."[5] The absolutely almighty Creator of whom he had learned from Ockhamist instructors had exercised his might, in Luther's view, through speaking. Thus in Luther's reading of scripture as he prepared his lectures in the 1510s, von Lüpke concludes, "a new definition of ontology took form, and within it decisively a new understanding of substance and relationship."[6] God's relationship to all things, including the human creatures shaped in His own image, provided the framework for understanding the origin, maintenance, and purpose of all things.[7]

Thus Luther's definition of God centered on His Person, His speaking, and His creative nature. To be sure, God's Word embraced more aspects than human words, but this recreative Word that renews and restores sinners to being God's children comes to human ears and eyes through the human words that the Holy Spirit puts to use in sacramental promises, in public preaching and private sharing of the gospel, and authoritatively in scripture. In fact, Luther believed that the Holy Spirit Himself remained present in and with the biblical text. He guides its reception just as he had guided its origin.[8] This perception of God and His Word, especially as it is present in the biblical text, enabled and enlivened a face-to-face relationship between Creator and human creature that shaped Luther's entire reading of scripture and his striving to fulfill his doctoral oath as summarized by his early biographer, Johannes Mathesius, "to study the Holy Scripture his entire life, to preach it, and to defend the

---

[5] WA40,2:230,20–25, 231,28; LW12:32–33.

[6] Von Lüpke, "Luther's Use of Language," 147. Cf. Hans-Martin Barth, *Die Theologie Martin Luthers. Eine kritische Würdigung* (Gütersloh: Gütersloher Verlagshaus, 2009), 147; Joachim Ringleben, *Gott im Wort: Luthers Theologie von der Sprache her* (Tübingen: Mohr/Siebeck, 2010), 92–112.

[7] Stefano Leoni, "Der Augustinkomplex. Luthers zwei reformatorische Bekehrungen," in *Reformatorische Theologie und Autoritäten. Studien zur Genese des Schriftprinzips beim jungen Luther*, ed. Volker Leppin (Tübingen: Mohr/Siebeck, 2015), 190–222.

[8] Robert Kolb, *Martin Luther and the Enduring Word of God. The Wittenberg School and its Scripture-Centered Proclamation* (Grand Rapids: Baker Academic, 2016), 75–97.

Christian faith in formal university disputations and in his writings against all heretics."[9]

Luther's understanding of God's creation of humanity—bound in space and time as human beings are, entrenched in place and history—and his perception of the historical nature of human life framed his thinking. These axioms compelled him to presume the necessity of passing on what God has said through new historical situations in new geographical and cultural settings. The reformer recognized early on that the nature of his task involved plumbing the depths of the biblical writers' use of words that convey God's reality to people. Furthermore, his calling required listening to his contemporaries' use of their own language to build the bridge that would enable the conversation between the apostles and prophets in their cultural setting and the Germans of his own time.

James Nestingen introduced his analysis of Luther's Small Catechism as an example of Luther's translating the medieval inheritance gleaned from his scholastic and monastic instructors by observing, "As eager as [Luther] was to find linguistic equivalents, he was just as intent on registering the historical witness of the faith in a culturally specific form." Nestingen found that the Catechism's translation of the essential elements of the faith was part of "a larger effort to move the altar from the church into the kitchen, bringing home the witness of the Christian faith at the family table."[10]

Luther as Translator of the Biblical Message

Luther was the consummate translator. His Bible translation still stands as a major accomplishment in the history of world literature.[11] Recent theological and linguistic discussion has, however, extended the concept of translation to the entire theological

---

[9] Johannes Mathesius, *Historien/Von des Ehrwirdigen in Gott Seligen thewren Manns Gottes, Doctoris Martini Luthers/anfang/lehr/leben vnd sterben* (Nuremberg: vom Berg and Neuber, 1566), VIIa.

[10] James A. Nestingen, "Luther's Cultural Translation of the Catechism," *Lutheran Quarterly* 15 (2001): 440.

[11] Kolb, *Enduring Word*, 209–38.

enterprise. Religion *is* translation, according to Michael DeJonge and Christiane Tietz, or—more precisely expressed—religion is always permeated by the translation of what stands in authoritative written or oral texts into language that addresses new situations.[12] All religions are always delivering past texts or other memories through a tradition into a new present. DeJonge labels this process *linguistic-historical contextualization*. Words must be rendered from one field of meaning to another, even within one's own language, as time and events give words new shades of meaning. Historically distinct situations must find a linking bridge in the "historical transplantation of ideas and experiences" (which are always related). Christianity, DeJonge argues, gives ultimate authority to what God has done in history as it is reported in Holy Scripture.[13]

Translation of individual terms always takes place in the context of a larger hermeneutical field, always in relationship to related concepts. Although they did not often use the term, on occasion Luther and his colleagues did describe the whole of biblical teaching as a *body*, a *corpus doctrinae*.[14] They used this term to designate something akin to the ancient term *rule of faith* (*analogia fidei*). It embraced basic components of the biblical message and set forth a standard for public teaching. Within the concept of *body*, in addition, we may note that the individual *members*—articles of faith, or topics in Wittenberg terminology—are all related. Adjustments to the understanding of one of these topics or members will affect others. This body functions as an organic whole. This proved to be the case as Luther began altering—deepening, broadening, reversing—his fundamental assessment of what it means to be Christian: his

---

[12] Michael P. DeJonge and Christiane Tietz, eds., *Translating Religion: What Is Lost and Gained?* (New York: Routledge, 2015), see esp. 1–12 and 169–73.

[13] Michael P. DeJonge, "Historical Translation: Pseudo-Dionysius, Thomas Aquinas, and the Unknown God," in *Translating Religion*, ed. Michael P. DeJonge and Christiane Tietz, 29–44.

[14] Irene Dingel, "Melanchthon and the Establishment of Confessional Norms," in *Philip Melanchthon: Theologian in Classroom, Confession, and Controversy*, ed. Irene Dingel, Robert Kolb, Nicole Kuropka, and Timothy J. Wengert (Göttingen: Vandenhoeck & Ruprecht, 2012), 161–79.

perception of biblical terms revolving around the concept of *righteousness* changed profoundly.

Because he perceived God as a person, a speaking person, a speaker whose word brought the worlds into existence according to Genesis 1, Luther's deepening of the understanding of the concept of God's Word stands as the framework for his entire reconceptualization of reality. This creative and recreative tool of God reveals His essence as steadfast loving-kindness and mercy. In the 1510s, this recreative Word was transforming the professor's life and his self-perception, as it redefined for him who he was while it hammered into form reconfigurations of other key concepts in his worldview. On the anvil of his experiences, he was forging new understandings of biblical raw material as he lectured and preached.

Luther's Revision of the Concept of Righteousness

Three decades later and less than a year before his death, in March 1545, Luther wrote that his understanding of the term *the righteousness of God* had stood in his way of loving the "intriguing" works of Paul in Romans and Galatians and also in the epistle to the Hebrews. A fundamental misunderstanding blocked his perception of what Paul was saying "because, according to the usage and idiom of all the teachers, I had been taught to understand it in philosophical terms,[15] that righteousness is a formal or active righteousness by which God is righteous and punishes sinners and the unrighteous."[16] Luther conceived of God's righteousness in terms of the law's judgment upon the human creatures' active performance of God's will. But somewhere after the completion of the Hebrews lectures in March 1518, Luther explains, "I began to understand that the righteousness of God is that by which the righteous person lives by the gift of God, namely by faith. And this is the meaning: the righteousness of God is

---

[15] As is often the case when he speaks of "philosophy," Luther here referred specifically to the anthropology of Aristotle, in which human performance defined the ultimate essence of the "*animal rationalis*," the human creature.

[16] WA54:185,16–20, LW34:336, *The Annotated Luther, Volume 4, Pastoral Writings*, ed. Mary Jane Haemig (Minneapolis: Fortress, 2016), 500–501.

revealed by the gospel, namely, the passive righteousness with which the merciful God justifies us through faith, just as it is written: the righteous person lives by faith. At this point I felt that I had been completely born again and had entered paradise itself through wide open doors."[17]

Luther's previous working definition of *righteousness* at the beginning of his career reflects the definition found in a standard theological dictionary of the time, that of Joannes Altensteig. In 1517, Altensteig, a Tübingen-educated priest in Mindelheim in the Allgäu who had studied with Luther's Augustinian mentor, Johannes von Staupitz, more than a decade earlier, published a dictionary of theological terms, which provides access to at least one strain of late medieval scholastic thinking. He defined a "righteous" (*iustus*) person as "one who keeps God's commandments" (*qui seruat mandata dei*). Citing the fifteenth-century Augustinian theologian Jacob of Valencia (1408–90), he posited that four things are necessary to be righteous, according to Psalm 15: being free of every blemish and all guilt, avoiding future sins and being cleansed should one commit a sin, doing good to God and the neighbor, and pleasing God and being accepted by Him for eternal life.[18] Altensteig's explanations of the verb *iustificare* and the noun *iustificatio* reflected the necessity of God's mercy playing a role in the sinner's attainment of righteousness but emphasized the role of human performance of deeds of love conforming to God's law as fundamental for understanding the term.[19]

In his lectures on the Psalms and Romans delivered between 1513 and 1516, Luther's definition of *righteousness* remained focused on human performance, even if he was gradually abandoning the idea that his performance made the critical difference in acquiring grace. At this time, he was absorbing Augustine's insistence that God's unconditional grace alone made it possible for Christians to perform God-pleasing actions or avoid having their sins counted against them. For Augustine, in the final analysis or judgment,

---

[17] WA54:186,3–9, LW34:337, *Annotated Luther*, 4, 501–2.

[18] Joannes Altensteig, *Vocabularius Theologie complectens vocabulorum descriptions* (Hagenau: Joannes Rynman, 1517), CXXVIIIa.

[19] Ibid., CXVIII.

righteousness still was measured in terms of obedience to God's commands. Commenting on Romans 1:29 in 1515, Luther defined unrighteousness: "disobedience is the essence of unrighteousness and the essence of sin," as Ambrose had taught. Luther was, however, already edging toward defining righteousness in terms of faith: "unrighteousness is the sin of unbelief, the lack of the righteousness that comes from faith," citing Romans 1:17 and Mark 16:16. Nonetheless, "a person who does not believe also does not obey, and he who does not obey is unrighteous." In the end, faith's fruits, not faith itself, defined human righteousness for Luther in late 1515.[20]

By mid-1516, Luther was linking righteousness more closely to faith and God's Word. As he compared the interpretation of righteousness (δικαιοσύνη) in the *Glossa ordinaria* with those of Desiderius Erasmus and Jacques Lefèvre d'Étaples,[21] he concluded that for Paul "total human righteousness leading to salvation depends on the Word through faith and not on good works through knowledge." Knowledge placed the matter under human control; faith was dependent upon the trustworthiness of the speaker of the Word. Nonetheless, Luther defined faith as "this most precious obedience," and God looks upon "the worth of obedience" in faith alone.[22]

Faith remained belief in the truth of the biblical report, not yet the trust that Luther would soon learn the biblical πίστις to signify. Because the measurement of conformity to God's law continued to shape his definition of righteousness, he viewed Christians as "unrighteous in terms of merit"—of what they deserved on the basis of their performance—but they pray for "the remission of our unrighteousness, or rather, for its nonimputation. For it is never remitted entirely, but it remains and needs nonimputation."[23]

---

[20] WA56:186,24–25, LW25:168.

[21] *Biblia Latina cum glossa ordinaria. Facsimile Reprint of the Editio Princeps Adolph Rusch of Strassburg 1480/81*, ed. Karlfried Froehlich and Margaret T. Gibson (Turnhout: Brepols, 1992), 279–81. The *Glossa* contained a definition of faith as belief in God's promises to his human creatures but tied the righteousness of faith to the performance of love.

[22] WA56:416,8–21, LW25:407–8.

[23] WA56:291,6–10, LW25:278.

The term *imputation* had played a relatively small role in late Medieval scholastic theology. Neither *imputatio* nor *reputatio* nor their verbal forms *imputare/reputare* occur in Altensteig's dictionary.[24] Imputation (*imputatio, imputare*), Augustine's translation of the Greek λογίζεται (the Vulgate used the synonym *reputare*), provided the divine complement to human righteousness. That righteousness proceeded no longer from human action but from God's view of whatever He was observing. However, God's appraisal of sinners as righteous had to come to terms with the experience of believers, who, though trusting in Christ, still were sinning. Luther began using this Augustinian term *imputare* to define righteousness while still focusing on conformity of performance to God's commands. He believed that God's regard for repentant, trusting sinners covered them *in spe*, in hope; divinely imputed righteousness ensured future salvation, but these believers were not *in re*, in "reality," righteous.

Luther's resolution of the tension between hope and fact came as his deepening concept of the power of God's Word as the ultimate determinative of reality brought him to view righteousness as twofold, expressed from two vantage points: the divine and the human. God's word of promise became more powerful—determinative of reality—as he perceived the parallel between the creative Word of Genesis 1 and the recreative Word of the gospel of Christ.[25] God's regard was no longer observation or promise of a future. This promise had immediate validity and the power to enact its future as present reality. It did so when it conveyed the Word that bestowed righteousness on sinners through the forgiveness of their sins and their liberation from bondage to Satan.

A decisive step in the development of Luther's mature understanding of righteousness occurred in 1518, as his apprehension of the reality-determining nature of God's regard or reckoning and His Word of promise developed. *On Three Kinds of Righteousness*[26] contrasted open sins, criminal acts, with outward conformity to God's

---

[24] Cf. Altensteig, *Vocabularius*, CXIIa.

[25] Johann Haar, *Initium creaturae Dei. Eine Untersuchung über Luthers Begriff der "neuen Creaturae"* (Gütersloh: Bertelsmann, 1939).

[26] WA2: 43–47.

law performed for other reasons than faith in God. This "civil" righteousness promotes societal order for the welfare of the neighbor
but plays no role in the sinners' relationship with God.[27] The second kind of righteousness, the opposite of original sin ("*peccatum
essenciale, natale, originale, alienum*"), permeates the entire person;
it is the very heart of true humanity, which Christ bestows through
the promise given in baptism ("*iustitia natalis, essencialis, origina-
lis, aliena*"). It is "that which determines who we are, our head, our
foundation, our cornerstone, our entire substance" ("*sors, capitale,
fundamentum, petra nostra et tota substancia nostra*"; John 3:5, 1:12;
1 John 3:9; Rom. 5:18–19). This righteousness comes through faith;
God's mercy covers believers even when they stray into sin because
their righteousness rests on God's regard or reckoning.[28] The third
kind of righteousness, contrasted with the unrighteous deeds of daily
life ("*peccata actuales*"), flows from faith, from the essential righteousness that God bestows out of his unconditional grace. Luther
labeled it "the righteousness that comes from the person" ("*iustitia
propria*"). It earns no merit in God's sight but is rather the product
of God's favor and the power of the Holy Spirit, who dwells in the
believer. Faith's conviction that trusts God's saying that the person is
righteous actualizes itself through the godly conduct of life.

Luther's treatise *Two Kinds of Righteousness,* composed in
early 1519, abandoned the "civil righteousness" of the earlier treatise, perhaps because he presumed that all his readers were baptized
and called to faith that produced good works or perhaps because he
regarded outward performance of the deeds prescribed by God's law
without faith as no more than a spurious righteousness according to
Romans 14:23: "Whatever does not proceed from faith is sin."

Luther's revolutionary redefinition of righteousness begins
with the observation that Christian righteousness has two aspects.
Luther's "*zweierlei*" is translated as "two kinds of righteousness" but
also as "twofold righteousness." Both translations capture part of his
intent. He contrasts two distinct forms of human righteousness: first
and foundational is God's gift of the new identity of the child of God,

---

[27] WA2:43,12–44,13.

[28] WA2: 44,32–45,33.

given from outside ourselves, of which we are passive recipients. The second is the performance or activities of the recreated child of God, who from inside his or her new-creature-self acts as God's righteous child. The two are quite distinct in regard to who is acting to produce each. The second translation, "twofold righteousness," is helpful because Luther viewed the two kinds of righteousness as inseparably united in the one person, coordinated in the trust in God's forgiveness that affirms God's identification of this sinner as righteous by demonstrating that righteousness in the deeds appropriate according to God's design for human life.

In this treatise of 1519, Luther retained the medieval language of "infusion," God's "pouring into" human creatures that which He gives. The first aspect of this divinely bestowed new identity "comes from outside the self and is poured into us from outside ourselves" ("*aliena, et ab extra infusa*"). This righteousness is Christ's righteousness, given to sinners through faith (1 Cor. 1:30; John 11:25, 14:6). Bestowed in baptism, renewed through true repentance throughout the Christian's life, this righteousness becomes the possession and property of believers. It marks them with the identity of the new creature recreated in Christ. This takes place in a manner that Luther illustrated with the analogy of the relationship of bride and bridegroom, applying passages where Paul speaks of the church to the individual believer (e.g., Eph. 5:25–30). The mutual sharing of all possessions paralleled Luther's use of Paul's statement in Romans 6:3–11 that in baptism, Christ buries the sinner's sin in his tomb and raises him up to new life, walking in the Savior's footsteps. Thus believers receive as their own Christ's innocence in the Father's sight.[29]

This righteousness rests on God's promise. It delivers new life. Trust in the promise transforms the orientation and practice of the believer. In 1519, Luther was building on his conviction, formed over the previous four years, that God liberated sinners from their sins through Christ's death and resurrection. In spring 1515, Luther had associated the gospel's power with God's nature as the powerful One—rather than with Christ's death and resurrection—as the core

---

[29] WA2:145,7–147,6. LW31:297–99.

of its content. Proclamation places the power in hearing words as the Holy Spirit's instrument or means of delivering it. When he came to Romans 4:25 in fall 1515, he focused on the salvation accomplished through Christ's being delivered up for sin and raised to restore righteousness: "Christ's death is the death of sin, and his resurrection is the life of righteousness because through his death he has made satisfaction for sin, and through his resurrection he has brought us righteousness. Thus, his death not only signifies but actually effects the remission of sin as a most sufficient satisfaction. His resurrection is not only a sign or sacrament of our righteousness, but it also produces righteousness in us, if we believe it. It is the cause of our righteousness."[30] Luther's treatment of the delivery of the Savior's death and resurrection in baptism in Romans 6 a few weeks later did not yet move from content to means of delivery and did not yet connect Christ's work to faith through the baptismal promise.[31]

But by mid-1519, as he edited his Galatians lectures of 1516–17 for publication, he concluded in comments on Galatians 1:2, "The person who presumes that he is righteous in any other way than by believing in Christ rejects Christ and considers Christ's passion and resurrection useless. On the other hand, whoever believes in Christ, who died, at the same time dies himself to sin together with Christ. The person who believes in the resurrected and living Christ rises by the same faith and lives in Christ and Christ lives in him. Therefore, the resurrection of Christ is our righteousness and our life, not only by way of an example but also by virtue of its power."[32] Jonathan Trigg's conjecture that Luther's understanding of justification emerged from his understanding of baptism as described by Paul in Romans 6 seems plausible on the basis of this passage.[33] The reformer's concept of justification did emerge out of his struggle to exercise the sacrament of penance faithfully once he perceived that the purpose of confession and absolution lay in

---

[30] WA56:296,17–22, LW25:284.

[31] WA56:321,23–328,26, LW25:308–16.

[32] WA2:455,17–23, LW27:168.

[33] Jonathan D. Trigg, *Baptism in the Theology of Martin Luther* (Leiden: Brill, 2001), 2.

the assurance of forgiveness in Christ and the mercy of God the Father on the basis of Christ's death and resurrection.[34]

This led Luther to compare attempts to attain righteousness—that is, an acceptable identity in God's sight—through the works of the law with the righteousness that comes through trusting the promise. In 1519, Luther labeled the righteousness that one seeks to attain through performance "a servile righteousness. It is venal, contrived, without foundation, external, temporal, worldly, produced by human power. It profits nothing for the glory to come but receives in this life its reward, glory, riches, honor, power, friendship, well-being, or at least peace and quiet, and fewer evils than do those who act otherwise." The righteousness of faith takes place when one "utterly despairs of this other kind of righteousness . . . and casts himself down before God, sobs humbly, and confesses that he is a sinner. This righteousness comes as the heart clings to the Word of Christ."[35] Galatians 3:15, comparing God's promise to a last will and testament, enabled Luther to reassert that true righteousness comes from a testamentary promise that is a pure, undeserved gift.[36]

Already in 1518, the Wittenberg professor affirmed that God's regarding us as righteous results in our "killing the flesh and crucifying our sinful desires" ("*mortificatio carnis et crucifixio concupiscentiarum*") and then to the practice of love, patience, and kindness and to joy and peace (Gal. 5:22).[37] In 1519, he noted that the discrepancy between the hope engendered by trust in the promise, which imputes righteousness to believers, and the fact that sin remains in the lives of believers did not prevent trust in God's promise of this righteousness or new identity in God's sight from having practical effects in the day-to-day living of Christ's people. "Faith in Christ loves God's law, which forbids lust, so it now does the very thing that the law commands. It attacks and crucifies lust."[38]

---

[34] Oswald Bayer, *Promissio. Geschichte der reformatorischen Wende in Luthers Theologie*, 2nd ed. (Göttingen: Vandenhoeck & Ruprecht, 1971).

[35] WA2:489,30–490,23, LW27:219–21.

[36] WA2:518,33–519,22, LW27:264.

[37] WA2:146,36–147,18.

[38] WA2:502,8–10, LW27:238.

As Luther put this perception of the Christian's righteousness as twofold to use, he changed his terminology. In 1518/1519 he had called these two sides or aspects of God-given righteousness "*iustitia aliena*" (the righteousness that comes from outside the self) and "*iustitia propria*" (the righteousness that believers exercise themselves through the Holy Spirit's power). In the 1520s, he began to label these two aspects of human identity "*iustitia passiva*" and "*iustitia activa*," passive and active righteousness. In 1535, at the beginning of his commentary on Galatians, he called the distinction between the two "our theology," the orienting understanding of what it means to be human and a key to understanding his doctrine of justification, of how God restores human righteousness while the presence of sin and evil continue to buffet believers' lives.[39] Here he contrasted the "righteousness of the law," which also false believers can produce, with the good works of believers, demonstrations of their "active righteousness" as the fruits of faith.

God's gift of this new identity as his child does not create two different persons, one passive, one active. It creates one righteous person, who trusts the Re-Creator, who has restored his chosen people to his family and enables his people to practice their identity in thoughts, words, and deeds. God has determined these actions that reflect this identity and their integrity as restored, justified human creatures. The motivation of this trust in Christ's death and resurrection and confidence in God's perception of them as righteous decisively distinguishes their proper practice of humanity from that of those who may do the right thing but for the wrong reason, not out of faith in Christ but for some other reason, base or noble as it may be.[40]

Luther's Revision of the Concept of Faith

Luther's altered definition of *iustitia* resulted not only from his altered perception of the nature and recreative power of God's Word but also from an altered understanding of faith. In Romans 1:17, he

---

[39] WA40,1:45,24.

[40] WA40,1:45,24–26.

had read, "The righteous shall live by faith." From Erasmus and from Melanchthon he learned that a medieval understanding of the Greek πίστις as "fides," "belief in the factuality of a statement," often summarized as "historic faith," was incomplete. The word should also be understood as *fiducia*, trust, a dependence on and confidence in what Christ has done and in the words that convey the benefits of his death and resurrection. The word *fiducia* does not occur in Altensteig.[41] The scholastic definition of the word *faith* (*fides*), according to Altensteig, among its several meanings, referred to believing what cannot be seen and believing without fear and with firm certainty. It includes assent to truth as revealed by God. Faith is an infused virtue, without which hope and love are not possible. Altensteig noted the distinction between unformed faith (*fides informis—sine charitate*) and formed or acquired faith (*fides formata/acquisita*), the latter of which pleases God.[42] Luther changed the framework within which the term was understood with recourse to biblical data and examples.

For Luther, Abraham served as the best example of faith. In 1531, he commented on Galatians 3:6, "Abraham believed God": "no distrust made him waver concerning the promise of God, but he grew strong in his faith as he gave glory to God, fully convinced that God was able to do what he had promised." Paul here "makes faith in God the supreme worship, the supreme reverence, the supreme obedience, and the supreme sacrifice. . . . Faith justifies because it gives God what is due him."[43]

In commenting on 2 Samuel 23:1 in 1543, in which, according to Luther's translation, David is called one who is trusting in the Messiah, he defines the Hebrew word הקם (*hukam*)—one who is "firmly set, constant, steadfast, certain"—in his dependence on Hebrews 11:1, "faith is the assurance of things hoped for." His German equivalent used the phrase "a confidence that is certain." Isaiah 40:8, "the word of our God will stand forever," aided him in explaining the certainty of this confidence. The Word is "steadfast,

---

[41] Cf. Altensteig, *Vocabularius*, XCa.

[42] Ibid., LXXXVIb–XCa.

[43] WA40,1:358,17–361,14, LW26:226–27.

certain, immovable; it does not soften, it does not quake, it does not sink, or fall, or let you fall." "It does not shake, it does not tremble, it does not quake nor wiggle, nor doubt." The Word enters the heart through true faith and "fashions it like unto itself, it firms it up, makes it certain and assured. It conforms the heart to him and is firm, certain, and sure. It stands up firmly, inflexibly, and steadfastly against all assaults, devil, death, and whatever its name may be." It rejects all that tends toward doubt, despair, anger, and rage. For it knows that God's Word cannot deceive. The object of this faith is the Messiah, whom David trusted as the coming one, whom Christians trust as the one who has come.[44]

Luther's Revision of the Concept of Original Sin

The opposite of this trust in this incarnate God is doubt. Luther also bound to his concept of faith his understanding of the traditional term *original sin* that theologians of the late Middle Ages had debated in the shadow of Augustine's emphasis upon it. Altensteig defined original sin (*peccatum originale*), citing Bonaventura and Hugo, as the origin of sins in Adam, from which human sins proceed. It is a weakness and impotence to resist certain motions and inclinations experienced by human beings, the tinder from which actual sins arise. Altensteig's authorities demonstrated that the gift of original righteousness liberates sinners from original sin.[45] Most scholastic theologians taught that baptism effected this liberation so that Christians had to contend only with actual sins and with the tinder of desire, concupiscence, from which the actual sins arose (though many scholastics regarded the mere desires as not being sinful in themselves). Luther deepened the definition and thus used it in the confrontation between sinful desire and trust in Christ that believers experience every day.

The reformer used several synonyms for the traditional "original sin," including "root sin," "inherited sin," "nature-sin," or

---

[44] WA54:32,15–33,14, LW15:272. Cf. John M. G. Barclay, *Paul & the Gift* (Grand Rapids: Eerdmans, 2015), 106–16.

[45] Altensteig, *Vocabularius*, CLXXXIb.

"person[embracing]-sin."[46] Already in 1516, Luther commented on Romans 10:6 that "by this trickery the ancient serpent deceived Eve, but not Adam, and to this day he is fooling all proud men. For he immediately called Eve away from the Word to works by saying, 'Did God say, etc.?' Then when she had begun to look at the meagerness of her work, she also began to despise the Word."[47] Both his sermons on Genesis 3 in 1523 and his lecture on the chapter in 1535 described the origin of the breach between God and his human creatures in Eden. Adam and Eve rejected God's Word and no longer trusted in him.[48] The professor observed that in Eden, the serpent assaulted God's will and His image in the human being by challenging his Word.[49] "When Satan had separated them from and deprived them of God's Word, nothing was not easy for him." A lie had separated Eve from God and His Word.[50] "The fountain from which all sin flows is unbelief, doubt, and abandonment of the Word," idolatry, denial of God's truth, the invention of new gods.[51] Luther's "Disputation on Justification" (1536) described original sin as "not a quiescent quality but a restless evil which labors day and night. . . . It is a restless animal, a beast which cannot stand still. . . . It moves human beings to avarice, disobedience, and other vices. . . . It always tries to move us away from God."[52]

In 1538, a new preface to his 1535 Galatians commentary defined original sin as the result of Satan's attacking trust in the God who would restore human righteousness through the liberation accomplished in Christ: "He persuaded our first parents to forsake

---

[46] Cf. WA51:354,20; 46:39–40, LW24:341–42, WA10,1:508,20, LW52:151–52.

[47] WA56:416,31–417,8, LW25:408.

[48] WA14:135,32–33;   24:91,11–13,   92,8–9,   27–32,   93,28–94,20.   Cf. WA42:110,5–116,29; 122,4–123,34; LW1:146–14, 162–64; Oswald Bayer, *Martin Luther's Theology: A Contemporary Interpretation*, trans. Thomas H. Trapp (Grand Rapids: Eerdmans 2008), 173–92; Bernhard Lohse, *Martin Luther's Theology*, trans. Roy Harrisville (Minneapolis, Fortress, 1999), 248–57.

[49] WA42:110,7–17, LW1:146.

[50] WA42:111,2–4, LW1:147.

[51] WA42:112, 20–22, LW1:149.

[52] WA39,1:112,15–113,9; LW34:182.

their faith in the God who had given them life and who promised enduring life; he induced them to try to become like God by means of their own wisdom and virtue."[53] For Luther, righteousness rested upon God's declaration of new life through the abolition of the sinner's status as sinner and consisted of the trust that grasped and relied on this divine declaration. Thus the root of all evil had sprung from the breach in trust in what God has said.

Conclusion

With the humanistic tools made available around 1500, Luther probed the language of the apostles and prophets within the context of his own confrontation with guilt and fear of God's wrath as well as his concern for pastoral care and the crisis of pastoral care that beset the late medieval church. As a person driven by these challenges, he delved into the biblical text and found there a God who was seeking him, desiring to call him to a repentance that would lead to trust in Christ. On the basis of his conviction that God's almighty Word not only created all that exists but also recreates sinners into God's children, the Wittenberg professor formulated a new definition of a number of significant theological terms—above all, "righteousness." The integrity of the forgiven sinner and the believer's identity as child of God rested on the recreative Word of God that pronounced God's chosen people righteous on the basis of Christ's death and resurrection. This new definition of righteousness connected with new definitions of other terms, including faith and original sin. His new definition of what it means to be a Christian thus launched a reformation and transformed the understanding of much of the terminology of the theological tradition he had inherited.

---

[53] WA40,1:34,1–15, LW27:145.

Martin Luther and Gustaf Wingren on Baptism

Dr. Mark D. Tranvik

(A personal note. Jim Nestingen was my doctoral advisor and a significant mentor as I deepened my understanding of Martin Luther and the Lutheran Confessions. When I first crossed paths with Jim, I was fresh out of Yale Divinity School and especially enamored of the theology of Karl Barth. While Jim appreciated Barth's many strengths, he also suggested that I needed a "Lutheran corrective" and pointed me to theologians from Sweden and Finland and the writings of Gustaf Wingren [1910–2000] in particular. Through Wingren, I came to see the limitations of Barth and his Calvinist Christology. Correspondingly, I now saw the deep wisdom in Luther's daring mix of the human and divine in his view of Jesus. I ended up exploring that further in the reformer's sacramental theology, particularly with reference to baptism.)

Baptism has had a curious history in the Lutheran church since the time of the Reformation. As I will suggest in this paper, Martin Luther elevated the sacrament to heights virtually unknown in the Christian tradition, with the possible exception of the early church. However, baptism quickly fell to second-class status in comparison with the attention lavished on the Lord's Supper. The seeds of this development can already be seen in the sixteenth century, and baptism's decline accelerated in the succeeding periods of orthodoxy, pietism, and rationalism. Only with the advent of the Luther Renaissance in the twentieth century can we see a new appreciation of baptism. Among the important thinkers in the rebirth of the sacrament is the Swedish theologian Gustaf Wingren.[1]

In this essay, I will provide an overview of Luther's understanding of baptism, being careful to underline how he saw a deep link between the sacrament and justification. I will also point to baptism as the best expression for Luther's conception of the Christian life. I will then move to Wingren's theology of baptism and investigate the degree of his dependence on Luther's understanding of baptism. I will also show how Wingren, building on the foundation provided by Luther and the early church fathers, uses baptismal language to shape his own distinctive proposal of the relationship between faith and daily life.

Luther on Baptism: An Overview

In his Large Catechism, Martin Luther says that "no greater jewel, therefore, can adorn our body and soul than baptism."[2] It is well known that Luther was prone to hyperbole in his writings. But the designation of baptism as an unsurpassable jewel is an accurate reflection of the reformer's estimation of the sacrament. Luther has discovered within the framework of baptism a "family" of words that are particularly well suited to his new understanding of justification. It is clear that nothing less than the language of baptism, the language of death and life, can do justice to the transformation wrought on one who trusts God's promises.

When one is baptized, says Luther, one should not understand this "allegorically" as the death of sin and life of grace but as "actual death and resurrection . . . for baptism is not a false sign." Similarly,

---

[1] For a good introduction to Wingren and his importance for Lutherans, see Marc Kolden, "Gustaf Wingren on the Christian Life," *Journal of Lutheran Ethics* 10, no. 9 (September 2010). Available online.

[2] Martin Luther, Large Catechism in *The Book of Concord*, ed. Robert Kolb and Timothy Wengert (Minneapolis: Fortress, 2000), 462 (hereafter cited as BC). For an expanded explanation of Luther's views on baptism, see Mark D. Tranvik, "Luther on Baptism," in *Harvesting Martin Luther's Reflections on Theology, Ethics, and the Church*, ed. Timothy J. Wengert (Grand Rapids: Eerdmans, 2004), 23–37.

he disdains those who speak of baptism as a "washing" away of sin, for that is "too meek and mild." Rather, "the sinner needs to die, in order to be wholly renewed and made into another creature."[3] Luther is stressing an event—the faith born out of trust in the promise—which is beyond all rational categories and therefore requires an eschatological terminology. Following Paul in Romans 6:4, Luther sees baptism as the way the cross and resurrection become contemporaneous with the believer. It might even be said that baptism effects the "joyous exchange" (*fröliche Wechsel*), a term Luther used frequently to express his understanding of the atonement.[4] As Ulrich Asendorf has made clear, this "exchange" is not merely an intellectual construct but rather something that effects a real transformation in the believer.[5]

When Luther says that "baptism is full and complete justification," this can be read as yet another protest against the Pelagianizing tendencies of the late medieval church. Rejecting any understanding of salvation that envisions a partnership of the human and divine wills, baptism for Luther effects an end of the old and a birth of the new, which rules out a segmented or progressive theology of justification. Simply put, baptism goes to the heart of justification—God's slaying of the sinner and God's resurrection of a completely new creature. As David Lotz suggests, for Luther baptism is justification "enacted."[6]

---

[3] Martin Luther, The Babylonian Captivity of the Church in *Luther's Works*, American ed., ed. Pelikan and Lehmann, 55 vols. (St. Louis and Philadelphia: Concordia and Fortress Press, 1955ff.), 36:58 (hereafter cited as LW). This translation is based on the Latin version found in *Luthers Werke*, Kritische Gesamtausgabe, ed. J. F. K. Knaake, et al., 57 vols. (Weimar: Böhlau, 1883ff.), 6:527 (hereafter cited as WA).

[4] See Heiko Oberman, *Luther: Man between God and the Devil*, trans. Eileen Walliser-Schwarzbart (New Haven: Yale University Press, 1989), 227. See also Luther's "Sermon at the Baptism of Bernhard von Anhalt" (1541): LW 51:320; WA 49:125.

[5] Ulrich Asendorf, *Die Theologie Martin Luthers nach seinen Predigten* (Göttingen: Vandenhoeck and Ruprecht, 1988), 366–70.

[6] David W. Lotz, "The Sacrament of Salvation: Luther on Baptism and Justification," *Trinity Seminary Review* 6, no. 1 (Spring 1984): 3–12.

Luther's early writings on baptism in particular also highlight his concern to merge the sacrament with penance. The latter was especially subject to abuse in his day, most notoriously in the indulgence controversy. Luther complained that penance, which had its foundation in baptism and whose function was to point to baptism, had degenerated into the "external pomp of works" and the "deceits of man-made ordinances." A specific target for Luther is the church father, Jerome, who said that penance is the "second plank after the shipwreck," thereby inferring that the power of baptism is broken because of sin. Luther, concerned to stress baptism's lifelong significance, turns this image on its head when he says, "The ship remains one, solid, and invincible; it will never be broken up into separate 'planks.' In it are carried all those who are brought to the harbor of salvation, for it is the truth of God giving us his promise in the sacraments."[7] Concerned to combat penance's tendency to supersede baptism, by the end of *The Babylonian Captivity of the Church*, he coalesces the two sacraments. Penance now becomes a way of talking about baptism: "Penance . . . is nothing but a way and return to baptism."[8]

Consequently, baptism is no longer just the sacrament of infancy or merely an "initiation rite" into the church. (The latter term, popular in many Christian circles, would appear to be ill-suited to a Lutheran understanding of the sacrament.) Now baptism spans the entire life of the believer. As Luther says in the Small Catechism,

> What does baptism signify? It signifies that the old creature in us, together with all sins and evil desires, should be drowned by daily sorrow and repentance and be put to death, and that the new person should come forth daily.[9]

Or he can say, "This whole life is nothing else than a spiritual baptism that does not cease until death."[10] The stress is on baptism's

---

[7] "Babylonian Captivity," 61, WA 6: 529.

[8] Ibid., 124; WA 6: 572.

[9] Martin Luther, Small Catechism in BC, 360.

[10] Martin Luther, "The Holy and Blessed Sacrament of Baptism" (1519) in LW 35: 30; WA 2: 728.

permanence and ongoing relevance. The believer lives in his or her baptism. It provides life with a sacramental horizon that shapes the beginning and end of existence as well as every moment in between.

Thus far in this essay, we have covered Luther's view of baptism and its vital link to justification and also the contention that the vitality of the sacrament extends until death, when the believer is reunited with Christ. A third point of Luther's baptismal theology also needs emphasis—his contention (for pastoral reasons) that the water itself, when joined to the promise, becomes charged with the presence of God.

In the second half of his life as a reformer, Luther confronted a wide-ranging array of groups who were reluctant to identify God too closely with the material world. Basic to this viewpoint was the belief that the Holy Spirit acted in an unmediated way.[11] Some of this was understandable given the superstitious or "magical" practices that plagued Christianity in this period. But undergirding this protest was also a metaphysical dualism between spirit and matter that inevitably relegated the sacraments to second-class status. Luther found this disturbing because he sensed that this emphasis on the "Spirit" and faith would ironically undermine and not undergird trust in God.

Luther is adamant that the sign cannot be dispensed with. When he says that God is present in baptism, he is not referring to some type of divine ether that hangs over the font. He is actually speaking of a divine presence *in* the water. The catechisms stress this in a number of different ways. The coming of the Word to the water makes the latter a "gracious water of life"[12] and a "divine, heavenly, holy and blessed water."[13] In his sermons, Luther can speak of Christ as having "stuck" (*gesteckt*) His death and life in the water[14] and says

---

[11] Luther's broad title for this group was *Schwärmer*, which tended to include everyone from Zwingli to the Anabaptists.

[12] Luther, Small Catechism in BC, 359.

[13] Ibid., 460.

[14] Otto Hof, "Taufe und Heilswerk Christi bei Luther," in *Zur Auferbauung des Leibes Christi. Festgabe für Professor D. Peter Brunner*, ed. Edmund Schlink and Albrecht Peters (Kassel: Johannes Stauda-Verlag, 1965), 227.

that the water is "mingled" or "mixed" with God's name.[15] He also suggests that the eyes of faith see not water in baptism but the "innocent, rosy-red blood of Christ." Mention might also be made of the seventh verse of Luther's baptismal hymn:

> The eye but water doth behold,
> As from man's hand it floweth;
> But inward faith the power untold
> Of Jesus Christ's blood knoweth.
> Faith sees therein a red flood roll,
> With Christ's blood dyed and blended[16]

Luther is not returning here to a sacramentalism where the distinction between heavenly and earthly realities is collapsed. But for faith's sake, this sign must not be dispensed with. For "faith must have something to believe—something to which it may cling and upon which it may stand." The water of baptism, enlivened by the promise, makes the death and resurrection of Christ personal and certain. It highlights the *pro me* character of the sacrament and makes clear why Luther would rely on his baptism ("I am baptized!") in moments of temptation and despair.[17]

Luther's emphasis on externality flows naturally from his view of the Incarnation. At the heart of the reformer's theology is a Christology that goes to daring lengths in its view of the divinity's extension into the humanity. Peter Brunner suggests a linkage between the communication of attributes (*communicatio idiomatum*) and baptism. As human nature shares the majestic power of

---

[15] Lorenz Grönvik, *Der Taufe in der Theologie Martin Luthers*, Acta Academiae Aboensis, Series A (Åbo: Åbo Akademi, 1968), 86.

[16] Martin Luther, "To Jordan When Our Lord Had God" (1541), in LW 53: 301.

[17] An excellent article that stresses baptism's role in providing comfort is John T. Pless's "Baptism as Consolation in Luther's Pastoral Care," *Concordia Theological Quarterly* 67 (2003): 19–32.

the divine nature, so the baptismal water shares in the divine power bestowed by the Word. It is no longer "simply water" (*aqua simplex*) but a "divine, heavenly" (*divina, celestis*) water by virtue of Christ's presence in it.[18]

The Baptismal Theology of Wingren

It is almost difficult to overemphasize the importance of baptism in Wingren's theology. The movement from death to life at the heart of the sacrament is also Wingren's hermeneutical key for understanding scripture and the nature of the Christian life. In the opening chapter of *Gospel and Church*, Wingren says that "in one sense all that follows in the subsequent discussion is an extended explanation of the meaning of baptism." Wingren clearly views himself in a line with Luther and the early church fathers in recovering a theme so central in the New Testament.[19] I will begin my analysis of Wingren with a brief summary of his theology and an outline of his context. Then proceeding on the conviction that baptism for Wingren is a river that flows through the entire landscape of Christian doctrine, I will examine the sacrament's relationship to Christology, creation, the fall, and the church.

Wingren's primary contribution to modern theology has been his recovery of the doctrine of creation. His main concern is to put the first article of the creed "back in its proper place." This emphasis on creation flows naturally from the order of scripture. Wingren believes a theology faithful to the Bible will take seriously the **order** of the Bible. Thus we must begin with creation. The entire prehistory of scripture (Gen. 1–11) is the story of "Everyman."[20] Our relationship with God is given with creation itself, even if we do not acknowledge it. Life from birth to the present is provided and

---

[18] Peter Brunner, *Die Evangelisch-Lutherische Lehre von der Taufe* (Berlin: Lutherisches Verlagshaus, 1951), 20.

[19] For example, references to Irenaeus and Luther far outnumber other figures in *The Living Word*.

[20] Gustaf Wingren, *Gospel and Church*, trans. Ross Mackenzie (Edinburgh: Oliver and Boyd, 1964), 6.

sustained by God. No matter what idolatry or ideology we may fall prey to, our relationship to God in **life** continues.[21]

In addition to this relationship with God bestowed in life itself, humanity also enjoys the distinction of being created in God's image, which is the same as Jesus Christ.[22] We are given dominion over the rest of creation. The fall results when we seek domination. Instead of being content with our role in the "natural order," we yield to temptation and turn creation into an idol. Only when we are restored in Jesus Christ (recapitulated) are we brought back into proper relationship with creation, the neighbor, and God. What is given in Christ is "life." This new existence in a sense is very old. As Wingren notes, "It never transgresses what God has already ordained and intended in creation."[23]

For Wingren, it then follows that the gospel is the death and resurrection of Jesus who reverses the pattern of "life unto death" set by Adam. Correspondingly, the church is the ongoing work of restoration that occurs when the gospel is proclaimed in preaching and the sacraments. The church's work continues until the future promised by Christ becomes present.

When we turn to Wingren's views on baptism, we find an impatience with the tendency to focus on the rite of baptism because it threatens what he sees as the biblical meaning of the sacrament.[24] To equate baptism only with a ritual reinforces the view "that the whole world and life of man . . . (are) a profane area which stands in no relation to God . . . by the side of the profane life the sacraments are set as some sort of holy substances, and we get lost in unending questions about how we are to fit divine activity into the normal life of man."[25] He acknowledges that in the ritual of the ancient church

---

[21] Gustaf Wingren, *Creation and Law*, trans. Ross Mackenzie (Edinburgh: Oliver and Boyd, 1961), 20.

[22] Ibid., 35.

[23] Ibid., 36.

[24] Gustaf Wingren, *Credo*, trans. Edgar M. Carlson (Minneapolis: Augsburg, 1981), 176.

[25] Gustaf Wingren, *The Living Word*, trans. Victor C. Pogue (Philadelphia: Muhlenburg, 1960), 152.

and the great drama of its baptismal liturgy, there was some approximation between the rite and the reality conveyed by the sacrament. But this has been lost by the "inroads which have been made on the baptismal ritual through the centuries." Today we cannot begin with the baptismal rite of the church and expect to arrive at an accurate understanding of baptism. (In fact, Wingren says one would have to go to a prison and witness an execution if one wished to comprehend what the New Testament has in mind when it speaks of baptism.)[26] Rather, our starting point must be the kerygma, the salvific event centered in Jesus Christ.

Fundamental to understanding Wingren's views on baptism is that the point of reference is always the death and resurrection of Christ and the corresponding death and resurrection of the believer. Here, of course, he is picking up on Luther and his explanation of the sacrament in the Small Catechism.[27] Wingren refuses to budge from this center and speculate on "metaphysical" questions surrounding the sacrament. This kind of thinking is foreign to scripture and it especially detracts from his notion of the sacrament as an "event."[28] Reflection on baptism always begins with *the* baptism, what Wingren calls "baptism in its definitive form"—the death of Christ on Calvary.[29] Relying on the biblical exegesis of Oscar Cullman's *Baptism in the New Testament*, Wingren views Jesus' death at Golgotha as the "general baptism" or the "true and proper baptism for all humanity."[30] He reminds his readers that this way of thinking about baptism is Scriptural. In Luke 12:50, Jesus speaks of his impending death as a baptism he has to be baptized with. Or again in Mark 10:38, referring to the cross, Jesus asks his disciples if they are able "to be baptized with the baptism with which I am baptized." The early church, most notably in Romans 6, also assumes this linkage between baptism and the crucifixion.[31]

---

[26] Wingren, *Credo*, 177.

[27] Luther, Small Catechism in BC, 360.

[28] Wingren, *Gospel and Church*, 3.

[29] Wingren, *Credo*, 177.

[30] Wingren, *Gospel and Church*, 7.

[31] Ibid.

We now turn to how Wingren links the sacrament with the story of creation and the fall. Humanity is created in the image of God. However, this fellowship with the Creator is disrupted in the fall. Men and women put ultimate trust in something created instead of their Creator. This sets in motion a chain of events whereby the neighbor is neglected or harmed and the charge to have dominion is warped and twisted. Having cut itself off from the life-giving activity of the Creator, humanity is now involved in a dominion of death.[32] The effect of baptism is to bring humanity back into a relationship with Christ. Wingren juxtaposes the great Christological hymn of Philippians 2 with the account of Adam in Genesis 3, who exalted himself and fell.[33]

It should be noted that what is restored in baptism is the "image of God" in which we were originally created. To be "in Christ" is not to be elevated to some vague supernatural status or to become more "spiritual." Wingren's view is that Adam "fell upward" when he attempted to claim more than what was rightfully his. Baptism plants Adam's feet firmly back in the earth. As Wingren says, "To become like Christ is to conform to God's rule in creation. The life which Jesus gives to the world through his victory is the life which Adam lost."[34]

Being restored in Christ through baptism points to the significance of the church in Wingren's theology of the sacrament. The church exists because God's goal for humanity (being refashioned in the image of God) has only been achieved in Christ.[35] He conceives the church's mission as reaching out to the world so that humanity may become truly human. This can happen only in baptism, for only here does "man truly become man."[36] Baptism thus has an "open character"; it is the gateway to the world and the means by which the church "multiplies greatly."[37] Wingren's emphasis on baptism as

---

[32] Wingren, *Creation and Law*, 49.

[33] Wingren, *Gospel and Church*, 8.

[34] Wingren, *Creation and Law*, 35.

[35] Wingren, *Gospel and Church*, 10.

[36] Ibid., 59.

[37] Ibid., 11.

the primary sacrament keeps the church's mission activity front and center: "The church exists for the sake of the unredeemed who are outside it."[38]

Of course, Wingren's argument for baptism as the "first sacrament" does not mean it is the last. Once you pass through the gateway, you must be nurtured within the church: "If baptism is the door of the church, it is also the entrance into a continually new hearing of the word, renewed study, renewed communion, and renewed prayer and praise day by day."[39] However, nothing can be added to baptism within the fellowship of believers. Rather, all that we receive is a renewal and continuation of baptism.[40]

Wingren believes that when baptism is blunted and muffled, problems are quick to follow. Indeed, he argues that this is precisely what has happened in much of Western Christianity. When baptism is regarded as a "mere formality," Wingren sees a direct line of disintegration to a more inward-looking church, a preoccupation with the Eucharist, and an elevated view of the ministry.[41] If baptism ceases to be the overall paradigm for the way the church thinks about itself, then the result is introversion and irrelevance.

Furthermore, Wingren underlines a strong connection between baptism and ethics. By participating in Christ's reversal of Adam, Wingren says that baptism is the starting point for ethical instruction. By "putting on Christ" in baptism, the believer's life becomes drawn into an imitation of Christ. Not, however, as "imitation" has often been understood—a type of self-transcendence that merits favor before God. Rather, Wingren sees the "imitation" as leading directly to the neighbor: "Baptism points beyond itself to the relationships into which it brings the baptized. It is the reverse of the acquisitive attitude which clings for dear life to what is created. . . . In Christ death has become life and our neighbor part of

---

[38] Ibid.

[39] Ibid., 138.

[40] Ibid., 131.

[41] Ibid., 129.

the humanity for which he suffered death, and which His body, the Church, now prays for and cares for."[42]

Wingren's death-life hermeneutic and his insistence that baptism is a reality in every moment of life remove any need for the so-called third use of the law. The baptismal paradigm simply makes this impossible: "The Gospel is not a first stage, marked by conversion, after which he (the believer) is to submit to certain commandments and be governed by these rather than the Gospel. On the contrary, the Gospel is his daily sustenance."[43] In other words, the source of new life is the gospel alone and not some supposed eternal law existing outside the baptismal framework.

For Wingren, placing baptism front and center in a Christian ethic allows for a dynamism often missing in other theologies. Here he has Barth in mind, a favorite target. Wingren says that Barth makes the distinction between the present and the future solely a matter of *insight*. For Barth, the eternity that will be revealed is that of the incarnation. The line stretching from now to Christ's return affords no new victories, for the victory has already been won.[44] For Wingren, such a view is far too arid and static. If one places baptism on the line between the present and the future, a certain vitality is recovered: "Those who are baptized are put to death and raised to life, and this double action is a present reality." The believer's movement in Christ from death to life assumes that the Christian life will be a constant cleansing or what Wingren calls "purification."[45] It is important to note that this movement does not take place external to the relationship with Christ but *within* it. It is a confession about what happens to one who is "clothed in his baptism."

Wingren also comments on the relationship between baptism and vocation, saying that "our baptism is realized in our earthly vocation."[46] By this, he is stressing that baptism drives a person of

---

[42] Ibid., 209.

[43] Ibid., 213–14.

[44] Ibid., 212.

[45] Ibid.

[46] Ibid., 53. See also his comments in Gustaf Wingren, *Luther on Vocation*, trans. Carl C. Rasmussen (Philadelphia: Muhlenberg, 1957), 28–31.

faith out into the world. But the very act of going out into the world is fraught with loneliness and temptation (hence the popularity of the "sect" mentality). However, the suffering that always accompanies a mission when it meets resistance has the effect of drawing the believer back to his baptism, where he is again renewed and given the strength to go forward. It is in vocation that the dynamism implicit in baptism is realized and experienced. During the time of the church, the Christian is perpetually on the way from death to life.

Some Concluding Remarks

As we compare Luther and Wingren, it might be said that their baptismal theologies need each other. While both have a robust understanding of the sacrament, there are shades of difference in each writer.

As we have seen, Luther makes the closest possible link between baptism and justification. Baptism is the place in time where God's promises are enacted in the life of the believer. In an age where so many people are deeply afflicted with anxiety, pointing to the baptismal promises made over the font can be a word of great comfort. In the place of loneliness, meaninglessness, and a loss of purpose, the church can remind believers that a Word has been pronounced in the midst of their lives that draws them away from self-preoccupation and into the hands of God, whose love remains steadfast. Luther's cry in the midst of his own temptation, *"baptizatus sum"* ("I am baptized!"), needs to be echoed throughout the church.

While Wingren would never deny the consolation to be derived from baptism, for him the accent falls elsewhere. Expanding on Luther's view of baptism as the sacrament for daily life, Wingren takes great care to point to the significance of the sacrament as Christians live out their callings in a complicated world. Grounded in baptism, now understood as Christ's very death and resurrection, he sees the Christian life as dynamic venturing forth into the future. Christ's death and rising propel the believer forward and are reenacted daily in the warp and woof of life. No longer is baptism merely a little-remembered liturgical ornament from one's past. Rather, it joins the believer to the living Christ and his mission in God's own world.

That I May Be His Own

The Necessary End of the Law

Dr. Jason D. Lane

"Bargains, bargains, El-ahrairah," he said. "There is not a day or a night but a doe offers her life for her kittens, or some honest captain of Owsla his life for his Chief Rabbit's. Sometimes it is taken, sometimes it is not. But there is no bargain, for here what is is what must be."

—The Black Rabbit of Inlé,
in Richard Allen's *Watership Down*

In this essay, I take on the topic of necessity as a possible way to reexamine certain aspects of the current debate on Law and Gospel.

I.

We think of necessity in a legal way. "Good works are necessary for salvation." "Repentance is necessary for forgiveness." "You must do this or that." Talk of necessity runs the risk of theological abstraction and legal structures for how God works and must work. Firm theories about why the Son of God needed to die led to what Gustav

Aulen called the "legal order" of the atonement.[1] Yet in the gospel accounts, the necessity of Christ's death and resurrection takes center stage as the Old Testament promises are fulfilled. Peter is rebuked during Jesus' arrest for using a sword, because man's will cannot change the course of God's plan. Jesus refuses to use His power to call down legions of angels from His Father. God's mercy triumphs over His omnipotence. All this, because the Son of Man goes as it is written of Him; it is necessary (Matt. 26:53).[2] Necessity, we assume, is legal, but this necessity is different. Christ makes clear that it must happen this way; there is no other way.

Part of the difficulty in understanding this necessity of Christ's redemptive work has been our tendency to interpret it with legal or fatalistic definitions. St. Anselm (1033–1109) most clearly raised the question of necessity concerning Christ's incarnation, passion, and death in the Latin Church, but he is largely blamed for circumscribing the atonement of Christ within a legal framework.[3] Although I believe this is due more to our inattentive reading of Anselm, the adoption of his perceived line of argument has had an effect on preaching.[4] The way that we have embraced Anselm's thought limits

---

[1] Gustav Aulen, *Christus Victor: An Historical Study of the Three Main Types of the Idea of the Atonement*, trans. A. G. Herbert (New York: Macmillan, 1969), 91.

[2] All Bible citation are from the *English Standard Version* (Wheaton: Crossway, 2001), unless otherwise noted.

[3] See, for example, the popular critique of Aulen, *Christus Victor*, 84–95. For his critique of Melanchthon and Lutheran Orthodoxy, which both veer from Luther on the atonement, see 123–33.

[4] Steven Paulson and Nicholas Hopman, "Christ, the Hated God," *Lutheran Quarterly* 30, no. 1 (Spring 2016): 15. Paulson and Hopman describe what Anselm's view of the atonement has become in modern preaching: "The crucifixion is told as if it were fulfilling God's own desire or maintaining his eternal essence by somehow completing work that sinners left undone. In short, a sinner needs the cross as the last chance of completing the law. Or, more subtly, God needed the cross for his own self in the form of a sacrificial offering. Yet, when the story of Christ is reversed God neither needs the law, nor the cross within the law. Sinners were the ones who crucified Christ, not the Father's inner need or the law's external demands. For that reason we say that

the redemptive work of Christ to the law. Christ fulfills law to bring us back to the law, which reestablishes the original relationship between God and man. To save humanity, it is supposed, God must act in a particular way because justice and His own honor require it. External forces or at least abstract eternal principles appear to be at work. Sin required the death of man, and God became man to satisfy God's wrath and fulfill the righteousness that the law demands vicariously for sinners.

Gerhard Forde explains that Anselm and later the Lutheran dogmaticians, many of whom followed his logic concerning the vicarious satisfaction, were faced with a dilemma concerning God's freedom toward man. If God justifies man without any merit based on the law, it would mean that God is entirely free in justifying man and acts only according to His own good pleasure. To avoid attributing to God an ultimate and yet arbitrary freedom (which Calvinists assert), the Lutheran dogmaticians circumscribed God's absolute freedom by saying that God acts freely, "but only in accordance with the inner law of His own essence."[5] What this inner law is is not entirely clear. But it appears a quality of God's essence that self-imposes a stricture on His ultimate freedom. God, who created the law for man, is now restricted by His own law. His mercy then can only stem from His legal righteousness to satisfy justice and fulfill the law that was beyond the power of sinners to fulfill. Here Christ must do what the law requires and pay for sin, but only because justice requires it and God's honor demands it. Necessity, as it is conceived here, is entirely legal. For those familiar with Luther's sharp distinction between Law and Gospel, that the law and its threats ends whenever and wherever Christ reigns or "the law . . . until Christ" (Gal. 3:24), this description of the atonement as a legal transaction within the bounds of an eternal law robs St. Paul's statements, such

---

God was not forced by his own inner necessity or essence to express his wrath at sin. God's wrath does not emerge from within him, but from without among sinners. Neither is wrath quelled by mere punishment for sin. God does not need catharsis in order to accept sinners into his kingdom, nor is he waiting for sinners to fulfill the law before he can act."

[5] Gerhard Forde, *The Law-Gospel Debate* (Minneapolis: Fortress Press, 1969), 4.

as "now the righteousness of God has been manifested apart from the law" (Rom. 3:21) and "Christ is the end of the law for righteousness to everyone who believes" (Rom. 10:4) of their freeing power to those under the law.[6] Thus far we have the typical reading of Anselm on the atonement and the Lutheran orthodox view.

The neat picture of Anselm and later orthodoxy on the legal scheme, however, needs further examination, especially since it ignores a very important passage in Anselm's discussion of necessity where he asserts God's absolute freedom in regard to man's salvation[7]. He explains that we can offer no further account concerning the necessity of God becoming man and dying for sinful humanity except to deal with what is revealed and say that what is is what must be, once God has freely willed it. In other words, God does not fit into a legal scheme. Anselm explains,

> There is an antecedent necessity which is the cause of a thing, and there is also a subsequent necessity arising from the thing itself. . . . By this subsequent and imperative necessity, it was necessary—since the belief and prophecy concerning Christ were true, that he would die of his own free will—that it should be so. For this reason he became man; for this reason he did and suffered all things undertaken by him; for this reason he chose as he did. Therefore they were necessary, because they were to be, and they were to be because they were, and they were because they were; and, if you wish to know the real necessity of all things which he did and suffered, know that they were of necessity, because he wished them to be. But no necessity preceded his will.[8]

In other words, once God decides to show mercy, He cannot do otherwise. He is as He does and He does as He wills. For Anselm, the antecedent necessity is God's free choice to rescue humanity. To

---

[6] See James Nestingen, "Speaking of the End of the Law," in *The Necessary Distinction: A Continuing Conversation on Law and Gospel*, ed. James Arne Nestingen, Albert B. Collver III, and John T. Pless (2017), 169–84.

[7] *Cur Deus Homo* II, 17.

[8] Anselm of Canterbury, *Cur Deus Homo*, ed. Hugo Laemmer (Berlin: G. Schlawitz, 1857), 82–83.

know the antecedent necessity is to know God's will for humanity. From our perspective, however, we cannot comprehend the antecedent necessity, the choice, unless the occurrences of subsequent necessity are set forth in Christ. Anything else is whimsical speculation. Once the deed is done and God has become man and died to rescue us, there is no use in speculating about alternatives: "Was there another way?" What is actually the case is what must be, not according to abstract concepts of divine attributes but because "He has mercy on whomever He wills" (Rom. 9:18) as we learn in Christ.

In this way, Anselm follows St. Paul's argument in Ephesians 1, although he does not say it as beautifully. Paul sets up the two necessities. First, the antecedent necessity, "He chose us in him before the foundation of the world, that we should be holy and blameless before Him" and "in love He predestined us for adoption to Himself as sons through Jesus Christ, according to the purpose of His will" (1:4–5). Paul begins with God's plan in eternity that we should be His forever. The eternal plan is not strictly to make us obedient but to have us through adoption, to make us children who are and who were in Christ always meant to be His own. This is what Luther is getting at in his explanation of the second article of the Creed (II, ii, 4), "that I may be His own." What we were made for at creation and lost as a result of sin and the curse of the law has become reality again in Christ. Christ's past tense work is then delivered in time by the Holy Spirit through His church and brought to completion on the day of resurrection.[9] No inner law drives Him to it, nor does the outbreak of sin force Him to save humanity to restore His honor. Humanity's

---

[9] James Nestingen, "Changing Definitions: The Law in Formula VI," *Concordia Theological Quarterly* 69, no. 3–4 (July/October 2005): 265–66. Dr. Nestingen says it better: "Yet at the same time, what is now realized goes on into the future. So the explanation of the second article concludes with the words, 'All this he has done that I may be his own'" (SC II,ii,4). And the use of the present perfect in the third article explanation indicates that what has begun continues in a way that as justified the believer remains a sinner who confesses: "'I believe that I cannot by my own understanding or effort believe in Jesus Christ my Lord or come to him' and who therefore depends on the ministry of the church, in which 'day after day, he fully forgives all my sins' until the last day, 'when he will raise me and all the dead'" (SC II,iii,6).

sin strangely is not the cause of God's plan in Christ, and therefore
the gospel cannot be seen as a last-ditch effort to rescue humanity.
According to Anselm's definition of antecedent necessity, only the
gracious and eternal will of God is the cause of Christ's incarnation, passion, death, and so on. It must be because it must be, and
it must be because He willed it. Paul recognizes the oddity of the
logic and therefore calls it "the mystery of His will [τὸ μυστήριον τοῦ
θελήματος αὐτοῦ]" (Eph. 1:9).

Paul then establishes the second or subsequent necessity: "In
Him we have redemption through His blood, the forgiveness of our
trespasses, according to the riches of His grace, which He lavished
upon us, in all wisdom and insight making known to us the mystery of His will, according to His purpose, which He set forth in
Christ as a plan for the fullness of time, to unite all things in Him,
things in heaven and things on earth" (Eph. 1:7–10). The concrete
expression of God's will in Christ is the limit and boundary of knowing the "mystery of His will." The free choice in eternity, however,
"in the fullness of time," is *now* made known, "set forth in Christ" in
the concrete form of the forgiveness of sins (Eph. 1:7). All this is necessary because God willed it—this way, and in no other way. Instead
of immutable principles, we get immutable promises.

The mystery of His eternal will is not an eternal law in the
divine mind.[10] His will is mercy and His very nature is that of a loving father, as Luther's hymn, "Dear Christians One and All Rejoice,"
so vividly portrays: "But God had seen my wretched state / Before
the world's foundation, / And mindful of His mercies great, / He

---

[10] See, for example, Joachim Mörlin, *Disputationes Tres de Tertio Usu Legis
Contra Fanaticos* (1566), who defines the law (II:64) as the eternal rule of
the divine mind: "The perfection and immovable rule in the divine mind
[*illa perfectio cuius norma et immota regula in mente divina est lex*]." For a
summary of his disputations and the text, see Irene Dingel, *Der Antinomis-
tische Streit (1556–1571)*, Controversia et Confessio: Theologische Kontro-
versen 1548–1577/80 Kritische Auswahledition (Göttingen: Vandenhoeck
& Ruprecht, 2016), 305ff. This stands in contrast to the careful wording of
FC VI:4, where the problematic definition of the Law in FC VI:3 that equates
God's immutability (and thus eternality) with the Law. "For the Law is a mirror
in which God's will and what pleases Him are exactly portrayed" (FC VI:4).

planned for my salvation / He turned to me a father's heart; / He did
not choose the easy part / But gave His dearest treasure."[11] Or as Paul
Gerhardt would have us sing, "Love caused your incarnation; / Love
brought you down to me."[12] God's eternal and loving heart toward us
is the cause of all that happens, and what has happened happened
"for us and for our salvation" (Nicene Creed). Love, however, should
be understood not as the principle to which God conforms but as
the expression of His eternal nature made known to us and for us in
Christ (Eph. 1:9).

So far, then, we can see that the necessity of Christ's redemptive work is based on His eternal promise to have us as His own
and not an abstract notion of the law. What is left to sort out is the
revelation of His gracious will in time and all that, according to His
promise, is necessary. As I mentioned, the revelation of God's eternal
will is often cast within the legal language of principle, order, and the
divine mind, rather than seeing with St. Paul the mystery of His will
as His merciful desire to make us His own no matter the cost. But
with what remains of this essay, I want to explore the scope of this
necessity in Christ. Specifically, I want to suggest that God's plan to
make us His own includes the necessary end to the law in Christ.

II.

At the end of Luke's gospel account, the language of necessity (δεῖ)
appears again. We tend to focus on the necessity of the cross, insofar
as Christ pronounces the end of sin and the law's accusation against
us: "It is finished" (John 19:30). Yet Christ also had in view His

---

[11] Martin Luther, "Dear Christians, One and All, Rejoice," in *Lutheran Service Book* (St. Louis: Concordia, 2006), 556. The original German emphasizes
that the will of God to save is "in eternity," and also it demonstrates more
clearly than the English that for Luther, the antecedent necessity is God's own
mercy that He cannot forget. "Da jammert Gott in Ewigkeit / Mein Elend
übermaßen / Er dacht an sein Barmherzigkeit, / Er wollt mir helfen lassen. /
Er wand zu mir das vater hertz, / Es war bei ihm fürwahr kein Scherz, / Er ließ
sein Bestes kosten." WA 35:424 (with modernized spelling).

[12] Paul Gerhardt, "O Lord, How Shall I Meet You," in *Lutheran Service
Book*, 333.

resurrection. It was necessary to defeat death and the power of the devil forever, and it was necessary because "it was not possible for Him to be held by [death]" (Acts 2:24). After His resurrection, however, when everything had been accomplished in His death and resurrection, the redemptive δεῖ reappears: "These are my words that I spoke to you while I was still with you, that everything written about me in the Law of Moses and the Prophets and the Psalms must be [δεῖ] fulfilled" (Luke 24:44). Some may want to emphasize the death and resurrection as the objective, historical event of man's redemption and the fulfillment of the scriptures. Although this certainly gets the facts right, it misses the delivery *pro me* or *pro nobis* that Paul is so concerned with in Ephesians 1, Romans 10, and elsewhere. The fulfillment comes when the gifts are delivered and the goal of God's plan is complete. "Thus it is written, that the Christ should suffer and on the third day rise from the dead, and that repentance for the forgiveness of sins should be proclaimed in his name to all nations, beginning from Jerusalem" (Luke 24:46–47).

Necessity is here paired with fulfillment. In a real way, Christ fulfills what was necessary under the law. He bears the weight of sin and the law's condemnation and thus silences the law's curse (Gal. 3:13). But this fulfillment, though complete in Him and in history, is not yet fulfilled *in us*.[13] Sinners are locked in a web of accusation as long as their flesh remains. As long as sin clings to them in this life, the law accuses, threatens, and kills. This is how Luther understood the law.[14] But whenever the Holy Spirit works repentance and faith

---

[13] See Luther's second set of disputations (II:26) in WA 39.1, 349, 1. "Cum autem Christus venerit, non solvere, sed implere legem, frustra venit, si nulla sit lex *in nobis* implenda" (my emphasis).

[14] Naomichi Masaki, "Luther on Law and Gospel in His Lectures on Galatians 1531/1535," in *The Necessary Distinction: A Continuing Conversation on Law and Gospel*, ed. James A. Nestingen, Albert B. Collver III, and John T. Pless (St. Louis: Concordia, 2017), 153–54. "For Luther, the Law was not a description of what man is supposed to do within the structure of the eternal order. Instead, he viewed the Law as what it actually does. It kills. Luther observed how man in his weakness and sinfulness is capable of reducing the Law to a mere command, a rule, a system, a structure; a neat little package that is not threatening. He lamented that not only the sophists and monks but also

in Christ, He brings the law to its proper end. James Nestingen has
been of great help on this point: "The Law can only end when it is
fulfilled."[15] So the Holy Spirit brings the law to a necessary end by
delivering Christ into the conscience to reign as its new Lord. The
necessity for both remains: "*Opus alienum, ut faciat opus proprium*"
(FC V:11). Nestingen describes the undoing of the law's reign in us
with Luther's language of the blessed exchange:

> Christ finishes the Law in two ways. He enters the conscience through
> the absolution, through the proclaimed Word and the administered
> Sacrament to effect the forgiveness of sins. This is the true substitu-
> tionary atonement, happening here and now. Christ Jesus takes upon
> Himself the sinner's sins, the sinner himself or herself, and in a mar-
> velous exchange, as Luther calls it, becomes the victim for us so that
> while He bears our sins and our death, we arise in His righteousness.[16]

The second fulfilling of the law in us is what the Formula calls
"walking in the Law . . . yet without compulsion" (FC VI:18). This
fulfilling of the law after justification is not merely a response of the
will to a command but also living in the resurrection ahead of time
by faith. The law that we walk in is, as Nestingen notes, "not eternal
in the sense of Augustine's *lex aeterna* doctrine. . . . But it is eternal in
the eschatological sense. . . . The significance of the Law is that it

---

the majority of those who hear the Word do not struggle with sin, death, and
the devil. The Law, indeed, does give requirements. But beyond the commandment, the Law exercises power and force. Man can no longer make use of the
Law to organize his life and take control of his way of living. The Law kills and
condemns, and it does so in a number of ways."

[15] Nestingen, "Speaking of the End of the Law," 174.

[16] Ibid. The language of the atonement here points to the inseparable nature
of redemption achieved and redemption delivered in the forgiveness of sin.
One might call it the relationship between content and function. See James
Nestingen, "Distinguishing Law and Gospel: A Functional View," *Concordia
Journal* 22, no. 1 (January 1996): 27–34. St. Paul assumes a similar relationship
between redemption/atonement and forgiveness in Ephesians 1:7: "In him we
have redemption through his blood, the forgiveness of our trespasses, according to the riches of his grace."

points ahead to the shape of life when God completes what He has begun in Christ Jesus."[17]

Because God's purpose is to make us His own in Christ, the preaching of both Law and Gospel remains a temporal affair. It is needed this side of the resurrection, until the work of the law is complete in us forever—namely, in our death and the destruction of our sinful flesh—and until the gospel has reached its end in us, in the resurrection of our bodies. The final passage from the Formula of Concord VI captures this most clearly:

> For the old creature, like a stubborn, recalcitrant donkey, is also still
> a part of them, and it needs to be forced into obedience to Christ not
> only through the law's teaching, admonition, compulsion, and threat
> but also often with the cudgel of punishments and tribulations until
> the sinful flesh is completely stripped away and people are perfectly
> renewed in the resurrection. Then they will need neither the procla-
> mation of the law nor its threats and punishment, just as they will no
> longer need the gospel, for both belong to this imperfect life. Instead,
> just as they will see God face-to-face, so they will perform the will
> of God by the power of the indwelling Spirit of God spontaneously,
> without coercion, unhindered, perfectly and completely, with sheer
> joy, and they will delight in his will eternally.

The necessary end of the law means finally the end of sin and the bringing to completion of what is already ours by promise in Holy Baptism. Death has already occurred, and the hope of the resurrection is ours now by faith and then in reality, when both Law and Gospel cease and we see with unveiled eye the face of Christ and what God has made us to be. This is nothing other than "to be His own and live under Him in His kingdom and serve Him in everlasting righteousness, innocence, and blessedness, just as He is risen from the dead and lives and reigns to all eternity" (SC II, ii, 4).

---

[17] Nestingen, "Speaking of the End of the Law," 175.

Concluding Thoughts

Anytime we get into the language of "doctrine," we move in the way of abstract thinking. Nothing wrong with abstract thinking, as it goes, but Christ of course is not a doctrine; He is a person, and more specifically, as we learn to confess from the catechism, He is "my Lord." Yet the doctrine of Christ is necessary to confess because I must know who my Lord is—namely, "true God, begotten of the Father from eternity, and also true man, born of the Virgin Mary." Abstract thinking is necessary in the discipline of dogmatic theology and certainly in confessing the person and office of Christ. Without stepping back to consider what is true from scripture and what the great cloud of the church's witnesses has confessed, we are drastically limited in what we can say. Pious effusions of the heart are hardly trustworthy and rarely pious. Christian doctrine is sturdy, objective, and universal. And yet when we confess, for example, the atonement of Christ from outside the experience of God's concrete word of repentance and forgiveness, we venture inevitably into legal structure to which the mind must give assent. We make the rough places smooth by giving legal context to the death of Christ, without realizing that the cross is one subsequent necessity among a string of others for our salvation in Christ, according to the definite plan of God: His incarnation, death, resurrection, the preaching of repentance and forgiveness of sins, our resurrection, and the eternal innocence of the children of God who enjoy pleasures forevermore at God's right hand. For this reason, our biblical consideration of God's salvation and what was necessary for man's redemption must keep the entire plan of salvation before our eyes. All was necessary not according to some inner logic in God but because He chose us in Christ (Eph. 1:4). What I have learned from Dr. Nestingen is to start with the concrete word of absolution to sinners, to let Christ reign in the heart by faith and give us His righteousness. Theology beyond this is, as Luther would say, error and poison. The forgiveness of sin brings the law to its necessary end and makes known the mystery of God's will, which is and in Christ always has been to have us as His own.

Bibliography

Anselm of Canterbury and Hugo Laemmer. *Cur Deus Homo*. Berlin: G. Schlawitz, 1857.

Forde, Gerhard O. *The Law-Gospel Debate*. Minneapolis: Fortress Press, 1969.

Hagen, Kenneth. "Luther on Atonement—Reconfigured." *Concordia Theological Quarterly* 61, no. 4 (October 1997): 251–76.

Hopman, Nicholas. "Luther's Antinomian Disputations and the Lex Aeterna." *Lutheran Quarterly* 30, no. 2 (2016): 152–80.

Lutheran Service Book. St. Louis: Concordia, 2006.

Masaki, Naomichi. "Luther on Law and Gospel in His Lectures on Galatians 1531/1535." In *The Necessary Distinction: A Continuing Conversation on Law and Gospel*, edited by James Arne Nestingen, Albert B. Collver III, and John T. Pless, 135–67. St. Louis: Concordia, 2017.

Nestingen, James. "Distinguishing Law and Gospel: A Functional View." *Concordia Journal* 22, no. 1 (January 1996): 27–34.

———. "Speaking of the End of the Law." In *The Necessary Distinction: A Continuing Conversation on Law and Gospel*, edited by James Arne Nestingen, Albert B. Collver III, and John T. Pless, 169–251. St. Louis: Concordia, 2017.

Paulson, Steven, and Nicholas Hopman. "Christ, the Hated God." *Lutheran Quarterly* 30, no. 1 (Spring 2016): 1–27.

The Chicken or the Egg?

Michael J. Albrecht

Jim is my *Doktorvater*, and the title of my thesis was "The Faith-Life Legacy of a Wauwatosa Theologian—Prof. Joh. Ph. Koehler, Exegete, Historian and Musician."

The Wauwatosa Theology flourished in the Wisconsin Synod during the first three decades of the twentieth century. Chapter 2 of my thesis provides my "Description of the Wauwatosa Theology."

There are at least five different aspects of the Wauwatosa Theology: (1) fresh, independent exegetical study of the Holy Scriptures, (2) historical study of the interplay between the church and the world, (3) rigorous self-criticism, (4) comprehensive understanding of *Verstockung*, and (5) appreciation for art in all its many forms, including music (especially the Lutheran chorales), painting, literature, poetry, and architecture. The order in which these five elements are listed is not intended to imply a hierarchy of importance. Each of these five aspects is an essential component of the Wauwatosa Theology.

In its original historical context, the Wauwatosa Theology was set in contrast to the dominant role played by dogmatics in the Missouri Synod. The pulpit was one place where this contrast became evident. Professor Koehler neither claimed nor implied that preaching based on the orthodox Lutheran dogmaticians of the seventeenth century would result in false doctrine, but the Wauwatosa Theology insisted that preaching the doctrine learned in dogmatics class was not the same as sermons based on the preacher's own direct encounter with the Holy Scriptures.

Koehler anticipates a legitimate question from students and pastors who admire the orthodox Lutheran theologians from whom they have learned so much. How about the respect for our fathers and teachers whom we are to follow? I expect of my students that they do not accept one word from me without examination but that they under all circumstances permit themselves to be guided by the truth. I have the same opinion of the fathers. But that is something external. The esteem and reverence for the teachers is a much deeper, more delicate matter that cannot be satisfied with such externalities.[1]

It is in this spirit that I want to thank Jim and honor him with this consideration of the first aspect of the Wauwatosa Theology listed earlier, the proposal to do fresh, independent exegesis, unencumbered by dogmatic presuppositions.

The question goes back at least as far as Aristotle and Plutarch: Which came first, the chicken or the egg? You can find a video on YouTube that purports to settle this perennial question.[2]

We can ask a similar question about dogmatics and exegesis. Which comes first? If a dogmatic system is constructed for purposes of catechesis or seminary training, exegetical study must provide both the foundation upon which everything rests and the plumb line by which the builder checks to make sure the corners are square and the lines are true. At the same time, the good and faithful exegete will bring certain dogmatic assumptions to his task. It is neither possible nor desirable to banish dogmatic presuppositions absolutely. The exegete does not come to his task as *tabula rasa*.

Rather than pretending to approach the text with scientific objectivity, the exegete will be much better served by tuning his ear to listen for the music of the gospel. The melody of the good news can touch the heart in a way that transcends prose. The Word of God speaks both to the head and to the heart, and the music of the gospel conveys the message in a way that is both pleasant and profound.

---

[1] J. P. Koehler, "The Analogy of Faith," in *The Wauwatosa Theology—Volume 1* (Milwaukee: Northwestern, 1997), 268.

[2] https://www.youtube.com/watch?v=1a8pI65emDE.

For example, in an unpublished and undated[3] conference essay that is handwritten in English, Koehler presents his exegesis of Ephesians 1:3–14. An extended quotation is given here to demonstrate that Koehler is not merely making a few preliminary remarks. He is laying the foundation that he considers to be *sine qua non*.

A grand picture rises before the inner eye of the apostle in which are encompassed all thoughts of God with all that has come to pass in the universe from eternity before the foundation of the world and that will be henceforth to the consummation of God's grace in heaven forevermore. This St. Paul, near the end of his life, views with the highest emotion of awe and wonder, and his love and thankfulness rise to words and expressions that exceed all human comprehension but raise in the heart of the impressionable reader the same awe and wonder with the desire to learn the meaning of this revelation. That makes Paul a poet in the highest sense of the word. It is not enough for him to find words that give to our intellect notions and concepts of what cannot be comprehended, but he must even change his voice, as in Galatians 4:20, into song to touch the hearts of his readers. He sings, that the readers can hear it with their inner ear, for alone with the faith of the heart can they conceive of the glory of God's grace, which is the real subject of Paul's swan song.

I don't know of any commentary on the Epistle to the Ephesians that takes note of this poetic character of the letter in due manner. That must not embarrass us in our appreciation of it as though it were superfluous or useless or even dangerous to dwell on it at length. The remark has been made that our way is a sort of romanticism that may endanger the true care of correct interpretation of the scriptures, laying too much stress on the external form of the apostle's speech. That criticism is far beside the mark. On the contrary, where there is a sense for music and poetry as we find it everywhere in Holy Writ and also especially with Paul, this appreciation of it will find

---

[3] The essay is written on the back of what appear to be galley proofs of two articles by W. F. Beitz on "The Gospel of Nahum" and "The Gospel of Habakkuk." These two articles appeared in *Faith-Life* in the May 1931 and June 1931 issues.

response in such hearts, because that sense for gospel music also is with the Christian, εν Χριστω, in Christ.

So also the sense for art where it is found in scripture becomes a means of entering deeper into the meaning of the Spirit's word by understanding his mode of moving the spirit of the holy writers. Thereby it becomes a means in the hand of the Holy Ghost to win the heart for the Savior and to help fulfill the prayer of Paul, "that you may know what is the hope to which He has called you, what are the riches of His glorious inheritance in the saints, and what is the immeasurable greatness of His power toward us who believe" (Eph. 1:18–19 [ESV]).

The lack of understanding and appreciation in question seems to prove our contention that there is a tendency also among us, which approaches the scriptures with an undue intellectualism, which harps on the *Wortlaut* without the necessary knowledge of the origin and compass of any *Wortlaut*. I fear that the full understanding of what scripture means when it speaks of Inspiration is lost to such minds. They forego the pleasure and profit of understanding not only the working of the Holy Spirit in the heart of the holy writers but also the depth of their message, which is conveyed to us in poetical language through the Spirit.[4]

The music of the gospel has a way of crossing over cultural boundaries. Consider the impact of the music of Johann Sebastian Bach in contemporary Japan.[5] This also illustrates how music continues to speak to human hearts generations and even centuries after it was composed. Bach's music has been called "the fifth gospel." The Gospels of Matthew, Mark, Luke, and John have crossed even more boundaries and touched many more generations than the music of J. S. Bach. The followers of Jesus have grown from a small band of Galilean fishermen into the largest religion in the world today.

One of my beloved teachers at Wisconsin Lutheran Seminary said that dogmatics really should be taught and studied as church history—specifically as the history of exegesis. What can we learn

---

[4] Concordia Historical Institute, Koehler Family Collection, box 8, folder 137.

[5] Uwe Siemon-Netto, "J. S. Bach in Japan," *First Things*, no. 104 (June/July 2000): 15–17.

from our fathers in the faith? How did St. Augustine understand this portion of scripture? How did Martin Luther preach on this text?

In the study of theology, dogmatics and history occupy parallel positions: the former presenting the inner connection of the divine purpose of salvation and its revelation in the Word of God, the latter telling the story of the working out of the divine plan on Earth through the ages. The center of study is the exegesis of the scriptures, which forms the basis for both doctrinal theology and the teaching of history. Luther knew what he was saying when he urged that the study of the languages be fostered. The immediate word or words of the scriptures are more important than dogmatical terms. Likewise the human means of communication and assimilation of language, which are God's gifts too. The lexicon, grammar, logic, and psychology are not to be lightly brushed aside. But above all ranks the supreme and supernatural gift of the Spirit, faith, which through love leads us to understand God's thoughts to us-ward and to understand each other. That fact has been exemplified in history at different times and places, and we ought to learn to appreciate it. It is significant that such a great part of the scriptures is devoted to history, which fact alone should suffice to assign history its rightful place alongside dogmatics as a theological study.[6]

Neither dogmatics nor exegesis is best done in isolation. The interpenetration of exegesis, dogmatics and church history can protect the individual exegete or the individual dogmatician against himself. Listening to the *viva vox evangelii* in the Holy Scriptures and entering into conversation with our fathers and brothers in the faith (both reading what they have written and speaking to them in person) may help us avoid the temptation to fall in love with our own insights and passions. The old adage warns that if it is new, it probably isn't true, and if it is true, it probably isn't new—even though it may be new to you. Those who fail to learn from history are likely to repeat it.

Our Christian faith is historical. The Bible did not drop from heaven in our own time as a finished product. Both the dogmatician

---

[6] John Philipp Koehler, *The History of the Wisconsin Synod*, 3rd ed., ed. and largely trans. Karl Koehler (St. Cloud, Minnesota: 2004), 208.

and the exegete must be alert to the immediate and wider contexts in which a particular *sedes doctrinae* is found.

J. P. Koehler demonstrates how this can work in his examination of *Die Analogie des Glaubens*, which was published serially in the first three issues of the *Theologische Quartalschrift* in 1904.[7]

The Election Controversy had divided the Synodical Conference (which included both the Missouri Synod and the Wisconsin Synod) from the Ohio Synod and the Iowa Synod. In the aftermath of the controversy, a series of free conferences tried to bring the two sides back into conversation with each other. Both sides appealed to the analogy of faith in support of their positions, but there did not seem to be a clear definition of the analogy of faith on either side. Koehler observed,

The concept "mystery" and the approach to that was really at the bottom of the differences. Walther left the mystery of election alone; Schmidt and Stellhorn thought they could solve it. The old shop-worn idea of the analogy of faith, indeed, along the lines of the later 17th-century dogmaticians, was a mischief-maker on both sides, although in Walther's approach there was more of the freedom of Luther's exegetics than Melanchthon's way of handling the Scriptures. Franz Pieper's statement, that the doctrine of justification constituted the analogy of faith, calls this to mind. But Luther was a free spirit who cannot simply be parroted.[8]

The first free conference took place April 19–20, 1903, in Watertown, Wisconsin. It was open to pastors of all synods who subscribed to all of the Lutheran Confessions. There were between fifty and seventy-five men in attendance. The purpose of the meeting was "by the grace of God to bring about thru such frequent free conferences, if possible, unity of doctrine."[9]

The discussions were rather haphazard, since there was no definite program; the speakers talked at random, and because of the divergent conception of all the essential theological premises, there was

---

[7] The English translation cited here is by E. E. Sauer and was published in *Faith-Life* 62, no. 6 (1989) and 63, no. 1 (1990).

[8] Koehler, *History of the Wisconsin Synod*, 242.

[9] Ibid., 211–12.

no meeting of the minds. Toward the close of the last session, Pastor Doermann (an Ohio Synod pastor from Chicago) alluded to the analogy of faith, which had been given a different interpretation in the original Election Controversy by practically every one of the various spokesmen. Professor Franz Pieper declared that it was the doctrine of justification, meaning that all Lutheran teaching of scriptural truth must be in conformity with that doctrine. There was no time for further discussion, so Koehler, who had not taken the floor until then, moved that this hermeneutical principle called the analogy of faith be threshed out at the next meeting before the differences concerning Election were again taken up. That meeting was scheduled for September of the same year at Milwaukee.[10]

The men who participated in the second free conference were mainly Synodical Conference men from Milwaukee and the surrounding area. There was no debate on the analogy of faith and no exegetical study of Romans 12:6. Koehler's most vivid memory of the deliberations was a speech delivered by Dr. Adolf Hoenecke (director of the Wisconsin Synod seminary in Wauwatosa) "because it shows how the man worked in distinction from most of his contemporaries." Koehler summarizes Hoenecke's presentation with obvious appreciation.

Theological procedure in establishing Scriptural doctrine starts out with assembling all the passages that expressly deal with a certain doctrine. These are arranged according to the essential elements of the teaching as they appear in the Scriptural statements. Next is the study of this detail according to the wording of the scriptures. That wording comprises the meaning of the individual words according to their etymology and usage in the particular context. After these details have been established, they are assembled; then it will appear that, again and again, there are such utterances of the Spirit that remain paradoxical to our human reason or that we cannot adequately express. For the doctrine deals with the divine, eternal truths of salvation that on practically every count is beyond our comprehension and human concepts. And in want of the conception, our expression and language are likewise lame, so scripture itself time

---

[10] Ibid., 241.

and again resorts to figurative and parabolic speech. The dogmatician's business then is not to try to reconcile the Scriptural truth to
our human mind and make it plausible; that is the way of rationalism. For that reason, Paul in Romans 12 addresses himself to faith
that is wrought by the Holy Ghost. Faith can grasp what our human
mind rejects, which also remains a mystery because of the individual
differences of mental and spiritual makeup.[11]

Although Koehler had proposed a discussion of the analogy of
faith, Dr. Hoenecke chose to address biblical hermeneutics without
any specific reference to the analogy of faith. Koehler surmises that
Hoenecke "thereby, very likely unintentionally, showed that he had
no truck with it."

Since no one else seemed to be eager to provide a clear definition of the analogy of faith based on an exegetical study of Romans
12:6, Koehler proceeded to publish his exegetical article in the inau-
gural issues of the *Theologische Quartalschrift*.[12]

Koehler begins by drawing a contrast between the positions of
the two sides in the Election Controversy. The Synodical Conference
spokesmen (with whom Koehler aligns himself) maintain that
there must be no deviation from the grammatical-historical sense
of the Bible passages that speak to the doctrine in question. If there
are two passages that seem to contradict each other, one may not
modify the clear grammatical-historical meaning of either passage.
When purely human reason is not able to bring the clear and simple
sense of a passage into harmony with other doctrines of scripture,
the honest and humble exegete will report the difficulty and presume that the problem lies in himself and not in the Holy Scriptures.

Koehler calls the spokesmen for the Ohio Synod and the Iowa
Synod "the opponents," but he also says, "I hope that people have
enough confidence in me so that they do not believe that I am making a personal insinuation, but am seeking to set forth the contrast

---

[11] Ibid., 243.

[12] What follows is a free paraphrase of Koehler's article with occasional
footnotes to guide the reader who wishes to consult the original article. See footnote 1.

factually and bring it to an issue in order that the matter becomes clear."[13]

The opponents maintain that not all doctrines of scripture are expressed with the same measure of clarity. Justification by faith, the doctrine on which the church stands or falls, is absolutely clear. That is not the case with the doctrine of Election. All doctrines of scripture must be in harmony with each other, so it is the task of the theologian to discover this harmony. When a less clearly revealed doctrine appears to contradict a clear doctrine, the former must be interpreted according to the latter. This does not mean that the clear doctrines are the source from which other doctrines evolve, but it may mean that the clear and simple sense of certain passages will have to be adjusted to bring them into harmony with the clear doctrines.

Both sides claimed the term *analogy of faith* for their position. Both sides were convinced that their position was in agreement with the best teachers of the Lutheran Church. Koehler grants that the opponents can appeal to the seventeenth-century Lutheran dogmaticians, but he insists, "The stand of our Lutheran fathers is a question of only secondary importance." Koehler immediately explains, "There is in this order of presentation no lack of respect for our fathers or a deviation from what has hitherto been our theology. On the contrary, in it we are in full accord with the principle that always has been authoritative in such questions within the Lutheran church during the best of times."[14]

Romans 12:6

With chapter 12, the Apostle Paul begins the second (the practical) part of his letter with general admonitions to live in Christian sober-mindedness, σωφροσυνη. Koehler calls it "the first virtue of a Christian, especially in congregational life." In the Greek text of verse three, there is a play on the words φρονειν, υπερφρονειν, and σωφρονειν that we cannot imitate in German or in English. In one

---

[13] Koehler, "The Analogy of Faith," page 242.

[14] Ibid., 222.

way or another, some part of the original idea will be lost in trans-lation. In addition to the relationship between these three verbs, the comparison to the members of the human body in verse four and Paul's list of examples in verses 6–8 also come into consideration.

English Bible translations render υπερφρονειν as "think more highly of yourself." This fits the context, but in contrast to σωφρονειν, it also expresses a disposition that aims at greater things without recognizing any restraints or limitations. It is not necessary (as the English translation seems to indicate) that this unrestrained ambi-tion be consciously in a person's mind—although it often is.

The members of the human body differ from each other in out-ward appearance and in function, which may lead us to value some members more than others, but the diverse members of the human body are not independent of each other. It is the combination of diverse functions that leads to a higher goal.

Paul's list of examples begins with prophecy, followed by three items (service, teaching, and exhortation) that are limited by the gift itself, and the list concludes with generosity, zeal, and cheerfulness to stress the manner in which the gifts are to be used.

The context, therefore, indicates the breadth of meaning in Paul's use of υπερφρονειν. Unbridled ambition will transgress the limits set by God in a twofold way: by ignoring the diversity of gifts in the church and by going beyond the limit set by the gift itself.

The limitation for φρονειν so that it becomes σωφρονειν rather than υπερφρονειν is the μετρον πιστεως. "Faith" is always justifying faith in Christ Jesus, but "the measure of faith" is an expression Paul uses as a synecdoche, a part for the whole, to refer to the special gift God has given to the individual, different in kind and in degree from that given to any other. This trustful condition of the heart is the basis for every gift of faith.

Koehler paraphrases verse three as follows: "In his thoughts and actions, especially in his position as a member of the congrega-tion, a Christian is not, in using his special gift, to be so unrestrained that something of his own, his natural manner, which has not been created by the Holy Spirit, enters into his use of the gift."[15]

---

[15] Ibid., 227.

Luther's German translation of verse six is an interpretation that can only be understood in one way: that prophecy is to have its criterion in the faith, *fides quae creditur*. This is how the objective faith becomes the analogy of faith. The church fathers understood it this way, as did Calvin and Beza. Whenever the analogy of faith is discussed in the sixteenth and seventeenth centuries, it is understood as a norm of interpretation. It should not surprise us to find this presupposition reflected in Luther's German translation. But Koehler asserts, "I am convinced that our passage does not deal at all with a rule of interpretation, indeed, not even with something that might furnish a parallel to a rule of interpretation."[16]

The question is, What does Paul mean by προφητεια? From Luther on, the fathers understand this word as the interpretation of the Old Testament. They find a hermeneutical rule here that is easily applied to the interpretation of the whole Bible. But the Apostle Paul contrasts the gift of prophecy with the gifts of speaking in tongues and interpreting tongues (1 Cor. 12:10 and 14:18–19, 22). Unlike the one speaking in tongues, the prophet remains clearly conscious of himself and his surroundings and speaks directly to those who are present, especially the unbelievers who may come to see what is going on.

Prophets were not totally under the control of the Holy Spirit, and listeners were warned to listen critically (1 Cor. 14:29 and 1 John 4:1). This may explain why Paul admonishes the prophet to use the gift of prophecy κατὰ τὴν ἀναλογίαν τῆς πίστεως.

Remembering that the Apostle Paul is the author of both 1 Corinthians and Romans, it is reasonable to expect him to use the term προφητεια in a consistent manner, unless the context indicates otherwise. The context in Romans 12 is a list of spiritual gifts, which can easily be understood as linking prophecy with service, teaching, and exhortation. Koehler concludes, "Every other explanation appears to me to deviate unnecessarily from the immediate meaning of the words and context. . . . It is almost generally conceded that in verse 3 subjective faith is meant. One cannot see why in so close a

---

[16] Ibid., 228.

context this meaning is to be dropped in verse 6, especially since in the second instance the article is added."[17]

Koehler sees no need to understand "faith" in the objective sense as *fides quae creditur*. The meaning of this word is established by Greek etymology, the corresponding Hebrew word, and the way New Testament authors use the word. Koehler insists, "I am convinced that πίστις occurs in only one sense in the New Testament, in the subjective sense, and designates the saving faith. The distinction between *fides quae creditur* and *fides qua creditur* is justified in the later Church Latin, but not in the use of the word πίστις in Scripture."[18]

A historian can understand how the Latin word *fides* came to mean "the doctrine of the faith" in the Middle Ages. Roman influence on the intellectual life of the church brought about an externalized understanding of what scripture calls πίστις. Today we are the heirs of this development, and both German speakers and English speakers tend to take the Latin understanding for granted.

Koehler considers two passages often cited as examples of faith in the objective sense. Paul says, "Before faith came, we were held captive under the law" (Gal. 3:23). People were saying that Paul "is now preaching the faith he once tried to destroy" (Gal. 1:23). Koehler explains,

> Faith is not something that exists for and by itself, something that in the first passage *came into being* at the time of the apostles and in the other was *exposed to persecution*. No, in Paul's lively language the term is *personified* to a certain degree. In the first passage the *new economy* is meant in which *faith* is everything, it is the subject of preaching, all value is placed upon it over against the *previous economy of the law* in which *works* outwardly played a more important part. In the second passage the thing that Paul at first persecuted, and now was preaching, is the fact "*that people believe on Christ*," hence subjective, personal faith.[19]

---

[17] Ibid., 229–30.

[18] Ibid., 231.

[19] Ibid., 233.

Accordingly, the faith mentioned in Romans 12:6 is best under-stood as the subjective faith of the one who has the gift of prophecy. This passage furnishes no hermeneutical rule.

Since Romans 12:6 does not provide a biblical basis for the analogy of faith as a rule of interpretation, Koehler goes on to con-sider whether Christ Jesus employs or teaches any such principle. When the devil tempts Jesus, for example, by quoting scripture, "He will give his angels charge over you, and they will lift you up in their hands so that you do not strike your foot against a stone," Jesus responds with another Bible passage, "You shall not tempt the Lord your God." Jesus uses scripture to interpret scripture. How does this apply to the Election Controversy?

Repeatedly our opponents have affirmed that they desire of us no more than that we are not to overturn the doctrine of the uni-versal counsel of grace with our explanation of the passages dealing with predestination. This demand is justified, and we believe we are meeting it. But when our opponents in turn, with the doctrine of the universal counsel of salvation, weaken the contents of the passages dealing with predestination, they are assuredly falling into the same error. They are not doing what Christ is here practicing; they are not interpreting scripture with scripture in the manner in which this expression has hitherto always been understood.[20]

In the Sermon on the Mount, Christ reveals the deeper mean-ing of the law (Matt. 5:21–22, 27–28, 31–32, 33–37, 38–42, 43–48). He used a Bible story about David to explain the deeper meaning of the Sabbath (Matt. 12:1–8). He used the story of Moses at the burn-ing bush to teach the doctrine of the resurrection to the Sadducees (Matt. 22:23–32).

We have to acknowledge that it is not the purpose of these words in the Old Testament to proclaim this doctrine. But Christ and the Pharisees, too, did not invent this doctrine. It is the teaching of the Old Testament from its very beginning and stands in the most immediate relationship to the doctrine of redemption, as Paul writes to the Corinthians. What meaning does the gospel of him who was to bruise the serpent's head have in contrast to the punishment, "You

---

[20] Ibid., 245.

will surely die," if the resurrection is not the outcome? It is true, Christ does not say that God is revealing this doctrine in the words quoted, but He reminds the Sadducees that without this connection of thought, they are robbing the words of a part of their contents so that the words then have very little meaning. God had promised Abraham and Isaac not only that their seed was to possess Canaan but also that all generations on Earth were to be blessed through their seed. What can these words mean without connection with the first gospel?[21]

When Christ reveals the deeper meaning of a Bible passage, he does not change or adjust the meaning of the passage. He does not wield an analogy of faith to force disparate passages into harmony with each other. He simply testifies to the truth that the scripture cannot be broken because it is the very word of God.

The preaching and teaching of the apostles sounds like they have learned from Jesus. Peter says the Old Testament prophets studied their own writings to discover what the Spirit of Christ was predicting about the death and resurrection of Jesus (1 Pet. 1:10–12). Peter confidently asserts that the prophets were inspired by the Holy Spirit to give us the Holy Scriptures (2 Pet. 1:19–21).

The book of Hebrews is replete with exegesis that applies Old Testament types to the doctrine of our redemption by Christ Jesus.

The aged Apostle Paul commands Timothy, "Follow the pattern of the sound words that you have heard from me, in the faith and love that are in Christ Jesus" (2 Tim. 1:13). The fathers saw this as a parallel passage to Romans 12:6. They understood "faith and love" as a short summary of the doctrine Paul taught Timothy to preach. They speculated that Paul might even have written a brief digest for Timothy and referred to it when he said, "What you have heard from me in the presence of many witnesses entrust to faithful men, who will be able to teach others also" (2 Tim. 2:2).

Even if Paul speaks of words that are sound and certain, he is referring neither to clear passages of scripture in contrast with obscure passages nor to passages of scripture that contain the chief doctrine of Christ in contrast with more obscure doctrines or

---

[21] Ibid., 246.

something similar. On the contrary, he is referring to the *teaching* of the gospel in contrast to the *false doctrine* that deviates from the gospel and is an invention of man. Thus far, then, exegesis is not his subject. False teaching, however, adorns itself with the authority of the Old Testament. Therefore the apostle adds the warning against profane and old wives' fables, endless genealogies, vain jangling, doting about questions and strifes of words, perverse disputings, and supposing that godliness is gain.[22]

Koehler mentions Paul's distinction between the letter and the spirit (2 Cor. 3:6) and his warning against philosophy (Col. 2:8), but neither of these provides a hermeneutical rule akin to the presumed analogy of faith. Koehler concludes, "Thus I find in Scripture no explicit direction for what is called scientific exegesis. Scientific exegesis is always the result of learned studies which became necessary through temporal distance from Scripture. The studies have as their goal to *understand* Scripture, to *find* its meaning. The apostles, on the contrary, proclaim the word with divine power and on the basis of immediate revelation."[23]

Koehler calls the final section of his article "The Correct Method of Interpretation." He considers it "a matter of prime importance" to keep it simple so that the interpreter does not have to have a seminary education to understand the scriptures correctly. The "natural simplicity" of Christ and his apostles, later adopted by Luther and his colleagues, is to read the Bible the way you would read any other book, with only one special consideration—that the Bible is the infallible word of God.

Everybody concedes that exegesis must be in harmony with the chief doctrines of sin and grace. Luther often makes this demand. But . . . Luther is not expressing the hermeneutical rule that exegesis is thus dependent on dogmatics. He is more interested in a *practical* criterion for the unskilled too, by means of which they can easily recognize false doctrines. In this sense, Melanchthon even calls the Small Catechism the analogy of faith.[24]

---

[22] Ibid., 248.

[23] Ibid., 249.

[24] Ibid., 260.

The correct position of the Lutheran theologian is that he is a believer. As such, he assumes that Holy Writ is God's Word. That is not the result of his investigation, but *it is the foundation of his theology*. He also knows the teaching of the gospel, and this teaching is certain for him. This is also a dogmatic assumption. But we cannot conclude from this fact that he is now incapable of carrying on exegetical labors in an unbiased way and incapable of opening wide the ears of his understanding in order to learn clearly and without additions from other sources what the Holy Spirit has to say to him. On the contrary, an unbeliever will always inject his unbelief and will not be able to hear and understand without bias. On the other hand, it is indeed a difficult art (and yet again it is so simple but just for that reason so difficult) for the believing theologian to remain unbiased. Not everyone learns it. But hermeneutics must make this demand, and with God's grace we can also succeed in meeting it.[25]

It seems safe to say that the doctrine of Election is not a burning issue in most of our churches today. It is likely more neglected than controverted. And the analogy of faith is not a familiar concept to most churchgoing Lutherans anymore. So why bother with this topic? Two brief stories come to mind.

On a road trip from Wisconsin to California, I traveled with a brilliant young man who was a doctoral student at Notre Dame. He knew New Testament Greek much better than I did. We had plenty of time to discuss theology. I don't recall exactly what the topic was, but I still vividly remember quoting a Bible passage to him, confident that he would understand the clear and simple meaning of the passage, and he responded, "It means whatever the pope says it means."

I used to preach once a month at the Presbyterian Home, where I met a dear elderly lady of Baptist persuasion who told me that she enjoyed my sermons, but it bothered her when I made it sound like baptism saves us. I pointed her to 1 Peter 3:21, "Baptism doth also now save us." I knew she loved the good old King James Version,

---

[25] Ibid., 261.

but her response was, "It can't mean that!" She was convinced that only Jesus can save us, and to her that meant that baptism can't save anyone.

Aged King Solomon said it a long time ago, "There is nothing new under the sun" (Eccles. 1:9).

Luther's Heidelberg Disputation

A Little Course on Preaching

Dr. Ken Sundet Jones

Introduction

In April 2018, I sat down with a student who would soon walk across a stage, with parents and grandparents looking on, to receive a degree, a Grand View University diploma and a handshake from my university's president. Following a summer on staff at one of our Lutheran Bible camps, he'll head off to seminary in Austin, Texas, eager to soak up all the theology and biblical material they can throw his way and, we hope, be on the receiving end of an external call to ministry that matches the internal call already in place. But in April, we two sat across a table in our campus coffee shop to take up Luther's sixteenth-century equivalent of twenty-eight tweets about what makes for faithful theology and preaching. It seemed an appropriate conversation for us that day, because of a looming five-hundredth anniversary a couple weeks later.[1]

With a freshly minted master of arts and philosophy, Wittenberg Augustinian friar Leonhard Beier set out on a journey from Wittenberg with Martin Luther in April 1518. The university town in Saxony had begun to be the locus of fomenting change within

---

[1] This article is written not only with my student Joel Timmons in mind but also with fond memories of many such conversations with my own dear teacher and mentor, James Nestingen, through the years.

the Roman church and the Holy Roman Empire.[2] This journey
took the two black-robed and tonsured monks through Leipzig,
on to Coburg and Würzburg, and finally to Heidelberg.[3] There the
Augustinian hermits of Luther's order had gathered at the university
for their General Chapter. After the controversy on indulgences that
led to the Ninety-Five Theses almost six months earlier, the controversial university professor had been asked to present a summary of his
teaching, and Beier had been given the honor of providing a defense
of the new set of theses Luther presented.[4] The audience on April 26
included those in authority in the order as a matter of course but
was also open to university students, citizens of the city on the
banks of the Neckar, and invited dignitaries from the Palatinate and
beyond.[5]

What those in attendance heard from Luther—and presumably from Beier (in particular in the twenty-eight theological theses)[6]—in Robert Kolb's words "constituted a paradigm shift" in our
understanding of God's relationship with human creatures[7] and for
those with discerning minds marked the first appearance of the

---

[2] Dennis Bielfeldt, "Heidelberg Disputation: 1518" (henceforth Heidelberg), in *The Annotated Luther, Volume 1: The Roots of Reform*, ed. Timothy J.
Wengert (Minneapolis: Fortress, 2015), 67ff.

[3] Andrea van Dülmen, *Luther-Chronik: Daten zu Leben und Werk* (Munich:
Deutscher Taschenbuch Verlag, 1983), 34.

[4] Martin Luther, "Heidelberg Disputation," in *The Annotated Luther, Volume, 1: The Roots of Reform*, ed. Timothy J. Wengert (Minneapolis: Fortress,
2015), 80.

[5] Attendees included Luther's university classmate and friend Johannes
Lang, his own university professor Bartholomew Arnoldi, Heidelberg stu-
dent and later Strasbourg reformer Martin Bucer, and Johannes Brenz of
Schwäbisch Hall. Heidelberg, 71, 79.

[6] In the theological theses, Luther discussed matters that inform the pastoral calling of proclamation of the gospel—his ultimate concern—while the
philosophical theses that followed showed how the Aristotelian philosophical
traditions he received from Scholastic theology served to limit that proclamation. See Heidelberg, 73ff.

[7] Robert Kolb, "Luther on the Theology of the Cross," *Lutheran Quarterly*
16 (2002): 443ff.

full theological program that matured into what we've come to call the Reformation. This was an anthropological and Christological as well as a homiletical and pedagogical point of view that drove what happened during the next two and a half decades of Luther's career. It was placed in the hands of Beier's generation and set the parameters that guided their own preaching and teaching. For us who exist in a church and wider culture in an equally fractious age that faces its own Babylonian captivity,[8] Luther's Disputation serves as a primer that establishes metrics by which the faithful—whose primary calling, Luther later argued, was to judge doctrine[9]—might assay the truth and purity of the church's preachers, teachers, and adjudicatories, not to mention our own delivering of the goods in the mutual conversation and consolation of the saints.[10] Luther in Heidelberg defined and defended what Melanchthon in Article V of the Augsburg Confession would label the Office of Preaching.[11]

In Jesus' parable of the mustard seed (Luke 13:18–19), our Lord points to the seed's *telos* as a tree in whose branches many birds may make their nests. It is not too great a leap to argue that in contemporary North American Christianity, the birds on the Lutheran branch may have found a comfortable perch, but their song has become

---

[8] See Martin Luther, "The Babylonian Captivity of the Church," in *The Annotated Luther: Volume 3, Church and Sacraments*, trans. Erik H. Herrmann (Minneapolis: Fortress, 2016), 9ff. Luther's title refers to the ancient Israelites' defeat by Babylonian forces and forced removal to exile in their enemy's land—all of which came about because of God's judgment on their own faithlessness. The best scriptural passage to show the effect of life in exile is the angry lament of Psalm 137.

[9] Martin Luther, "Das eyn Christliche versamlung odder gemeyne recht und macht habe, alle lere zu urteylen und lerer zu beruffen, eyn und absusetzen, Grund und ursach aus der schrifft," in *Luthers Werke*, Kritische Gesamtausgabe, ed. J. F. K. Knaake, et al., 57 vols. (Weimar: Böhlau, 1883ff.), 11, 401ff.

[10] Martin Luther, "Smalcald Articles" III:4 "Concerning the Gospel," in *The Book of Concord: The Confessions of the Evangelical Lutheran Church* (henceforth BoC), ed. Robert Kolb and Timothy J. Wengert (Minneapolis: Fortress, 2000), 319.

[11] Philip Melanchthon, "The Augsburg Confession," *BoC*, 40.

garbled by the taint of works righteousness on the one hand and libertinism and licentiousness on the other. The situation not only leaves the church and its public proclamation in a position of weakness and often unfaith; it also leaves the sinful and the broken flying in a ceaseless murmuration[12] because potential life-giving perches offer a series of either inauthentic and empty promises or untenable demands. If the church in North America faces its own Babylonian captivity, the way out comes not through human endeavors that fulfill the hope of a utopian dream of either liberal or conservative justice nor by mystical practices, by the descendants of Ignatius Loyola and his spiritual disciplines, or by an extension of Philipp Jakob Spener's pietistic conventicles.

Instead, if we are to be true to Luther, who was himself steeped in Paul's assertion of justification by faith, then in an age when "steeples are falling,"[13] what is called for is the only thing that has ever had the power to change hearts and raise people to new life. Less than two years after the general chapter in Heidelberg, as Luther endured the sixty days following a messenger's delivery of the papal bull of excommunication that demanded his recantation, he penned "Freedom of a Christian," in which he asserted,

> One thing and one thing alone is necessary for the Christian life, righteousness, and freedom, and that is the most holy word of God, the Gospel of Christ. . . . Therefore, we may consider it certain and firmly established, that the soul can lack everything except the word of God. Without it absolutely nothing else satisfies the soul. But when soul has the word, it is rich and needs nothing else, because the word of God is the word of life, truth, light, peace, righteousness, salvation,

---

[12] The murmuration of flocks of starlings usually occurs without any leader and as a defense mechanism against a nearby predator such as a falcon. The metaphor works well in describing human creatures beset by the evil one. See Andrea Alfano, "How Do Starling Flocks Create Those Mesmerizing Murmurations?," The Cornell Lab of Ornithology: All About Birds, accessed April 3, 2018. https://www.allaboutbirds.org/how-do-starling-flocks-create -those-mesmerizing-murmurations/.

[13] Nikolai F. S. Grundtvig, "Built on a Rock the Church Shall Stand," in *Lutheran Book of Worship* (Minneapolis: Augsburg, 1978), hymn #365.

joy, freedom, wisdom, power, grace, glory, and every imaginable blessing.[14]

If this is so, then we may inquire how this word actually happens, how it can possibly render the transformation of the faithless, how it can ever bring about God's declaration in Deuteronomy 32:39: "See now that I, even I, am he, and there is no god besides me; I kill and I make alive; I wound and I heal."[15] Luther's continual and abundant outflow from his desk to Herr Kinko's local print shop reveals him organizing his thinking, for the task of writing is a matter of organized thinking. In the Heidelberg Disputation, he ordered his thoughts into a series of theses that, for us, are in turn able to organize our own language in a way that it becomes a living word from God that accomplishes this killing and raising act.

Apart from the gospel that took on such cussed sinners as the two us, one of the things that initially bound Jim Nestingen and me together was the fact that we came from prairie stock: Jim from North Dakota and Saskatchewan and me from West River country and the Black Hills in South Dakota. We knew the land, brooked no fussiness, and ran close to the ground. My grandparents were cattle ranchers, and the menfolk on our family's ranch faced the constant task of mending fences. The "bob wire," as we called it, needed to be restretched, retacked to fence posts, or replaced from pasture to pasture across all four seasons. The reason for fence lines and the energy spent to keep them in good shape was to protect our ranch's costly investment in livestock. One night, my grandfather drove home after playing banjo at a country dance, and he hit a stray heifer, killed the cow, and totaled the vehicle. A significant investment in beef and Buick was lost, spread across the twenty-foot width of the gravel road. Our God seeks to protect a similar and considerable divine

---

[14] Martin Luther, "The Freedom of a Christian," in *The Annotated Luther, Vol. 1: The Roots of Reform*, trans. Timothy J. Wengert (Minneapolis: Fortress, 2015). 490–91.

[15] Harold W. Attridge, ed., *The HarperCollins Study Bible* (San Francisco: Harper One, 2006). All further scriptural references will be taken from this source.

investment made when God in Christ spent Himself on the cross in order that the good news might be delivered. What the Heidelberg Disputation does is provide a fence line within which the church's public proclamation and God's investment are protected and profitable. It proffers guidelines within which sinners might hear the word in its truth and purity[16] and functions as Luther's little preaching course.

The Perils of Pulpit Advice

I live in a city with a daily newspaper that has an august and much-vaunted history. Its Pulitzer Prizes are proof of the kind of journalism its reputation was built from. Sadly, it is no longer an independent publication but is now owned by a media conglomerate whose flagship has led the charge in simplifying news, decreasing the depth of analysis, and pandering to ever-shortening reader attention spans. The paper has been reduced to running stories that are mere lists of recommendations of bars in the metro where you can drink green beer on St. Patrick's Day or "30 Places to Land Mexican Fare" (egregiously ignoring my favorite). The state of preaching one encounters in the church today has fared little better. What ought to be a keen-edged proclamation is instead a set of advice for successful suburban religion, a mere presentation of information about the Bible and its times, or, worst of all, the delivery of biblical principles for growing your inner spirit. The implication of all of it is that by being offered easily digestible homiletical crumbs, the ill-informed sermon audience can assemble a personal concatenation of ideas and fashion a pleasant future for themselves, their children, and their community. Such a sermon recommends that the sin-sick soul find a balm not in the Gilead present in Christ crucified and risen but in the soothing ointment of the self.

All of it stems from an unholy attraction to the law as the vehicle for salvation and cannot find a way to leap from the letter to

---

[16] Martin Luther, *Luther's Small Catechism* (Minneapolis: Augsburg, 1940), 14.

the Spirit.[17] Thus we can never leave the realm of the law's ceaseless yammering, and, neglecting its accusation, we avoid its judgment and never truly require Christ's benefits. All the bromides and nice words about the righteous causes we might take up in the world wind up being a fervent to-do list for a religious in-group. In the Heidelberg Disputation, Luther begins with a word designed to stop such preaching in its well-worn tracks: "The Law of God, the most salutary doctrine or life, cannot advance human beings on their way to righteousness, but rather hinders them."[18] Luther argued from the start in the Disputation that good works, while good, can't do the actual work of justifying sin-sick souls.[19] Here's how it often floats off a preacher's tongue: "God is love. Vote Democrat." Or "God is good. Ban abortion." I confess that whenever a pulpiteer gives me a task, I either think I can't possibly attain such holy ranks of true believers or think, "Been there, done that, didn't even get a t-shirt for it." I spent my college years at a good Lutheran school praying to become more, to do more, to be a really religious person. But I never spoke in tongues, and praising the Lord never became my *lingua franca*. I just wound up more worried, more anxious, and more aware of my sin. Pulpit advice and trying to get people to choose to be better and more worthy recipients of God's love is a fruitless endeavor. Progress in attaining goodness and achieving self-repair is an illusion.

For Luther in the Disputation, the law is a good (salutary) thing—quite helpful for working toward safety, peace, security, and order in God's kingdom in this world. But the problem with the law is that I want to apply it to God's other realm, where Christ alone is the hinge. So when preachers urge me to look to the law to gain righteousness, they wind up dissing Christ and what he did on the cross. Which sounds like blasphemy and adds sin to sin. Trusting in

---

[17] In his commentary on Psalm 83:10, Luther distinguished between the letter and the spirit, "or the judgment of the cross by which the flesh is to be crucified, judged, and condemned, indeed, by which the world and its prince are judged." LW 39.

[18] Heidelberg, 81.

[19] Thesis 3: "Although the works of Human beings always seem attractive and good, it is nevertheless probable that they are mortal sins." Ibid., 82.

the law and the good works they demand leads me to turn away from Christ and toward either my own navel or my *curriculum vitae*.

Luther wants to disabuse me of this by undercutting the law. As he says in his Romans commentary, the first task of a true theologian is to eliminate the good[20]—that is, to trash my idea of gaining goodness anywhere other than at the foot of the cross. To put it another way, by eliminating the law as a means for attaining righteousness before God, Luther begins God's two-part process of killing and making alive, wounding and healing. If Luther is right in "The Freedom of a Christian" that we have two selves in us (an old outer person of the flesh and a new inner person of the spirit),[21] then destroying the law (and the attendant good works that it requires) as the agent of salvation will destroy the old person in me. When that happens, I'll finally have ears to hear (Mark 4:9), and I'll be ripe for the proclamation of the gospel. And now we've landed in the territory of Luther's theology of the cross, where we discover God most active in death and brokenness, weakness and despair.[22] When I've got "plenty of nothing,"[23] no good deeds, no pleasant pieties, no claim on righteousness, then Christ who has all that good stuff will sign it over to me.

The take-home for preachers then is to remember Luther's words later in the Disputation that "the Law says, 'Do this,' and it is never done."[24] In preaching law, religious do-gooder-ism, pious pronouncements, and Christian job descriptions, the preacher places

---

[20] "The chief purpose of this letter [to the Romans] is to break down, to pluck up, and to destroy all wisdom and righteousness of the flesh. This includes all the works which in the eyes of people or even in our own eyes may be great works. No matter whether these works are done with a sincere heart and mind, this letter is to affirm and state and magnify sin, no matter how much someone insists that it does not exist, or that it was believed not to exist." Martin Luther, "Commentary on Romans" (1:1), LW 25:135.

[21] Luther, "Freedom," 489ff.

[22] See section "Preachers of the Cross."

[23] George Gershwin (1898–1937), "I've Got Plenty of Nothing," *Porgy and Bess*, 1934.

[24] Thesis 26, Heidelberg, 84.

the sermon's hearers in an untenable position. What's more, as Luther declared in Thesis 3, they have propelled the sinners before them into "mortal sins."[25] In the meantime, Christ, who is eager to bestow mercy on the godless and despairing, sits waiting in the wings never to walk on stage and speak his word. *Caveat proclamator!* The Lord will not be hindered. If a preacher prefers to present wisdom and law, Christ is not above descending to lesser venues where less holy orators not only know their lack of worldly wisdom but in spite of such lack also are willing to deliver the inheritance from the First-Born. Pulpits are not the Sondheim Theatre on Broadway, and if a preacher seeks only to speak brilliant wisdom, Christ is likely to show up in a ratty community theater instead, where clumsy thespians miss cues but understand what the playwright is up to.

The Farce of Free Will

In probably his most challenging thesis in the Disputation, Luther said that the idea of free will is a farcical idea. It "exists in name only."[26] So much of what passes as preaching makes the fatal assumption that those who hear the preacher's words will act on them—that is, if the preacher might only convince them to use their free will to accomplish the task laid out from the pulpit. This follows right in the footsteps of our first parents in the Garden, whose fall into sin depended on this desire for free will. I like thinking of my will as free, because it allows me autonomy and the chance to occupy my own godly throne. But that idea works only apart from God's sovereignty. If God is God, then all things happen apart from my puny attempts to wring change out of the world around me. It's what Paul is talking about in the discussion of predestination in Romans 8.[27] Only if my will is captive and bound would there be any reason for

---

[25] Thesis 3: "Although the works of human beings always seem attractive and good, it is nevertheless probable that they are mortal sins." Ibid., 82.

[26] Thesis 13: "Free will, after [the fall into] sin, exists in name only, and when 'it does what is within it,' it commits a mortal sin." Ibid., 82.

[27] "For those whom he foreknew he also predestined to be conformed to the image of his Son, in order that he might be the firstborn within a large family."

something as utterly drastic as God predestining the cross, my Lord's
death on it, my own death, and my resurrection brought about by
preaching the gospel. Thus if a preacher's words hinge on me ginning
up my will and choosing a better path, then there will be little room
for Christ's work in this scheme. While the words will sound good,
they will blaspheme the cross because they will imply that Jesus' final
breath on Calvary was powerless, and what is required is something
I add to it.

In Thesis 13, Luther speaks of the so-called free will doing
"what is within it" to do and in Thesis 16 goes further: "The person
who believes that one can obtain grace 'by doing what is in oneself' adds sin to sin and thus becomes doubly guilty." When it rolls
off the tongue of a preacher, the idea of free will always involves
good works and implies what Scholastic theologians in the generations before Luther, including his own teachers at the University
of Erfurt, asserted as the job of a serious Christian in the Roman
church. "*Facete quod in te est*" (Do what is within you to do).[28] If I
attempt to do these things with my free will, my unfaithful desire
to seize my autonomy is revealed, and the preacher has asked me to
seize something that belongs to Jesus. "Do what is within you" feeds
my penchant for coveting what is the Lord's. So thinking I can step
up to the divine judge's banc and present a *curriculum libero arbitrio*
of my good works and the many times I've sent Jesus' body and blood
down my gullet and, in return, get some grace doled out as a result
of this evidence, just makes things worse. Luther called this "going
to God's judgment seat."[29] If I'm moved to follow this preacher's dictum, God doesn't have a problem with me trying that, but Luther

---

And those whom he predestined he also called; and those whom he called he
also justified; and those whom he justified he also glorified" (Rom. 8:29–30).

[28] See E. Jane Dempsey Douglass, *Justification in Late Medieval Preaching: A
Study of John Geiler of Keiserberg* (Leiden: Brill, 1966), 142.

[29] "Righteousness consists of this, that having known and judged ourselves,
we do not despair before God's judgment seat, before which we plead guilty in
this petition, but that we seek refuge in God's mercy and firmly trust that he
will deliver us from our disobedience to his will. He who humbly confesses his
disobedience and sin, who admits that he deserves the sentence and sincerely
asks God for mercy, not doubting that it will be granted, is righteous before

knew from his own painfully rigorous experience that it won't work. So his admonition to preachers in the Disputation is to say, in so many words, "Let me save you some trouble. Quit telling people to do the *facete* stuff all together." Instead, preachers ought to assume their hearers' will is captive to themselves in sin. When that happens, preachers can begin to see that their hearers' attempts at doing anything are useless flailing before the judgment seat of God and, perhaps, will instead point in a new direction: to the mercy seat of God.

The Gift of Despair

Our contemporary culture has a veneer that is regularly polished to a fine sheen in pulpits on Sunday morning. The culture has taught us to seek glory, success, and status, and we don't much like a preacher who denies Nike's dictum to "Just do it." Preachers fear that sermons become audience downers by not presenting people the possibility of improvement. Despair is a homiletical *persona non grata*. But in the Heidelberg Disputation, Luther was unafraid of despair— although a specific kind of humble despair he called *Anfechtung*[30]— "for it arouses the desire to seek the grace of Christ."[31] In Romans, Paul uses a trope that appears frequently in diatribes of the day— the assumption of an imaginary audience asking him questions as he makes his argument. After Thesis 16 in the Heidelberg Disputation, Luther seems to do the same thing. Thesis after thesis he's been

---

God." Martin Luther, "An Exposition of the Lord's Prayer for Simple Laymen," LW 42:43.

[30] This German idea with many different meanings all rolled into one word is notoriously difficult to translate into English. *Anfechtung* can mean trouble, turmoil, temptation, terror. What Luther is getting at, however, is moments when our sense of our self in relation to others—particularly God— is brought into question and pushes us to question the why and wherefore of the Hidden God. In his autobiographical summary in the introduction to his Latin Works, he refers to his experience as a friar before understanding justification as having had a "troubled conscience." LW 34:336.

[31] Thesis 17: "Nor does speaking in this manner give cause for despair, but rather for humility, for it arouses the desire to seek the grace of Christ." Heidelberg, 82.

knocking out the struts that support my reasonable, free-willing, reward-demanding, glorious self. By Thesis 16, Luther has brought us to a point where we might want to sing the musical *Avenue Q*'s "It Sucks to Be Me."[32] When preachers don't allow us a single move of our own, and our first reaction is despair. Like the disciples following Jesus' admonition to the rich young man to sell everything and give the money to the poor, we have to ask who could possibly do it (Matt. 19:25–26). But in this thesis, Luther bids the hearers of such preaching to hang on, to know that this feeling is one side of the coin of God's justifying word.

The promise here is that faithful preaching will make something happen. Luther calls it desire, which is the same human action as willing, but now those who hear such preaching are set up—compelled—to act counter to their own will. With my own will made nothing and the universe despising a vacuum, God's own will can move into my impious heart. I've known God's will all along (both in divine law and in God's working in the structures of society), but I have broken every bit of law between bookends one and ten of the Commandments. The law simply hasn't worked. It doesn't have the ability to grab my heart. I'm so captured by my own autonomy that God has wrenched it from me. Like he did with the sacrifice of Isaac, the yearned-for son of Sarah and Abraham, he takes my will and gives it back as it should be, in line with his own. Luther's Disputation now begins to look an awful lot like a law/gospel sermon in its structure. In this thesis and the next few, there is a turning point. A good sermon will not give the old sinner in me an inch and will instead take me to the verge of despair. The preacher is not to take all hope from me but to give me the one thing, the only thing, the only person who is my hope. Jesus. Thus Thesis 18: "It is certain that one must utterly despair of oneself in order to be made fit to receive the grace of Christ."[33]

---

[32] Robert Lopez and Jeff Marx, *Avenue Q, the Musical: The Complete Book and Lyrics of the Broadway Musical* (Milwaukee: Applause Theatre & Cinema Books, 2010).

[33] Heidelberg, 83.

Lest the preacher be afraid of people's despair, there's a big difference between utterly despairing, which most who read the thesis think of, and despairing of yourself, which is what Luther actually wrote. He's been harping on "do what is within you to do." He's not after my despondency but my relinquishing the idea that I can do the justifying deed. There are all kinds of benefits Christ is ready to dole out, but I won't desire them, at least not under his terms. They're either completely free or not for me. To despair of myself is to know the futility of my pious gestures, my insistence on my will's autonomy, and the taint of sin that sticks to my every good intention. I've walked my own dark road of clinical depression and have been known to pop a Wellbutrin for good measure. Luther doesn't want anybody to follow that trail. Jesus is intent on pouring Himself out for me, but if I'm full of myself (the goal of much preaching), I make a poor vessel for holding his life.

Preachers ought to take note that preaching with the Heidelberg Disputation at its core will place them directly in Opposite Day. In this thesis, Luther takes the preacher right into Christ's promise that the last will be first (Matt. 20:16) and that those who lose their life will gain it (Mark 8:35). Thesis 18's talk of despair and desire is riddled with grace and mercy but only when a sermon's hearers know how riddled *they* are with sin and its payout, death. When my students finally hear what Luther is saying, they become big fans. And they become impatient with the same old self-improvement schemes and dreary requirements of religion, including those dished up by both well-meaning Unitarians and limp Lutheran preachers. To despair of ourselves is to become steeped in the last half of Romans 8, where the apostle says out loud what I know in my bones: when it comes to the world's incessant demands, I'm like a sheep to be slaughtered. But Luther's kind of despair is also the moment where a sermon's hearers can at last be persuaded to believe that nothing's going to snatch them away. Not things above, nor angels, nor principalities, nor depression, nor demons, nor my inability to get things right. Jesus has his eye open for empty-handed sinners.

The preacher's penchant to avoid this kind of despair and instead dole out life lessons isn't much different from the reaction of Erasmus of Rotterdam to Luther's teaching. The great Humanist would have given preachers props for thinking about lessons to be learned. Luther, however, in spite of cherishing Aesop's Fables,[34] wasn't on board with lessons, morals, philosophy, or worldly wisdom. Erasmus was out to create a program that would educate people into righteous behavior. For Luther, it was a good move for life in this world but not at all in regard to matters of faith. Worse, if the lesson comes with God as the teacher, then God is capricious and pernicious, inflicting terrible demands on me. Luther argued that apart from Christ, this is the bottom-line God you'll get with life lessons. Which is what set him completely at odds with Erasmus[35] several years later, and which is also the problem with preachers who insist on delivering "biblical truths" as if a sinner like me will gladly and successfully put them into practice.

But if a preacher can be weaned from lessons and proclaim a revealed God crucified and risen, then adages, bromides, and morals to the story can be left in the infertile soil they were planted in with the fruits of the Spirit that only need Christ's death and my despair to sprout and become part of God's intended harvest. This is what makes a preacher who is a true theologian.

Preachers of the Cross

We need to be careful when we talk about theology and preaching. In Thesis 19, Luther argued, "That person does not deserve to be called a theologian who perceives the invisible things of God as understandable on the basis of those things that have been made [Rom 1:20]."[36] "Theologian" is as misunderstood a word as "evangelical." Thesis 19 begins Luther's attempt at clarifying matters and staving off preaching that presents ideas that are well-considered and philosophically

---

[34] "It is a result of God's providence that the writing of Cato and Aesop have remained in the schools, for both are significant books. . . . Aesop contains the most delightful stories and descriptions. Moral teaching, if offered to young people, will contribute much to their edification." Martin Luther, *Table Talks*, LW 54: 210.

[35] E. Gordon Rupp and Philip S. Watson, eds., *Luther and Erasmus: Free Will and Salvation* (Philadelphia: Westminster, 1959).

[36] Heidelberg, 83.

reasonable—what my ranch country kin would call "thunk through." But when we use our reason to search out what lies beyond the chasm between the *deus absconditus* and us, we are tempted to treat the results of our quest as the *Ding an sich* of preaching.

Yet such theological reasoning is the human work, the "natural principle" in Thesis 2, that accused me of thinking of it as pristine. So in this thesis, Luther sets up a pit for us homiletical Wile E. Coyotes to fall into. We don't get to call ourselves theologians because true theologians don't get the title through their own understanding or effort.[37] Instead, it happens when God kills off the old self-satisfied and self-justified sinners in the pulpit and in the pews. It's going to take a cross (his and ours) to make us into theologians. However brilliant a preacher's reasoning is, in its ability to justify sinners, it hasn't even reached the bottom step of the pulpit. In fact, it is something utterly unreasonable (yet similarly and inversely attractive to the despairing in Thesis 18) that does this work: "The person deserves to be called a theologian, however, who understands the visible and 'backside' of God [Exod. 33:23] seen through suffering and the cross."[38]

This last winter, my cup of hate for the season and much more had runneth over. Month after month of snow and ice, storm after storm approaching from the west is only the surface of my hatred. I hate preaching from the same lectern in the same nondescript funeral home for three funerals—my father, sister, and aunt—in sixteen months. I hate grading. I hate that half the people in my marriage will one day be widowed. And lots more. Most of all, I hate that these things are the *only* way to become a true theologian and ever know something of Christ's mercy. With the stark contrast of Thesis 19, Luther halts a preacher who attempts to know God through speculative reasoning or analogies with worldly things. God certainly wants to be found . . . but only where God wants to be revealed.

The only place it's safe to be revealed that won't result in the incineration of this sinner with almighty goodness or the explosion

---

[37] See explanation of Article III of the Apostles' Creed: Martin Luther, "Small Catechism," *BoC*, 35.

[38] Ibid., 84.

my prideful ego is in thin places of life. These are places of emptiness and sorrow. It's through disregarded things that seem to have
no power. It's in the suffering servant who was despised, rejected
(Handel lovers may now sing the aria). It's in His word that arrives
in ephemera—water, bread, wine, and air moving across the lips of a
preacher to announce absolution. And it's in my suffering and death.
What all these things have in common is that life there is so thin
that I have lost my agency; I have had my power wrenched away,
and what's reasonable is turned over like the merchants' tables at the
temple in Jerusalem (Matt. 21:12). This is why the best preachers
are those who've both suffered themselves and had a preacher in the
midst of it. The place to best learn and most easily hear the gospel (and, in turn, preach it) is in the middle of life's crucible: in our
brokenness, failures, and death. In other words, if preachers want
people to become the strongest witnesses of the gospel and the ones
who have come to know what's what, then people suffering under
the cross must be the primary target of their preaching.

The same is true for identifying and shaping budding preachers. Coming out of a family just nominally connected to the church
and certainly coming to seminary with a lame German major and
never having taken a philosophy course or understood the meaning of hermeneutics and eschatology, I was an unlikely candidate to
become a pastor. But what I did have was the cross of growing up
amid dysfunction and violence, not to mention a growing awareness of what I think of as my own crapitude. When I sat in a classroom my first term of seminary and heard Gerhard Forde declare
the deed of salvation done for me, I was hooked. I had those "ears
to hear" (Mark 4:23). I wanted more. And I wanted to know how to
speak this same word. It occupied me for the rest of my seminary
days and through six years working on a doctorate. When preachers
preach the gospel to people under the cross, sinners hear the Lord's
voice as Jesus promised that His sheep would (John 10:27). They
won't mistake glory and success and prosperity and morality as the
gospel. Those things can't heal. They can't change hearts. And they
can't raise the dead. These are the theologians of the cross Luther
described in Thesis 21—those who discern God's hand at work in
their *Anfechtungen*. We ought not call pastors without seeing if they
know how to do this. Better yet, don't call anyone to be a preacher

who hasn't discovered their own ears to hear in the midst of trials and turmoil.

Luther has already established the doing of good works for salvific reasons as an evil that compounds sin, so it follows logically that he throws shade at preachers and teachers (he puts them in the category of a "theologian of glory") who lay the burden of fulfilling the law on those who are desperate to be relieved of it. They call evil good and good evil, not imagining that their free will's striving could be anything but salutary (see Thesis 1). These preachers are true Pelagians, and that might just be the most dangerous and prevalent heresy of our own day. Once again, let the proclaimer beware! Do not trust your instincts, wisdom, or advice-rendering abilities, for God's mercy is to be found under the sign of its opposite—the works of God that "always seem unattractive and evil."[39] Luther points preachers in this direction in Thesis 21: "A theologian of glory calls evil good and good evil. A theologian of the cross calls a thing what it actually is."[40] Yet we ought not take this thesis as permission to be the kind of theologians whose every move is to call BS on any idea we don't agree with. Having served a congregation across the street from a state capitol, I know the temptation to expound on the spiritual implications of proposed legislation from across the political aisle. But preachers have no particular wisdom on politics, economics, or "who wore it best." To call a thing what it is refers specifically to good works (helpful in this world but something on the order of manure for gaining ground in the next) and the masks of suffering and death (totally helpful in both of God's realms) behind which God is working an alien work.

One Little Word

Luther's "A Mighty Fortress Is Our God" includes a phrase that should come as a great and defiant hope for Christ's proclaimers. After first detailing the Evil One's machinations and power, Luther declared,

---

[39] Thesis 4: "Although the works of God always seem unattractive and evil, they are nevertheless really immortal merits." Heidelberg, 82.

[40] Ibid., 84.

"One little word subdues him."[41] The gospel seems like such a little thing, and this word appears to have no power over the forces that are arrayed against it, but as it sneaks up to deliver an unsuspecting world, it is truly the only thing that has any power at all. While this "little word"—the promise in proclamation and the sacraments— seems to be nothing at all, preachers must trust that this little noth- ing is the very thing the Spirit uses to gain what it desires. In the Heidelberg Disputation, Luther declared that God's love does not find, but creates, that which is pleasing to it.[42] God's love is the sword protruding from the mouth of the pale rider at the denouement of Revelation (19:15), bringing the word to bear. This love, this word, this rider named Jesus *is* Aristotle's unmoved mover who creates what it desires: New Eves and New Adams.

When I sit in a pew on a Sunday morning and in too many waking moments the rest of the week, I long to be made new. I have this damnable and undeniable history I drag along in my wake, long- ing that something will change and knowing I can't do it myself. I sit there not caring a whit about a clergy shortage but only that there be *one single preacher* with the guts to declare it to me. If I am to fear and love God, as Luther's explanations of the Commandments in the catechism declare,[43] my fear and love must come from something external, from a word outside of me that gives what it says.[44] My love of God—my true love, that is, and not some sham sentimentality that raises a hand in worship toward things above—is created when the word comes to me from without. It snatches away my captivation with myself and instead captivates me with something altogether new and pleasing to the Lord. If I've walked into the sanctuary that

---

[41] Martin Luther, "A Mighty Fortress Is Our God" (1529), *Evangelical Lutheran Worship* (Minneapolis: Augsburg Fortress, 2006), hymn #504.

[42] Thesis 28: "God's love does not find, but creates, that which is pleasing to it. Human love comes into being through that which is pleasing to it." Heidel- berg, 85.

[43] "Small Catechism," *BoC*, 352ff.

[44] Ken Sundet Jones, "The Ten Commandments," in *By Faith: Conversations with Martin Luther's Small Catechism* (Minneapolis: Augsburg Fortress, 2017), 43ff.

Sunday morning, asking with Paul, "Who will deliver me from this body of death?" (Rom. 7:24), as a sheep to be slaughtered (Rom. 8:36), what good news it is that instead of a packing plant cutting floor, I'm destined to be salt spicing up an insipid world![45] And when that happens, I'm totally sent. Over. The. Moon.

In spite of the state of preaching in the church, we ought to be encouraged by the power of this evangelical word. The father of lies wants us to be worried and seeks to undo the New Jerusalem built brick upon brick by the word. In the face of worrisome things and of threats from within and without, the word of the Lord comes on the lips of a preacher of old, the prophet Isaiah (41:14–16):

> Fear not, you worm Jacob,
>   you men of Israel!
> I am the one who helps you, declares the Lord;
>   your Redeemer is the Holy One of Israel.
> Behold, I make of you a threshing-sledge,
>   new, sharp, and having teeth;
> you shall thresh the mountains and crush them,
>   and you shall make the hills like chaff;
> you shall winnow them and the wind shall carry them away,
>   and the tempest shall scatter them.
> Then you shall rejoice in the Lord;
>   in the Holy One of Israel you shall glory.

There's not a preacher in the church who isn't a worm or an insect hoping against hope that the word they preach will bring life to dry bones. The Lord's promise to make you a threshing sledge, with teeth sharp and new, is a promise to make preachers who can judge doctrine, theologians of the cross who know how to call a thing what it is. When we catch onto that kind of proclamation, the presence of Luther's little preaching course on our transcript will have depth and meaning.

---

[45] Mark 9:49–50. See Robert Farrar Capon, *Kingdom, Grace, Judgment: Paradox, Outrage, and Vindication in the Parables* (Grand Rapids: Eerdmans, 2002), 183.

Catechetical Discipleship

John T. Pless, MDiv; LLD

James Arne Nestingen has a history with Small Catechism. Parents, grandparents, and the faithful congregations served by his father wove the grammar and vocabulary of Luther's little handbook into the fabric of Jim's life. Later on as a pastor and teacher of the church, the Small Catechism would find an extraordinary advocate and expositor in Jim's work. He would team up with his mentor, colleague, and friend Gerhard Forde to write *Free to Be*, a book structured around Luther's Catechism for confirmation instruction. There would also be scholarly articles opening the nuances of the Small Catechism for a new generation of pastors and teachers.[1] There is no schism between Jim Nestingen "disciple of Christ Jesus" and Jim Nestingen "the theologian." They are *simul*. I am delighted to offer this essay exploring how discipleship itself is catechetical and how Luther's Small Catechism is itself something of a "field manual" for disciples whose lives are now cruciform in shape as they follow the crucified Lord Jesus Christ, breathing the air of the promise made certain in His resurrection.

---

[1] See, for example, James Nestingen, "Luther's Cultural Translation of the Catechism," *Lutheran Quarterly* (Winter 2001): 440–52; "Graven Images and Christian Freedom," *Lutheran Theological Journal* (May 2015): 27–33; "Preaching the Catechism" *Word & World* (Winter 1990): 33–42; "The Catechism's *Simul*," *Word & World* (Fall 1983): 364–72; "The Lord's Prayer in Luther's Catechism," *Word & World* (Winter 2002): 36–48.

Discipleship is a good New Testament word that has enjoyed a resurgence of usage in recent years. It has become part of the name of one denomination, Disciples of Christ, and in some church growth literature, it has become fashionable to distinguish between members and disciples. In a recent article on "Discipleship in Lutheran Perspective,"[2] Mark Mattes suggests that in American Christianity, discipleship is broadly understood in two ways. On the one hand, there is the approach of American Evangelicalism, where the tactics of neorevivalism are employed to provide nominal church members with disciplines that will lead to an experience of God and make for a more effective personal spiritual life. On the other side of the aisle, there would be the mainline churches associated with the Social Gospel movement, where discipleship is defined as moral deliberation that leads to the embrace of a liberal agenda for global justice, peace, and ecological awareness. The approach of American Evangelicalism would fix the church while the Social Gospel approach would fix the world. Mattes asserts that Lutherans have a completely different take on discipleship, and it has to do with repentance and faith, death, and resurrection. Discipleship is about death to the old Adam and the resurrection of a new man who lives before God by faith and before the world in love that is turned outward in the service of the neighbor.

Discipleship is catechetical. It is coherent with the shape and content of the Small Catechism authored by Martin Luther. Friedrich Mildenberger aptly says, "A catechism is not primarily a book. . . . Rather, catechism is training in a certain body of knowledge."[3] Prior to the Reformation, the term *catechism* was used in a variety of ways inclusive of the core Christian texts of the Creed, Lord's Prayer, and Commandments and the ways in which these texts were taught. We

---

[2] See Mark Mattes, "Discipleship in Lutheran Perspective," in *The Mercy of God in the Cross of Christ: Essays on Mercy in Honor of Glenn Merritt*, ed. Ross E. Johnson and John T. Pless (St. Louis: The Lutheran Church-Missouri Synod, 2016), 501–18.

[3] Friedrich Mildenberger, *Theology of the Lutheran Confessions*, trans. Erwin Lueker (Philadelphia: Fortress, 1986), 140.

can observe this usage also in Luther. For example, in his Preface to the German Mass (1526), Luther writes,

> The German service needs a plain and simple, fair square catechism. Catechism means the instruction in which the heathen who want to be Christians are taught and guided in what they should believe, know, do, and leave undone, according to the Christian faith. This is why the candidates who had been admitted for instruction and learned the Creed before their baptism used to be called *catechumenos*. This instruction or catechization I cannot put better or more plainly than has been done from the beginning of Christendom and retained till now, i.e., in the three parts, the Ten Commandments, the Creed, and the Our Father. These three plainly and briefly contain exactly everything that a Christian needs to know. (AE 53:64–65)

Then Luther goes on to suggest how these texts should be taught in the homes in order "to train as Christian" (AE 53:65) children and servants.

In his lectures the next year (1527) on the Book of Zechariah, Luther complains that there are so few preachers who properly understand the Lord's Prayer, Creed, and Commandments and are able to teach them to the ordinary folk. Then he goes on to say, "One ought, however, to regard those teachers as the best and paragons of their profession who present the catechism well—that is, who teach properly the Our Father, the Ten Commandments, and the Creed. But these teachers are rare birds. For there is neither great glory nor outward show in their kind of teaching; but there is in it great good and also the best of sermons, because in this teaching there is comprehended, in brief, all Scripture. There is no Gospel, either, from which a man could not teach these things if he only were willing and took interest in the poor common man. One must, of course, constantly prompt the people in these brief things—that is, insist on them and urge them upon all people in all Gospels and sermons" (AE 20:157).

Catechism sermons were a regular feature of church life in Wittenberg in the 1520s. These sermons reflect the aim of the first of Luther's "*Invocavit* Sermons" preached after Luther returned from the Wartburg to do damage control on Karlstadt's ill-fated attempt to accelerate reform. In a stunning sentence, Luther sets the reality of death before the congregants: "The summons of death comes to us all, and no one can die for another. Everyone must fight his own battle with death by himself alone. We can shout into another's ears, but everyone must himself be prepared for the time of death, for I will not be with you then, nor you with me" (AE 51:70). Then Luther makes the point as to the necessity of catechetical instruction if disciples are to face death in faith: "Therefore everyone must himself know and be armed with the chief things which concern a Christian" (AE 51:70). These chief things that concern a Christian are the stuff of the catechism. While not catechism sermons in the narrow sense of that genre, the Invocavit sermons are surely catechetical in that they teach Christians how to live in faith and love, exercising patience in suffering and being well-versed in the scriptures in order to endure the devil's attacks.

Luther's third series of sermons on the catechism preached from November 30 to December 18, 1528, prefigures the content of the Large Catechism even as it demonstrates the seriousness with which Luther took the tasks of teaching disciples of Jesus Christ. In the first of these sermons, Luther reminds his hearers that those who want to be Christian should know the catechism "And one who does not know them should not be counted among the number of Christians" (AE 51:137). Those who do not know the catechism are not to be admitted to Holy Communion. In this sermon, Luther also accents the responsibility of parents in partnering with pastors to catechize the young. "Every father of a family is a bishop in his house and the wife a bishopess. Therefore remember that you in your homes are to help us carry on the ministry as we do in the church" (AE 51:137). Luther suggests that the words of the Ten Commandments, the Creed, and the Lord's Prayer can be learned "easily enough by praying in the morning when you rise, in the evening when you go to bed, and before and after meals" (AE 51:137). Learned by heart, these core texts can then be fleshed out with additional biblical passages and the content made explicit in preaching, as we see Luther doing in the catechism sermons.

The recognition of the need for a catechism and competent catechists—that is, preachers who could prepare the head of the family to teach the faith to his household—became even more urgent with the Saxon Visitation. Along with other Wittenberg colleagues, Luther participated as a "visitor" in the Saxon Visitation of 1528. By his own admission, the bleak conditions in church life compelled him to prepare what we now know as the Small Catechism: "The deplorable, wretched deprivation that I recently encountered while I was a visitor has constrained and compelled me to prepare this catechism, or Christian instruction, in such a brief, plain, and simple version. Dear God, what misery I beheld! The ordinary person, especially in the villages, knows absolutely nothing about the Christian faith, and unfortunately many pastors are completely unskilled and incompetent teachers. Yet supposedly they all bear the name Christian, are baptized, and receive the holy sacrament, even though they do not know the Lord's Prayer, the Creed or the Ten Commandments! As a result they live like simple cattle or irrational pigs and despite the fact that the gospel has returned, have mastered the fine art of misusing all their freedom" (SC Preface 1–3, K-W, 347–48). Luther recognized that both pastors and people needed a form of basic instruction in discipleship, for disciples are those who continue in Christ's Word (see John 8:31) and so live not in fleshly bondage to any idolatry but in the freedom that He gives.

Luther holds pastors accountable for teaching. In the Preface to the Small Catechism, he challenges pastors and preachers, begging them for God's sake to take up their office, have mercy on their people, and "help us bring the catechism to the people, especially the young" (SC Preface 6, K-W, 348). Preachers are themselves to not only teach the catechism but also grow in their knowledge of it. Like all disciples, pastors are to be "eternal students" who grow ever deeper in the words that they are called to proclaim. In his 1530 Preface to the Large Catechism, Luther confesses, "But this I say for myself: I am also a doctor and a preacher, just as learned and experienced as all of them who are so high and mighty. Nevertheless, each morning, and whenever else I have time, I do as a child who is being taught the catechism and I read and recite word for word the Lord's Prayer, the Ten Commandments, the Creed, the Psalms, etc. I must still read and study the catechism daily, and yet I cannot master it as I wish, but must remain a child and pupil of the catechism—and I also do so gladly. These fussy, fastidious fellows would like quickly; with one reading, to be doctors above all doctors, to know it all and need nothing more. Well this, too, is a sure sign that they despise both their office and their people's souls, yes, even God and his Word. They do need to fall, for they have fallen all too horribly. What they need, however, is to become children and again begin to learn the ABCs, which they think they have long since outgrown" (LC Preface 7–8, K-W, 380–81). Recognizing that the Spirit works only through the external words of God to make and sustain disciples of Jesus Christ, Luther is incessant in his insistence that pastors use the catechism to teach the faith.

Perhaps Luther is so strong in this insistence because he recognizes how multidimensional the catechism actually is, and this increases its *usefulness* for the life of discipleship. The Small Catechism is multifaceted. Eric Gritsch has called it a "whetstone"[4] for the church, as it sharpens basic distinctions necessary for Christian proclamation and life. Kirsi Stjerna identifies it as a "compass,"[5] for it navigates the Christian's reading of scripture. Charles Arand says that the Small Catechism is a "theological Swiss Army knife,"[6] for it can be used for several tasks. The Small Catechism is a handbook in doctrine, summarizing the scriptures teaching of human sin and God's mercy in Christ. It serves as a prayer book. Ludwig Ihmels opined that "the Catechism is not only a school book, and not only a confessional book but it is a life book."[7]

The catechism (that is, the Decalogue, Apostles' Creed, Lord's Prayer, and Words of Institution for Baptism, and the Lord's Supper) are seen by Luther as a digest and summary of the entire Bible. Already in the "Booklet for the Laity and Children" prepared in Wittenberg in 1525, the Ten Commandments, Creed, Lord's Prayer,

---

[4] Eric Gritsch, "Luther's Catechisms of 1529: Whetstones of the Church," *Lutheran Theological Seminary Bulletin* 60 (1980): 3–14.

[5] Kirsi I. Stjerna, "The Large Catechism of Dr. Martin Luther, 1529," in *The Annotated Luther*, ed. Krisi I. Stjerna, vol. 2: Word and Faith (Minneapolis: Fortress, 2015), 285.

[6] Charles Arand, *That I May Be His Own: An Overview of Luther's Catechisms* (St. Louis: Concordia, 2000), 57.

[7] Cited by J. Michel Reu, *Luther's Small Catechism* (Chicago: Wartburg, 1929), 366.

and Words of Institution for Baptism and the Sacrament of the Altar are identified as the "Lay Bible."[8] Later on, in 1577, the Epitome of the Formula of Concord calls Luther's Small and Large Catechisms "a Bible of the Laity, in which everything is summarized that is treated in detail in Holy Scripture and is necessary for a Christian to know for salvation" (FC-Epitome 5, K-W, 487).

Luther did not see the Small Catechism as a replacement for the Holy Scriptures but as the means to get to their heart and center, Jesus Christ, God's Son in human flesh crucified for the sins of the world and raised from the dead for our justification. The Small Catechism navigates readers of the Bible, guiding them in a reading that is able to distinguish God's threats from His promises so that faith is anchored in Christ alone. Learning the catechism is not an end in itself but engagement with sound words of scripture geared toward repentance, faith, and a life of love within one's calling. All Christians are to be lifelong learners in this catechetical school, as they are constantly growing into this life defined by Christ Jesus. We can observe this pattern in Luther's Preface to the Small Catechism as he directs users to learn the words, move from the words to the meaning, and then take up a larger catechism.

In his Preface to the Large Catechism, Luther speaks of a single part of the catechism, the Ten Commandments, as a "brief digest and summary of the entire Holy Scriptures" (LC Preface 18, K-W, 382). The Reformer says that "those who know the Ten Commandments perfectly know the entire Scriptures and in all affairs and circumstances are able to counsel, help, comfort, judge, and make decisions in both spiritual and temporal matters" (LC Preface 17, K-W, 382). This is not a reduction of Holy Scripture but a way of reading the Bible from these core texts. Already in his "Personal Prayer Book" of 1522, Luther anticipated the ordering of the first three parts of the Small Catechism: "Three things a person must know in order to be saved. First, he must know what to do and what to leave undone. Second, when he realizes that he cannot measure up to what he

---

[8] For the text of "A Booklet for Laity and Children," see Robert Kolb and James Nestingen, eds., *Sources and Context of The Book of Concord* (Minneapolis: Fortress, 2001), 1–12.

should do or he needs to know where to go to find the strength he requires. Third, he must know how to seek and obtain that strength. It is just like a sick person who first has to determine the nature of his sickness, then find out what to do or to leave undone. After that he has to know where to get the medicine which will help him do or leave undone what is right for a healthy person. Then he has to desire to search for this medicine and to obtain it or have it brought to him" (AE 43:13). Just as an accurate diagnosis is a prerequisite for a therapeutic treatment, the law must do its work to expose sin, if the gospel is to be rightly received as God's own remedy to sin.

This would lead Luther to shift the structure of the sequence of the three core texts in catechetical instruction. Until the middle of the fifteenth century, the sequence of Creed, Our Father, Decalogue dominates. Around 1450, the Our Father takes the first position in catechetical handbooks. Johannes Surgant (1450–1503) gives a rationale for the medieval sequence of Our Father/Creed/Ten Commandments in his *Manuale curatorum*: "Since prayer that is not prayed in true faith is without power (for without faith no one pleases God), recite the Creed. Since faith without works is totally without any power and dead and comes to be alive only through obedience to the Ten Commandments, therefore obey the Ten Commandments and learn them."[9] The popular catechism by Dietrich Kolde (c. 1435–1515), *A Fruitful Mirror, or Small Handbook for Christians*, organized the parts of the catechism with penance in view. In *A Fruitful Mirror*, the Creed comes first as all Christians could confess it. The Creed was followed by the Commandments and other catalogs of sin as a preparation for confession to the priest. Finally, there is the Lord's Prayer as the prayer to be prayed in order to attain grace.[10]

---

[9] Gotfried Krodel, "Luther's Work on the Catechism in the Context of Late Medieval Catechetical Literature" *Concordia Journal* 25 (October 1999): 370.

[10] Timothy J. Wengert. "The Small Catechism, 1529," in *The Annotated Luther*, ed. Mary Jane Haemig, vol. 4: Pastoral Writings (Minneapolis: Fortress, 2016), 202.

Luther begins with the Ten Commandments as the summary of God's law that structures human life and shows sin. The Commandments are followed by the Creed as an exposition of the Trinitarian Gospel. Then comes the Lord's Prayer as the cry of faith in the midst of affliction, imploring God on the basis of His command and promise to deliver and save. James Nestingen observes, "Luther follows an experiential order. He begins with the commandments because this is where life begins, under the *nomos*, in the context of the demands and conditions that bear down from birth to death. As Luther understands and interprets them, the Ten Commandments codify and summarize the essential requirements of life in relation to both God and the neighbor. The gospel declares that Christ has broken into the world of the law to take it upon himself in his death and resurrection to make sinners his own, thereby freeing them from the powers of sin, death, and the devil. The Lord's Prayer follows the Creed, expositing the shape of life as it is lived out in the tension between the claims of the law and the gospel, teaching sinners to call out to Christ Jesus for his assistance. In this way each of the three parts of the catechism posts a defining part of the life of faith—demand, gift, and consolation in the struggles of life."[11] To this catechetical core, Luther will add material on baptism and the Lord's Supper and eventually on confession and absolution to teach not only what the sacraments are but also how they are to be used as faith lays hold of the treasures that God gives in them.

Disciples are those people who are called to faith by the gospel and now live by the promises of Christ to take up the cross and follow Him. Luther does not envision the Christian life—that is, the life of discipleship—without the cross. In his exposition of the Third Petition in the Large Catechism, Luther writes, "For where God's Word is preached, accepted or believed, and bears fruit, there the holy and precious cross will also not be far behind. And let no one think that he will have peace; rather, we must sacrifice all that we

---

[11] James A. Nestingen, *The Lutheran Confessions: History and Theology of the Book of Concord* (Minneapolis: Fortress, 2012), 76.

have on earth—possessions, honor, house and farm, spouse and children, body and life. Now, this grieves our flesh and the old creature, for it means that we must remain steadfast, suffer patiently whatever befall us, and let go whatever is taken from us" (LC III:448–49, K-W, 448–49).

Oswald Bayer has contrasted Luther's approach to theology with that of Anselm as it was configured in the medieval tradition. For Anselm, theology was faith seeking understanding. For Luther, it was faith enduring attack.[12] It is in this light that we see Luther's intention in preparing the catechisms and urging their use by disciples of Jesus Christ, ordinary Christians. In the words of Albrecht Peters, "Studying and praying the catechism takes place on the battlefield between God and anti-god; there is no neutrality here."[13]

This can be seen explicitly in Luther's Preface to the Large Catechism. Repeatedly Luther urges Christians not to take the catechism for granted or to believe that they have attained a sufficient knowledge of the faith. Not the least of Luther's concerns is that Christians are imperiled by the assaults of the devil, the world, and the sinful flesh and cannot withstand these attacks without God's Word: "Nothing is so powerfully effective against the devil, the world, the flesh, and all evil thoughts as to occupy one's self with God's Word, to speak about it and meditate upon it in the way that Psalm 1[:2] calls those blessed who 'meditate on God's law day and night.' Without doubt you will offer up no more powerful incense or savor against the devil than to occupy yourself with God's commandments and words and to speak, sing, or think about them" (LC Preface 10, K-W, 381). If the fact that the devil constantly ambushes Christians with his "daily and incessant attacks" (LC Preface 13, K-W, 381–82) is not enough to drive Christians to use the catechism, Luther says that we have God's command: "If this were not enough to admonish us to read the catechism daily, God's command should suffice to compel us. For God solemnly enjoins us in Deuteronomy

---

[12] Oswald Bayer, *Theology the Lutheran Way*, ed. and trans. Jeffrey Silcock and Mark Mattes (Grand Rapids: Eerdmans, 2007), 210–13.

[13] Albrecht Peters, *Commentary on Luther's Catechisms: Ten Commandments*, trans. Holger Sonntag (St. Louis: Concordia, 2009), 31.

6[:7–8] that we should meditate on his precepts while sitting, walking, standing, lying down, and rising, and should keep them as an ever-present emblem before our eyes and on our hands. God certainly does not require and command this without reason. He knows our danger and needs; he knows the constant and furious attacks and assaults of the devil. Therefore, he wishes to warn, equip, and protect us against them with good 'armor' against their 'flaming arrows,' and with a good antidote against the evil infection and poison. Oh, what mad, senseless fools we are! We must ever live and dwell in the midst of such mighty enemies like the devils, and yet we would despise our weapons and armor, too lazy to examine them or give them a thought!" (LC Preface 14, K-W, 382).

Preachers are warned not to become so vain as to imagine that they have mastered the catechism and already know all that they need to know. Luther urges preachers to study and meditate on the catechism so that they, in turn, are able to teach it to those committed to their care. Thus Luther returns to the neediness of common believers: "Let all Christians drill themselves in the catechism daily, and constantly put it into practice, guarding themselves with the greatest care and diligence against the poisonous infection or such security or arrogance. Let them constantly read and teach, learn and meditate and ponder. Let them never stop until they have proved by experience and are certain that they have taught the devil to death and have become more learned than God himself and all his saints" (LC Preface 19, K-W, 382–83). The catechism is the weaponry for spiritual warfare as disciples need to be trained in the use of the Word of God and prayer in the battle against the pressures of the world, the gravitational pull of fallen human nature, and the crafty tactics of the evil one designed to draw us away from the only true God and place trust instead in ourselves or some created thing.

The life of discipleship is oriented by the First Commandment; it is a life of fearing, loving, and trusting in God above all things. This God who is to be feared, loved, and trusted above all things is none other than the Triune God. He is the one God who is Father, Son, and Holy Spirit as confessed in the Creed. He is the God who has created us and all that exists, redeemed us with the suffering and death of His Son, sanctified us by the Spirit's gospel to live as His own. Each article of the Creed ends with Luther's signature line,

"This is most certainly true." This phrase becomes the platform for our calling Jesus' Father "Our Father" with boldness and confidence. In the Small Catechism, Baptism, Absolution, and the Sacrament of the Altar are not merely addendums to the catechetical core of Decalogue, Creed, and Lord's Prayer. They are necessarily connected to the confession of the Third Article, particularly the line that reads, "Daily in this Christian church the Holy Spirit abundantly forgives all sins—mine and those of all who believe" (SC II:6, K-W, 356). This is made even more explicit in the Large Catechism: "Further we believe that in this Christian community we have the forgiveness of sins, which takes place in the holy sacraments and absolution as well as through all the comforting words of the entire gospel. This encompasses everything to be preached about the sacraments and, in short, the entire gospel and all the official responsibilities of the Christian community" (LC II:54, K-W, 438). Then a few lines later, Luther writes, "Therefore everything in the Christian community is so ordered that everyone may daily obtain full forgiveness of sins through the Word and signs appointed to comfort and encourage our consciences as long as we live on earth" (LC II:55, K-W, 438).

Luther then adds as appendices to the Small Catechism daily prayers and the Table of Duties for it in daily life that disciples "thank, praise, serve, and obey God." It is within the time and places of life in the world that disciples live. Luther gives expression to this life with morning and evening prayers as well as mealtime prayers. Discipleship is not a withdrawal from this world into a rarified spirituality in a priestly or monastic order but life lived earthly estates of church, civil community, and household. In the words of Nestingen, with the publishing of the Small Catechism, Luther "moved the village altar into the family kitchen, literally bringing instruction in the faith home to the intimacies of family life."[14]

Luther recognized that the life of faith in the world is imperiled by false teachers and persecution from those who are enemies of Christ. Training in the catechism was seen as enabling Christians to distinguish the truth from false and pernicious doctrines that would

---

[14] James Nestingen, *Martin Luther: A Life* (Minneapolis: Augsburg Fortress, 2003), 76.

undermine faith. Teaching the catechism was also seen as a kind of pre-need pastoral care so that Christians would be ready for trials that might come with persecution. In his 1541 tract, "Appeal for Prayer against the Turks," Luther reminded his readers, "And finally, I strongly urge that the children be taught the catechism. Should they be taken captive in the invasion, they will at least take something of the Christian faith with them. Who knows what God might accomplish through them. Joseph as a seventeen-year-old youth was sold into slavery into Egypt, but he had God's word and knew what he believed" (AE 43:23). Disciples are to be prepared for whatever trials that yet await them in the future. If the catechism is engraved in the memory and embedded in the heart, then disciples will carry with them all they need to remain faithful to their Lord.

J. Michel Reu has documented how Luther's Small Catechism was taught and used from the sixteenth century into the early decades of the twentieth century. One aspect of the Small Catechism's usefulness was in mission work. Disciples are made by baptizing and teaching. The historian of Lutheran missions, Ingemar Öberg, notes, "Luther's Small Catechism soon became a standard book for basic Christian instruction in Europe. Its significance for evangelical Lutheran mission work to the present day cannot be overestimated."[15] The Swedish pastor John Campanius (1601–83), while serving colonists in New Sweden, south of Philadelphia, found time to learn the language of the Delaware Indians and translated the Small Catechism into that tongue in 1697. Bartholomew Ziegenbalg (1682–1719), the first Lutheran missionary to India, translated the Small Catechism into Tamil in 1707 and used it in his missionary efforts. No wonder then that church historian Mark Noll comments, "Much of the influence of Lutheranism around the world can be traced to the success of this catechism in expressing the profound truths of the faith in a language that all can understand."[16] Nestingen notes that Luther's was a cultural translation of the catechism in that

---

[15] Ingemar Öberg, *Luther and World Mission: A Historical and Systematic Study*, trans. Dean Apel (St. Louis: Concordia, 2007), 494.

[16] Mark Noll, *Confessions and Catechisms of the Reformation* (Vancouver: Regent College Press, 2004), 60.

he took "the defining elements of the ecumenical faith to exposit them in the mother tongue."[17] I would dare say that Jim has followed the Reformer's trajectory of providing a "cultural translation" of the catechism in our own day, a translation that resonates, that enlivens faith and confession.

Jim's work is a testimony to the fact that Small Catechism is not merely a relic of the sixteenth century. After nearly five hundred years, it has demonstrated its own resilience and durability in Lutheran churches throughout the world. It embodies the central truths of the Reformation in such a way that touches heart and mind, disciplining the Christian in the ongoing life of repentance, faith, and vocation. This is the life of discipleship.

---

[17] Nestingen, "Luther's Cultural Translation of the Catechism," 448. In a similar fashion, see the observation of Albrecht Peters: "The catechism enunciates the spiritual core of Scripture not as an insight gained by a spiritually gifted individual, but by means of those texts that have prevailed in Christendom and at the same time, within the context of the history of interpretation of these decisive texts. In this way, the catechism summarizes in a highly conscious manner the artisan and town privileges of Christendom. This is how the reformer circumspectly makes his confession a part of the witness of the Western Church" (*Commentary on Luther's Catechisms: Ten Commandments*, 20).

Sanctification Is Purely Passive

Dr. Marney Fritts

And because of [God] you are in Christ Jesus, who became
for us wisdom from God, righteousness and sanctification
and redemption.

—1 Corinthians 1:30

We must learn to understand sanctification as purely passive.[1] Jesus
Christ is our sanctification. Therefore, sanctification is not the active

---

[1] Gerhard Forde once observed a rare moment of clarity within the
Lutheran-Catholic Dialogues by the Roman Catholic Karl Peter. Peter conceded that it was evident that there was a "fundamental difference" between
Lutherans and Roman Catholics on the understanding of *what* is being medi-
ated through the office of ordained ministry. This fundamental difference,
Forde argues, ultimately reflects on the office itself. This fundamental theological difference, Forde contends, constitutes the ecumenical impasse still to this
day. Forde, "The Catholic Impasse: Reflections on Lutheran-Catholic Dialogue
Today," in *A More Radical Gospel: Essays on Eschatology, Authority, Atonement,
and Ecumenism*, ed. Mark C. Mattes and Steven D. Paulson (Grand Rapids:
Eerdmans, 2004), 197. In his recent article, "Speaking of the End to the Law,"
in *The Necessary Distinction: A Continuing Conversation on Law and Gospel*
(St. Louis: Concordia, 2017), Dr. Nestingen notes that in the 1530s, Philip Melanchthon departed from Luther's teaching of Christ as the twofold end of the

work of the Christian life following justification. Sanctification is a person who is God in the flesh, Jesus Christ. The question then is, If I am dead in my sin (Col. 2:13), and daily my sins are ever before me (Ps. 51:3), how is it that I am sanctified? How is Jesus Christ made to be sanctification for actual, present, kicking and screaming, yellow-bellied, rebellious sinners who either are filled with despair, unbelief, and other great and shameful sins or are well enough and are determined to be sanctified in themselves, working with the Holy Spirit? How does what is unholy become holy?

Third Article of the Creed: Sanctification Is by the Forgiveness of Sins

In both of Luther's Catechisms, he takes up the Holy Spirit in such a way that it is never to be confused as a power Christians harness, nor with the human spirit, nor especially with the "free-will." In Luther's explanation of the third article of the Creed in the Small Catechism, he explicitly negates the capacity of human faculties to contribute anything to belief. "I believe that by my own understanding or strength I cannot believe in Jesus Christ my Lord or come to him."[2] Here we can say two things about the passivity of the Christian in sanctification.

First, this makes belief in Christ the sanctifying deed of the Holy Spirit for sinners. It is not simply that belief is a foundation upon which

---

law (*telos* and *finis*) by developing the language of the third use of the law, convinced of the law's necessity in salvation (171). In a similar manner, Karl Peter observed a fundamental difference between the Lutherans and the Catholics; it appears there is a fundamental difference between Luther and Melanchthon on the law. Where Forde pressed Peter's observation that shows the deeper impasse in the understanding of the office of ministry itself, I am furthering Nestingen's observation of the departure of Melanchthon from Luther on the law by saying that what results is a fundamentally different understanding of sanctification. The discussion of the active life and the fruit of good works come under the locus of vocation.

[2] Martin Luther, "The Small Catechism," in *The Book of Concord: The Confessions of the Evangelical Lutheran Church*, ed. Robert Kolb and Timothy Wengert (Minneapolis: Fortress, 2000), 355.

the Christian must subsequently work out his or her salvation. Belief in Christ alone is salvation. What we "work out" regarding our salvation, as Paul urges in Philippians 2:12, is not the point at which now the "free-will" enters the equation to work with the Holy Spirit. This is not the call for Christians to align their wills with the will of God according to the law to be more like Christ. That is the mistake of Thomas à Kempis's *Imitatio Christi*, for it removes the clear proclamation of the cross as the end (*telos* and *finis*) of the law, sin, and death and replaces it with the desire to rehabilitate the will with Christ as an example. When you have Christ habitually as an example, Luther warns, you do not have Him as gospel, and when you do not have Him as gospel, He is no better than any of the saints who are all powerless to save sinners. The end of this particular Pauline verse is "with fear and trembling," which is to say that the sinner who desires to be righteous in the self, by the self, with the law as their guide, is confronted with the end of the self and the law as the means of salvation in the proclamation of Christ crucified. This fear is for sinners who tremble to have their destiny taken out of their hands. But for the saint, the one who has heard and in whom the Holy Spirit has worked belief in Christ alone as their righteousness, sanctification, and redemption, there is no more precious promise in the entire universe.

Luther writes of the comfort in the certainty that comes from hearing that his salvation has been taken entirely out of his hands:

> I frankly confess that, for myself, even if it could be, I should not want "free-will" to be given me, nor anything to be left in my hands to enable me to endeavor after salvation; not merely because in the face of so many dangers, and adversaries, and assaults of the devils, I could not stand my own ground and hold fast my "free-will" (for one devil is stronger than all men, and on these terms no man could be saved); but because, even were there no dangers, adversaries, or devils, I should still be forced to labor with no guarantee of success, and to beat my fists at the air. If I lived and worked to all eternity, my conscience would never reach comfortable certainty as to how much it must do to satisfy God. . . . But now that God has taken my salvation out of the control of my own will, and put it under the control of His, and promised to save me, not according to my working or ruling, but according to His own grace and

mercy, I have the comfortable certainty that He is faithful and will not lie to me.[3]

The old Adam in us is constantly battling God as the one who sanctifies. Therefore, Paul confesses of the war that rages within the Christian. This is because the Christian is, rightly speaking, *simul iustus et peccator*. The old sinner who hangs around our necks, like the five-year-old hanging on the back of the parent, remains until we rest in the grave. At the same time, we are saints in Christ, Who forgives all our sins. "For where there is the forgiveness of sins, there is life and salvation." These "two yous" are *totus totus*; you are totally sinner in yourself and, at the same time, totally saint. It is the *peccator* who has the habit of running back into sin and death and who then turns to blame Christ and make Him the minister of sin for freeing him from the law in the first place.

This accusation against Christ, however, has two false presuppositions. First, the law was given to make one holy. Paul repeats time and again that the law was given to reveal sin, not to remedy sin (Rom. 3:20, 5:20; Gal. 2:16). The second false presupposition in accusing Christ as the reason for sin is the belief that the Christian is no longer *simul, totus totus*, but *partum partum*, only partially sinner in the self and partially saint, progressing out of sinfulness up to saintliness in a zero-sum equation. This is also a consequence of thinking of justification and sanctification as a two-step, sequential stepladder to holiness. The *simul* is denied, and the old sinner has, presumably, escaped total death.[4] Rather, the relationship between

---

[3] Martin Luther, *The Bondage of the Will*, trans. J. I. Packer and O. R. Johnston (Grand Rapids: Baker, 1957), 313–14.

[4] Robert Kolb observes that Chemnitz does not "clearly develop Luther's emphasis on the necessity of death for sinners, rather than the necessity of satisfying an eternally existing law." "Human Performance and the Righteousness of Faith," in *By Faith Alone: Essays on Justification in Honor of Gerhard O. Forde*, ed. Joseph A. Burgess and Marc Kolden (Grand Rapids: Eerdmans, 2004), 133. This lack of emphasis appears to be closely linked to the different understandings of the law, which then is the root of the different understandings of sanctification because of the implications for the understanding of the *simul iustus et peccator*.

justification and sanctification or belief and holiness is "getting used to the unconditional justification wrought by the grace of God for Jesus' sake."[5]

The second point to note in the Small Catechism concerning the passivity of the Christian in sanctification is that Luther points to the Holy Spirit as the only actor in sanctifying. "Instead, the Holy Spirit has called me through the gospel, enlightened me with his gifts, made me holy and kept me in the true faith, just as he calls, gathers, enlightens, and makes holy the whole Christian church on Earth and keeps it with Jesus Christ in the one common true faith."[6] The Holy Spirit is the subject of all the verbs. "I" am the passive recipient of the working of the Holy Spirit. There is no synergism between the "I" and the Holy Spirit to call me into faith, to gather me into the communion of saints, to bestow on me His gifts of the forgiveness of sins, the promise of the resurrection from the dead and life eternal. Nor is there any cooperation of the will to make one holy. Not only does the human will or human spirit *not* cooperate with the Holy Spirit, but the human spirit or will is not to be confused with the Holy Spirit, such as a spark of the divine that remains after the Fall in the Garden of Eden. Rather, our human spirit is in rebellion with the Holy Spirit. The Spirit of God is the only one who is holy. Luther makes this clear statement in the explanation of the Large Catechism.[7]

Several years preceding his catechisms, Luther opposed Erasmus on this very point in *The Bondage of the Will* (1525) in a rhetorical fashion, "Does the Diatribe regard the 'free-will' as identical to the Holy Spirit?"[8] Even though the "free-will" (i.e., the bound will) is not the Holy Spirit, this does not mean it is active in salvation. Indeed, while the will is not active in sanctification, it is very active

---

[5] Gerhard Forde, "The Lutheran View of Sanctification," in *The Preached God: Proclamation in Word and Sacrament*, ed. Mark C. Mattes and Steven D. Paulson (Grand Rapids: Eerdmans, 2007), 226.

[6] Martin Luther, "Smalcald Articles," in *The Book of Concord: The Confessions of the Evangelical Lutheran Church*, ed. Robert Kolb and Timothy Wengert (Minneapolis: Fortress, 2000), 355–56.

[7] LC, 435.

[8] Luther, *Bondage*, 257.

in bondage to sin, actively opposing the Holy Spirit: "For I know that nothing good dwells within me, that is, in my flesh. For I have a desire to do what is right, but not the ability to carry it out. For I do not do the good I want, but the evil I do not want is what I keep on doing" (Rom. 7:18–19). It is indeed the case, as Paul confesses, that the human will has the active capacity for evil but only the passive capacity for good.[9]

Luther explains how it is that we are made holy by the holying Spirit, "Just as the Son obtains dominion by purchasing us through his birth, death, and resurrection, etc., so the Holy Spirit effects our being made holy through the following: the communion of saints or Christian church, the forgiveness of sin, the resurrection of the body, and the life everlasting."[10] The Holy Spirit places us in the bosom of Christ Himself, through whom we are made holy through word and sacrament. Once again, the Holy Spirit and Christ are the active ones in justification and sanctification, and the sinner is purely passive. The sinner is the one done unto by God Himself. The Holy Spirit does Himself to us when the Spirit makes us holy, which is accomplished through the proclamation of Christ crucified for the forgiveness of sins, "for you," in preaching and the sacraments. This is the "office and the work of the Holy Spirit, to begin and daily increase holiness on earth through these two means, the Christian church and the forgiveness of sins."[11] The old creature cannot but help see the words "begin," and "increase" as the point where "I" get a foot in the door, finally maturing such that I can and will work with God at least on this matter of sanctification. Imperceptibly, the subject of the sentence, the Holy Spirit, is replaced with the old creature.

This presumed swap of roles by the sinner is revealed when we attempt to wheel Luther's own words in the explanation of the third article against everything else he has already sufficiently explained. He writes:

---

[9] Gerhard Forde, *On Being a Theologian of the Cross: Reflections on Luther's Heidelberg Disputation, 1518* (Grand Rapids: Eerdmans, 1997), 54.

[10] LC, 435.

[11] Ibid., 439.

Meanwhile, because holiness has begun and is growing daily, we wait the time when our flesh will be put to *death*, will be *buried* with all the uncleanness, and will come forth gloriously and arise to complete and perfect holiness in a *new eternal life*. Now, however, we remain only halfway pure and holy. The Holy Spirit must always work in us through the word, granting us daily forgiveness of sins.[12]

Growth in sanctification is not a moral process but our progress to death. Holiness and immortality are not accomplished through morality but through death of the old and the resurrection to eternal life. As Dr. Nestingen's colleague Gerhard Forde writes, our growth is in "grace, not in our own virtue or morality. The progress, if one can call it that, is that we are being shaped more and more by the totality of grace coming to us. The progress is the steady invasion of the new."[13] It is God who is progressing in upon creation, upon individual sinners, not we who are progressing upward, out of this world, to God "somewhere out there."

The Center of the Hub

Dr. Nestingen is well known for teaching that the central presupposition of theology and, subsequently, proclamation is the *sola fide*. It is the "center of the hub," with the other theological *loci* radiating out from the hub like spokes on a wheel. We are justified by faith alone apart from works of the law. This captures Luther's theological claim in the Smalcald Articles that "here is the first and chief article. . . . On this article stands all that we teach and practice against the pope, the devil, and the world."[14] This is to say, then, that all other claims made on the sinner are registered and limited by this chief article. If Christ saves, the law cannot. If we are justified by faith alone, then the law has met its limit in Christ (Rom. 10:4). If we continue with the previous claim that sanctification is getting used to being justified, then sanctification is found to be the hub as well.

---

[12] Ibid., 438.

[13] Forde, "Sanctification," 241.

[14] SC, 301.

When Christ and Him crucified is made to be our wisdom, righteousness, sanctification, and redemption (1 Cor. 1:30), then our old sinful self that is ruled by the devil and bears his image is crucified, and a new creature of faith is raised from the dead. The Christian *qua* Christian is the new creature created by the Holy Spirit into the image of Christ. Paul says it this way in his letter to the Galatians: "Until Christ is formed in you," also, and importantly, "It is no longer I who live, but Christ who lives in me. And the life I now live in the flesh I live by faith in the Son of God, who loved me and gave himself for me" (Gal. 2:20). What the Holy Spirit wills and works is for Christ and Him crucified to be formed in us. It is Christ who lives in the saint, not a new Moses. Christ is our life, justification, and sanctification.

When Christ is formed in us, however, is not to have Him merely as a moral example. Christ as your life is not the revitalization of the old Adam to use the law better. The image of God in the Christian is not the law of God but of the gospel. As Luther says, "Paul wants to restore the image of God or of Christ in [the Galatians]. It had been deformed or distorted by the false apostles, and it consists in this, that they feel, think, and want exactly what God does, whose thought and will it is that we obtain the forgiveness of sins and eternal life through Jesus Christ, his son."[15] When Christ is formed in the sinner, He brings Aristotle to an end.

Aristotle will agree that something can be formed in you through your senses, as a picture in your mind, like a tree in the park, for example. But for Luther, Christ is not just a picture or an idea of Christ in our mind or heart but the entire person of Jesus Christ, human and divine, whole and complete, enters sinners. He invades sinners through the proclamation of His forgiveness of sins from the cross in preaching and the sacraments.

Aristotle, human reason (*ad modum Aristotelis*), indeed the entire sinner cannot abide this invasion of Christ because no two things cannot occupy the same space at the same time in the old wisdom of the world. Christ, however, does not abide by the laws of metaphysics and ontology but invades eschatologically to bring an

---

[15] Martin Luther, *Lectures on Galatians* (1535), 431.

end to the old and the beginning of the new. While we are yet philosophers and metaphysicians, or just physicians, He invades this particular strong man's house. He is intent on plundering us from the law,
for Himself by whom sinners are justified, sanctified, and redeemed.

The Apostle Paul, whose mission was to the Greeks, who were
steeped in the human wisdom epitomized in the laws of Aristotle
and Plato and their system of ethics, the hierarchy of being, metaphysical dualism of matter and spirit, the idea of the forms, life as
progress from potentiality to actuality, the eternal law, and the belief
in the immortality of the soul proclaimed Jesus Christ who is the
end of the law for faith, sanctification, and salvation. So Paul's letter to the Corinthians opens with a proclamation, once again, that
they are "those sanctified in Jesus Christ" (1 Cor. 1:2), who is the
Wisdom from God, over which they stumble time and again. At
the end of this first chapter, Paul restates this point, again without
equivocation. It is as if he is saying, "If Christ alone is your life, then
the ontological question of being is rendered moot; if Christ is your
sanctification, then your self-actualization is cut off by the arrival of
the Crucified and Risen One and not as moral reformation through
practice of the law and habit; if Christ is your redemption, then the
idea of eternal law and your ascent by means of it is not." The direction and the content of the Greek wisdom is reversed and inverted.
The direction is not from Earth to heaven but from heaven above to
Earth below. It is Christ who moves down and in upon sinners, not
we who ascend to God.

Paul speaks in similar explicit terms regarding sanctification
as a central matter when he writes to both the Thessalonians and
the Hebrews. Paul writes, "To be saved, through sanctification by the
Spirit and belief in the truth" (2 Thess. 2:13) and "we have been sanctified through the offering of the body of Jesus Christ" (Heb. 10:10).
While these notations are not an exhaustive list, it demonstrates that
Paul is not making justification and sanctification into a two-step
process toward being a Christian. He is not replacing the idea of the
law as an "eternal, ontological scheme,"[16] as though the law is like

---

[16] Gerhard Forde, *The Law-Gospel Debate* (Minneapolis: Augsburg, 1969),
200–15, especially 214.

an extension ladder up to heaven that one must ascend to the goal along with a new, Christian, two-step stepladder (justification first, sanctification second). The problem is not simply that the law was too difficult and simply needed to be limited and so made manageable for us.[17] It is not as though we are justified by faith alone as the first step and the sanctification of the Christian is the next step where the Christian shows through moral reformation that they are taking this Christian life seriously, finally. Paul does not separate justification and sanctification, because sanctification is this one man who is God, Jesus Christ.

Now for Christ to be any comfort to sinners and not someone the old creature shelves and steps beyond, he must be delivered, "for you," in peace, mercy, in the unconditional and repeated forgiveness of sins. In order for Christ to be anyone's actual sanctification in this old world, God sends us His preachers. Thus we have been given the ministry of the Holy Spirit.

The Holy Spirit's Categorical Proclamation of Christ

The Holy Spirit is not the inner voice of the human, and Christ is not our free will. God has chosen to use the external voice (*extra nos*) of Christ's preachers as the voice of the Holy Spirit to proclaim the Word, who is Jesus Christ. This Jesus Christ lacks no gift of the Holy Spirit, so, if we have the Son, we, too, are lacking in no Spiritual Gift (1 Cor. 1:5–8). Apart from this external preaching of the Word, you will not have the Holy Spirit or any spiritual gifts.[18] This is to preach Christ crucified and risen for you in the totality of grace, or as Luther says, to "preach Christ categorically." This is what Luther writes:

---

[17] Whether justification and sanctification is taught as a multiple-step progression in the Christian or two points of an ellipse (Ritschl), these are difficult to establish according to Paul. Two individuals who have identified in fuller fashion these two different ways of separating justification and sanctification as manufactured are David Lotz in *Ritschl & Luther* (Nashville: Abington, 1974), and Forde, "Sanctification," as noted earlier.

[18] Smalcald Articles III, 8: 3.

Christ is the way, the truth and the life (John 14:6) and that cate-gorically, so whatever is not Christ is not the way, but error, not the truth, but untruth, not life, but death, it follows of necessity that "free will" inasmuch as it neither is Christ, nor is in Christ, is fast bound in error, and untruth and death. . . . If all the things that are said of Christ and of grace were not said categorically, so that they may be contrasted with their opposites, like this: out of Christ there is noth-ing but Satan, out of grace nothing but wrath, out of light nothing but darkness, out of the way nothing but error, out of truth noth-ing but a lie, out of life nothing but death. . . . If you grant that the Scriptures speak categorically, you can say nothing of "free will" but that which is the opposite of Christ: that is, that error, death, Satan, and all evils reign in it. If you do not grant that the Scriptures speak categorically, you so weaken them, that they establish nothing and fail to prove that men need Christ; and thus, in setting up "free will," you set aside Christ, and make havoc of the entire Scripture.[19]

The purpose of proclamation is to make as much of Jesus Christ in our proclamation as the Apostle Paul does (*ad modum scripturae*) who gives everything to Christ: wisdom, righteousness, sanctifica-tion, and redemption. We preach Jesus Christ categorically, which is to say it is the Holy Spirit who is bestowing justification and sancti-fication that is this one man, our God, Jesus Christ for us. In matters of justification, sanctification, God does everything, we do nothing; sanctification is purely passive.

Bibliography

Forde, Gerhard O. "The Catholic Impasse: Reflections on Lutheran–Catholic Dialogue Today." In *A More Radical Gospel: Essays on Eschatology, Authority, Atonement, and Ecumenism*, edited by Mark C. Mattes and Steven D. Paulson, 189–99. Grand Rapids: Eerdmans, 2004.

———. *The Law-Gospel Debate*. Minneapolis: Fortress, 1969.

---

[19] Luther, *Bondage*, 307.

―――. "The Lutheran View of Sanctification." In *The Preached God*, edited by Mark C. Mattes and Steven D. Paulson, 226–44. Grand Rapids: Eerdmans, 2007.

―――. *On Being a Theologian of the Cross: Reflections on Luther's Heidelberg Disputation, 1518*. Grand Rapids: Eerdmans, 2004.

Kolb, Robert. "Human Performance and the Righteousness of Faith." In *By Faith Alone: Essays on Justification in Honor of Gerhard O. Forde*, edited by Joseph A. Burgess and Marc Kolden, 125–39. Grand Rapids: Eerdmans, 2004.

Kolb, Robert and Timothy Wengert, eds. *The Book of Concord: The Confessions of the Evangelical Lutheran Church*. Minneapolis: Fortress, 2000.

Lotz, David. *Ritschl & Luther*. Nashville: Abington, 1974.

Luther, Martin. *The Bondage of the Will*, translated by J. I. Packer and O. R. Johnston. Grand Rapids: Baker, 1957.

Concordia Publishing House. "Luther's Works." https://www.cph.org/c-2063-luthers-works.aspx.

Nestingen, James A. "Speaking of the End to the Law." In *The Necessary Distinction: A Continuing Conversation on Law and Gospel*. St. Louis: Concordia, 2017.

Honoring the Pastoral
Dimension to Theology

Dr. Mark Mattes

Well over thirty-five years ago, I began studies at Luther Seminary in St. Paul, Minnesota. Naturally, I was required to take courses in pastoral care. In these courses, I was exposed to various counseling theories of contemporary secular therapists. Those pastoral care professors surely were well intentioned, but learning secular psychological theories does not help anyone think like a pastor! If I wanted to think like a pastor, the one faculty member who was guaranteed to model that was not a professor of pastoral care but instead a historian, Jim Nestingen. Whether teaching history, confessions, or theology, Jim ever found ways to help his students develop a pastor's heart.

What is a "pastor's heart"? It cannot be reduced to what was so idealized among many seminarians as "caregiving," feeling another's pain with the attempt to fix people who are down and out. Instead, what Jim modeled throughout his lectures and his individual contacts with students was discerning Law and Gospel: when to comfort the afflicted and when to afflict the comfortable. It is that discernment, that wisdom (*sapientia experimentalis*),[1] that constitutes a pastor's

---

[1] WA 40/III: 63, 17; See Oswald Bayer, *Theology the Lutheran Way*, ed. and trans. Jeffrey G. Silcock and Mark C. Mattes (Grand Rapids: Eerdmans, 2007), 122.

heart. It is far more vital and relevant than the "caregiving" or the much-vaunted "ministry of presence" so highly esteemed by my peers. Unlike "caregiving," it can never be trivialized or sentimentalized. It does something. It has a bite. That the law kills and the gospel resurrects—the truth of our faith—is not amenable to the insipidity of contemporary therapeutic "caregiving," invariably the basis for a self-improvement spirituality, popular among mainline Protestants, which simply "gums" people to death (as Gerhard Forde put it).[2] The gospel is far more robust and powerful and thereby more "caring." Jim knew how to present the gospel promise such that the troubled conscience is liberated and so that one can then "thank and praise, serve and obey" God.[3] He was able to do this because he had so appropriated Luther's theology as his own. If we wish for renewal in the church and Christian theology, we should, like Jim Nestingen, hearken back to Luther's deeply pastoral approach to doing theology. "Pastoral theology" should not be simply one department among other departments, such as Bible or theology. Instead, it should be at the core of all theological inquiry.[4]

The Ubiquity of Theology

In the academy, theology has long found itself displaced as the "queen of the sciences." It is hard to say which discipline, if any, is governing the academy today, but it surely is not theology. Recently, a secular-minded colleague even suggested that my theology department should relinquish its calling to do specifically Christian theology and instead become an "interfaith" department, justifying its status in the

---

[2] Gerhard Forde, "Luther's 'Ethics,'" in *A More Radical Gospel: Essays on Eschatology, Authority, Atonement, and Ecumenism*, ed. Mark C. Mattes and Steven D. Paulson (Grand Rapids: Eerdmans, 2004), 145.

[3] Martin Luther, "The Small Catechism," in *The Book of Concord*, ed. Robert Kolb and Timothy J. Wengert (Minneapolis: Fortress, 2000), 355:2.

[4] In contrast, Friedrich Schleiermacher, who divides theological disciplines into the (1) philosophical, (2) historical, and (3) practical, does not accord privilege to Law and Gospel distinction. See his *Brief Outline on the Study of Theology*, trans. Terrence N. Tice (Richmond: John Knox, 1966).

university on the basis of its ability to foster religious diversity, advocating for tolerance of Islamic, Buddhist, or Taoist religious commitments. That will not happen, but it does indicate the perspective of many secular academics. In some universities, religion courses serve to fulfill general education requirements in the liberal arts curriculum. But hardly any university today positions theology as its center or purpose for existence.

It is no wonder that theologians ponder their status in the academy. In a world that values penultimate matters, such as the economy or politics, as primary or even replaces the ultimate with such penultimate matters, where do those of us who deal with meaning, meaningfulness, and truth fit in? Does theology make a difference in the world? Such challenges put theologians on the defensive. Most theologians believe an "apology" for their work is necessary.

The path less trod is the one that is less defensive but surprisingly more pastoral. Instead of trying to find theology's relevance for the modern world, perhaps the world—even the world of the academy—is far more religious than what many academics are willing to admit in spite of their protests and denials. That is, the world can only be understood from the perspective of some story or *mythos* that helps people make sense of the world and legitimates their behaviors. Such narratives include that of "democratic capitalism" or "democratic socialism" or various Marxist *mythoi*. We need not expend much energy defending the faith so much as exposing secular perspectives as themselves alternative, if not counterfeit, theories of salvation.[5] This is likewise true for those claiming to be "spiritual but not religious," which invariably is a form of Gnosticism. No matter what the discipline in the university, scholars want to preserve their discipline's place and justify its existence. In some way or another, scholars believe that their discipline furthers the human venture, in some sense *justifies* life. Push these scholars, regardless of their discipline, further, and chances are, you will find some theology embedded or hidden in their work.

---

[5] See Mark Mattes, "A Lutheran Case for Apologetics," *Logia: A Journal of Lutheran Theology* (Holy Trinity 2015), 25–32.

Scratch the surface of physics and you will find the metaphysical question of whether the cosmos is a result of design or chance.
Dig a little deeper into mathematics and you can hardly avoid the
truth that mathematics and theology share the same home ground:
infinity. (It is no wonder that on my campus, the mathematics
department is the one department outside of theology with the most
publicly self-professed Christians!) Ultimately, there is some kind of
intangible standard by which to legitimate specific scholarly inqui-
ries, whether that justification be "justice," "freedom," "creativity,"
"self-awareness," "consciousness raising," or (less frequently) "truth."
Such matters exude an aura of spirituality, and so theology is not far
behind and, in many cases, at the core of what all kinds of secular
people do, whether they acknowledge their theological underpin-
nings or not. Counter to secularist claims, religion is no mere ves-
tige, some kind of "add-on" to humanity, a cul-de-sac out of which
we are evolving. Instead, it deals with the core of human identity: the
heart. And what one trusts in, whether God or an idol, says everything about who one is.[6]

It takes a gospel-centered theologian, like a good detective, to
spot this truth. Whether or not they admit it, all academics, in whatever discipline—just like all other humans—are theologians, but
they are not all equally good theologians. What makes for a good
theologian is having the skill to discern Law and Gospel, knowing
when to comfort the afflicted and when to afflict the comfortable. For
this reason, Lutherans should not back down from Law and Gospel
distinction but, if anything, teach it, commend it, and demand it of
their pastors even more. No doubt, it is important that theology be
"systematic" and attempt to present itself in an orderly fashion by
finding the common thread between doctrines. It is crucial that theology be "constructive" and attempt to state its truths for today. It is
vital that theology be "contextual" and apply to where people are at.
But the most important task of theology is to be *pastoral*—centered

---

[6] "Therefore, I repeat, the correct interpretation of this commandment is
that to have a god is to have something in which the heart trusts completely."
See Martin Luther, "The Large Catechism," in *The Book of Concord*, 387:10.

on delivering the good news to those bound in sin, the promise that for Jesus' sake your sins are forgiven and that you are God's own.

Unaware theologians appear in all walks of life and in every situation. All people are theologians whether or not they admit or are aware of it. Even those who never attend a church, synagogue, or temple confess core beliefs about what's right or wrong, true or false, and upon what or in whom one ultimately should hang one's heart. That is, all humans have a deity whether or not they acknowledge the God who is self-revealing in the scriptures. But as Paul noted, not all "gods" or "lords" are benevolent (1 Cor. 8:5). Like Moloch of old, some demand sacrifice, as do our contemporary "global capitalist" gods of time, status, and control.[7] In contrast to such religious violence, so pervasive with so many alleged deities, we need a theology that is true to the gospel, one that is *pastoral*, discerning God's commands, most faithfully summarized in the Ten Commandments (although even nature itself testifies to their truth) and in God's promise, most clearly given in Jesus' resurrection from the dead but that is likewise also testified to in nature itself (such as the rainbow as God's covenantal promise of providential care for humankind, Gen. 9:13) and is clearly delivered in proclamation.

At the core of pastoral discernment is that God's law and promise in their structure or their content are not the same thing either. God's law commands us to do something and accuses us when we fail to do it. God's promise, however, commands nothing but guarantees that God will forgive, preserve, and sustain us. God's promise delivers gifts, while God's law delivers no such gifts but instead demands that we give of ourselves. To be sure, the afflicted and the comfortable are often one and the same person. But when the law does its deed in bringing sinners to an end, the preacher has a kairos moment, a time when the gospel can do its even more effectual deed of raising people to new life. At the center of a pastoral theologian's ministry is discerning where a sinner's conscience is at. No one more than Luther can help us in the task of retrieving a vital theology as inherently pastoral.

---

[7] See Craig M. Gay, *Cash Values: Money and the Erosion of Meaning in Today's Society* (Grand Rapids: Eerdmans, 2003).

Three Rules

From Luther, we have much to learn about becoming pastoral theologians, ones who discern where God's law hounds sinners to death and where sinners can receive God's liberating grace. In his "Preface to German Writings" (1539), Luther specifies "three rules" for "the proper way to study theology": (1) prayer (*oratio*), (2) meditation (*meditatio*), and (3) spiritual attack (*tentatio*).[8] These three rules teach us how to live as Christians in the church and the world. These three rules arise out of Luther's own response to the monastic spirituality that formed him but with a potent, surprising twist. As Vítor Westhelle notes,

> During the middle ages theologizing was largely accepted as comprising three steps: *Lectio, oratio,* and *contemplatio*. Luther changes the order of the first two. He starts with *oratio*, and then moves to *meditatio* (which includes *lectio*). But what is more significant and relevant . . . is that he totally changes the last step from *contemplatio* to *tentatio*.[9]

Westhelle further explains about *tentatio*, or in German, *Anfechtung*:

> *Anfechtung* means being in trial, probation, and tribulation, spiritual or otherwise. This is the "touchstone" because you cannot do theology without experiencing cross and suffering and persecution. Prayer and meditation ought to lead to *Anfechtung* only so we may know that the Devil and his minions are indeed being confronted.[10]

---

[8] Luther's Works, 34:285–87. My interpretation of Luther here is dependent upon Oswald Bayer's discussion of these three rules in *Theology the Lutheran Way*, ed. and trans. Jeffrey G. Silcock and Mark C. Mattes (Grand Rapids: Eerdmans, 2007), 42–66.

[9] Vítor Westhelle, *Transfiguring Luther: The Planetary Promise of Luther's Theology* (Eugene, OR: Cascade, 2016), 122.

[10] Ibid., 123.

In contrast to so many spiritual venues, from Buddhism to born-againism, contemplation—seen as a haven of spiritual ecstasy free from conflict with the flesh, the adversary, accusations of the law, and opponents of God's Word—is not to be expected in this life. In a word, Paul got it right: we walk by faith, not by sight (2 Cor. 5:7), because in the face of such opposition, such spiritual warfare, we cling to the goodness of God's promise that God (who raises the dead) will provide for us and take care of us, come what may.

It is through these three rules that we enter into the world of Holy Scripture, the most important habitation given for us to live. The world of the scriptures is not only one of depth, an encounter with God, but also one of breadth, in which the whole gamut of human life is expressed. In the scriptures, we have not only the Alpha and the Omega, a narrative structure that gives coherence to all life, the cosmic scope providing the beginning, middle, and end of everything, but also a hallowing of genuinely human experiences within that narrative, such as the celebration of romantic love in the Song of Songs, the crises of doubt voiced in Ecclesiastes, hunger for spiritual fulfillment as well as the encounter of dread in the face of God's absence in the Psalter, and an imperfect discipleship as is displayed in the gospels. In the scriptures, sometimes God is vitally present and, surprisingly, at other times significantly absent. And usually God allows the world to inflict a "thorn" in our flesh, as we see in Paul (2 Cor. 12:7–9). We surely have a God who is neither tame nor controllable. The center point of it all, defining the future of creation and the fate of sinners, of course, is the cross and resurrection of our Lord.

For Luther, it is spiritual attack (*tentatio*), God's own accusation against us in the law, resulting in what he called *Anfechtung*, or God's frightful opposition to us, as Jacob experienced the night he fought with an unnamed, mysterious foe at the ford of the Jabbok (Gen. 32:22–32), that leads us to bend our knees to pray (*oratio*) for illumination and finally to let scripture interpret us (*meditatio*). With our defenses down, God's Word speaks and reveals our identity both before God and with respect to the world. What these three rules do, among other things, is show us that it is not we who finally interpret scripture but scripture that interprets us.

The old Adam and Eve are far more apt to believe Desiderius Erasmus's defense of a "free will," that we contribute to our beatitude, or Thomas Jefferson's affirmation of autonomy, the usually consumerist "pursuit of happiness" as we see fit, provided no harm is done to others. In response to these two views, one Renaissance and the other modern (but both saturated in the theology of the "free will"), the only candidates ready for the gospel are those for whom such *autopoietic* (self-making) attempts to establish one's own life or happiness on one's own terms no longer work. Only those crushed by failure in their efforts at heroism will be open to the God who rescues.[11] What would have been implausible prior to the death of their ambition, that it is not we who hold authority over scripture but instead scripture that holds authority over us, now becomes plausible indeed. It is not we who define scripture but instead scripture that defines us. Scripture shows us our finitude, our dependence, our sin and guilt, our purpose, and gives voice to both lament and joy for us. In short, we have no clue about who we are or where we fit in the world apart from scripture's address and claim on us.

A pastoral theology knows that we are all theologians to some degree or another, that we all have an "ultimate concern," as Paul Tillich put it,[12] in which we trust and often for which we publically advocate. Even more to the point, it recognizes that every theology comes with its agendas. The first theological question asked in scripture comes from none other than the adversary, "hath God said . . ." When that question was asked in the Garden, it was to put God's Word in doubt and to encourage Adam and Eve to see themselves as adequate to serve as their own deities for themselves. Pastorally informed theology recognizes that we need to focus on the true content of theology, which for Luther is nothing other than the sinful human needing God's justification and the righteous God who for Jesus' sake justifies.

For many, theology is gaining a "God's-eye" perspective on reality, one that tidies up our experience so that it makes sense to us in

---

[11] For a study of heroism, see Ernest Becker, *The Denial of Death* (New York: Free Press, 1973).

[12] Paul Tillich, *Dynamics of Faith* (New York: Harper & Row, 1957), 1–4.

light of God. If our theology fails to square with metaphysics, the question of what's really real, then it is not grounded in reality. As noble as that goal is, a "God's-eye" view of reality is not something the human can pull off. It is not something given to us, at least in this life in which we only "see in a mirror dimly" (1 Cor. 13:12). Our scope is finite and limited, and so it will remain. Our thinking—this side of heaven—can only go so far. As Ecclesiastes 3:11 says, "[God] has put eternity into man's heart," and thus we cannot help but ask metaphysical questions, but the scope of getting at all reality is beyond our comprehension. On top of that, we are sinful and like to remain in control of our lives. The quest for a "God's-eye" perspective, which is the goal of most metaphysical systems, asks the question, What's really real? Outside or apart from the scriptures, this question can be indicative of a spiritual disease. No doubt, God is the most real of all reality. But metaphysics must ever be approached with caution: we all would wish we could establish our own divinity (what Luther called *ambitatio divinitatis*). But that is just our problem. We must eschew metaphysics when it is the attempt to justify ourselves in light of our insignificance and finitude or to offer an explanation that might console us when we encounter pain, which often seems so arbitrary and unmerited. Metaphysical categories are serviceable only when they are "bathed" in the truth coming from the scriptures.[13]

The Sinful Human and Justifying God

In that light, Luther in his interpretation of Psalm 51 (1532) defined theology as knowledge of God and humans (*cognitio dei et hominis*). For him, the only subject matter of theology is the knowledge that results from the relation between the sinful human who needs justification and the God who justifies.[14] Theology is not primarily

---

[13] See Mark Mattes, "Luther's Use of Philosophy," *Lutherjahrbuch* (2013): 110–41; see also Mattes, *Martin Luther's Theology of Beauty: A Reappraisal* (Grand Rapids: Baker Academic, 2017), 18.

[14] "The proper subject of theology is man guilty of sin and condemned, and God the Justifier and Savior of man the sinner." See "Psalm 51" in LW 12:311.

speculation that offers the grand narrative of cosmic and human history or a program for ethical or spiritual reform or reflection on the deepest yearnings of our inner life. In a word, it deals not primarily with metaphysics, morality, or mysticism. This is said not to disown the attempt to understand reality or to do good or to experience God. Rather, it is said to locate all such matters within the context of the scriptures and to deprive these goals of any bargaining chips of self-justification. The scriptures maintain that our theologizing is based on *where God meets us*—most clearly and specifically in the preached word and embodied in the sacraments but also as encountered in all creation, since God speaks to us in all things (Ps. 19; Rom. 1), though not always clearly. And here we should be unambiguous. Preaching at its best is not only a description of God's will and ways; rather, it actually *gives* the gifts it talks about. It does not merely enlighten but instead defines us as forgiven sinners. It was his mentor Johann von Staupitz and later his pastor Johannes Bugenhagen who "delivered the goods" to Luther, forgiving him his sins for Jesus' sake and so allowing him to resituate his life to be focused not on himself but instead on honoring God by trusting God's Word and seeking to help others in their needs.[15]

Luther came to these insights about a pastoral approach to theology via his monastic formation. Luther's spiritual formation can be traced to the influence of both the monastery and the university. The medieval university practiced *disputatio*, debating over theses offered by professors to students. Luther himself was a master at the art of disputation. However, Luther's spiritual background was in the "monastic" tradition, which treasured the practice of meditating the hours with the Psalter. This is a liturgical theology that honors a pastoral use of scripture coupled with a cultivation of the affects, including the emotions, senses, desires, and imagination. This monastic approach involves meditating on the text, listening to the scriptural word, allowing it to resituate our imaginations and do its work in us. Likewise, Luther was influenced, even in the monastery, by Humanism, which sought to return to the sources of faith

---

[15] See Franz Posset, "Staupitz and Luther," in *The Oxford Encyclopedia of Martin Luther*, vol. 3 (New York: Oxford University Press, 2017), 360–73.

(*ad fontes*) the scriptures in their original languages. While Luther honored the university method of *disputatio* to establish doctrine, his spiritual counsel is based on the monastic and Humanistic valuing of the scriptures. Both the monastic and the scholastic traditions influenced Luther's more systematic treatment of theology, which can best be described as catechetical, expositing the truth of the Ten Commandments, the Apostle's Creed, and the Lord's Prayer.[16]

A pastoral approach to theology means that theology must be discerning. Luther distinguishes between sinners who feel their sins (*peccator sensatus*) and those who are unaware of their sins (*peccator insensatus*).[17] This is one reason law must be distinguished from gospel. Some sinners are smug in their sin and confident of their ability to escape punishment. They need to hear God's accusing voice—said so paradigmatically in Nathan's rebuke to David: "*You* are the culpable one. *You* are the one who stands condemned! (2 Samuel 12:7)." Others are lost in both their sin and the feared consequences of their sin. Trapped in themselves, their life becomes a living hell, a nightmare. They know that they have been caught in the act. And they have no program that can free them. Instead, all their self-help merely feeds the centrality of the self and aggravates the problem. They need instead to hear God's promise of grace and mercy for Jesus' sake. As Luther put it, the penitent is "individuated" before God (*principium individuationis*),[18] meaning that he or she is exposed before God's scrutiny and so must confess to God: "Against you, you only, have I sinned." This person can and must hear that God is one who embraces the lost and welcomes them into His fold.

When in the early 1970s Karl Menninger asked, "Whatever became of sin?,"[19] the answer is that the modern world has repressed its very existence. We have valorized victims rather than help repentant perpetrators be delivered of their guilt. One movement stands

---

[16] What Bayer calls "Catechetical Systematics"; see *Theology the Lutheran Way*, 67–73.

[17] "Psalm 51" in LW 12:315 (WA 40/II:328, 1f.).

[18] See Bayer, *Theology the Lutheran Way*, 17.

[19] Karl Menninger, *Whatever Became of Sin?* (New York: Hawthorne Books, 1973).

out in contrast to modern repression of sin: Twelve-step groups of various sorts. Many struggling to overcome their addictions rely on the "twelve steps," where it is necessary to admit one's shortcomings and failures, in contradistinction to affirming one's victimization. Those who can own up to how they have contributed to hurt in their families, among their friends, and in their communities and admit "I'm an alcoholic" find the holding power of the addiction to lessen. It is not that the concept of sin has disappeared in North America and Europe but that it has been so repressed that one must seek a twelve-step group to actually encounter it. This is a shame because many do "feel their sins," but apart from confession and forgiveness, whether private or corporate, they have no outlet by which to come clean. Congregations evangelize through quaint "pet blessing" ceremonies and the like but also boldly broadcast, "Confessions Heard Today! Open to the Public." The church should take confession and forgiveness far more seriously than it has done recently. Those in recovery are simply the tip of the iceberg. And the church, at the behest of her Lord, actually has the office of the keys that can break the bondage of guilt far more powerfully than a decidedly nonsectarian twelve-step program can.

Hiddenness of God

As discerning, however, this pastoral theology realizes that some are not merely lost in their sin and guilt but also experience something other than guilt, "diffuseness," we might say, meaning that they have lost their compass or that they feel that God has abandoned them. They experience what Luther called the "hidden God" (*deus absconditus*).[20] Like the innocent sufferer Job experiencing God's abandonment, unjustly afflicted, they cry out, "Where is God?" This is more than simply the "dark night of the soul" described by various mystics.

---

[20] For distinguishing the law's accusation from the hidden God, see Mark Mattes, "Properly Distinguishing Law and Gospel as the Pastor's Calling," in *The Necessary Distinction: A Continuing Conversation on Law and Gospel*, ed. Albert B. Collver III, James Arne Nestingen, and John T. Pless (St. Louis: Concordia, 2017), 115.

In the experience of hiddenness, it is as if God Himself has been "absconded," stolen. Whether correct or not, those who experience such hiddenness feel abandoned by God. It is not so much that they feel accused by God's law. Instead, they encounter an emptiness, a gap, a hole, where previously God was. And so, such folks, like Job, look to accuse God and even seek a lawyer to put God on trial. Less burdened by guilt, it is more accurate to say that they experience confusion with respect to the justness of their experience, their place in the world, and deal with a diffuseness of self.

These people need to hear God's commitment of love to them and that God and his grace is sufficient for them in their trials. Even when God is hidden, we can appeal to the God whom we know is gracious and merciful in the love given in Jesus Christ. Whether as sinners brought low, even reduced to nothing by sin, or as those wondering where God has gone, we experience separation from God: a painful, even fatal, separation. Yet in such separation, Luther believes that the "naked God," as he puts it, "is there with humans in their nakedness."[21] No speculative or moral or mystical bridge can stand in the face of this "naked God." This naked God is God in His absolute majesty, the unapproachable God of light (1 Tim. 6:16). Without the word of absolution, we are brought to our end by this Absolute. With this God, we can have "nothing to 'do,' we cannot 'handle' him, we cannot 'deal' with him, we cannot 'speak' to him and, we cannot even believe in him."[22] This is why the name of Jesus—God's mercy and compassion—must be on the tip of every preacher's and confessor's tongue.

The End of the Law

Currently, the role of the law in the life of the believer, the law as parenetic or instructive for believers, the third use of the law, is hotly disputed among Lutherans. In the Formula of Concord, law exists for three reasons: (1) to curb sin so that social health will prevail, (2) to accuse sinners and lead them to Christ alone for salvation,

---

[21] WA 40/II:330, 1. See Bayer, *Theology the Lutheran Way*, 18.

[22] Ibid.

and (3) to instruct believers in how to oppose the flesh and so allow Christ to prevail in their lives.[23] Or, with respect to its third use, Luther put it, "The law is to be retained so that the saints know what works God requires in which they can exercise obedience toward God."[24] Charles Arand does a fine job describing this third use:

> As someone born anew by the Holy Spirit, the believer (the new creature) is eager to serve God willingly and spontaneously. But the old creature rises up and seeks to distract the believer by saying, "You want to serve God? I have a really good idea. You can serve God by going on a pilgrimage or by becoming a monk." At that point, the third use of the law enters by reminding the person of what God's will is for us, and thus channeling the believer's energies in a God-pleasing direction.[25]

Some Lutherans reject a third use because they cherish the truth that Jesus Christ is not only necessary for salvation but also sufficient for Christian living. For them, any talk of law in the Christian life is tantamount to legalism.

To my way of thinking, the current debate is due to different Lutheran responses to a fault line in the prevalent ethos of European and North American culture. This culture is "post-Christian," meaning that it is no longer structured along the lines of scripture but instead endorses the inviolability of individuals' quests for their own good provided no harm is done to others. Whereas at one time wider society endorsed an overall Christian ethos, that is no longer the case. In fact, distinctive Christian teachings about life and marriage are currently challenged by many in the academy, the media,

---

[23] The Formula of Concord, Solid Declaration, Article VI, in Robert Kolb and Timothy J. Wengert, eds., *The Book of Concord* (Minneapolis: Fortress, 2000), 587–91.

[24] Holger Sonntag, ed., *Solus Decalogus est Aeternus: Martin Luther's Complete Antinomian theses and Disputations* (Minneapolis: Lutheran Press, 2008), 227 (WA 39 I, 485, 22–24). See also WA 10 I/1, 456, 17–20.

[25] Charles Arand, "Law and Gospel," in *The Oxford Encyclopedia of Martin Luther*, ed. Derek R. Nelson and Paul R. Hinlicky, vol. 2 (New York: Oxford University Press, 2017), 98.

social work, and education. As if Christianity had never provided the dominant ethos of Europe and North America, many voices of these contemporary challengers surprisingly sound akin to ancient Epicureans who advocated that humans should seek pleasure in moderation provided no harm is done to others or ancient Gnostics who honored the divinity of the self, latent beneath layers of bodily existence, as well as the inviolability, but also necessity, of the self's right to explore all aspects and features inherent within it.[26]

The culture itself then creates a conundrum with respect to law. The prevailing ethos is *antinomian* in the sense that it denies any ultimate good or *telos* and so any objectivity in individuals' quests to measure or arbitrate whether or not they achieve their well-being. All "good" is relativized to individual taste. But surprisingly, the prevailing ethos is quite law-bound or *nomian* in the sense that individuals are compelled, driven, to "be all that they can be" based on "whatever turns their crank." Modern people are driven to fully explore all their desires and, in fact, *must* do so if they are to be their own self-creators. Paradoxically, they are "condemned to be free," as Jean-Paul Sartre put it.[27] There is no objective, universally recognized standard for the unencumbered self to measure whether or not it actually realizes its potential fully. Since it would clip the wings of individual self-expression, God's law is rejected. But it is replaced with an all-encompassing legalism that allows sinners no rest in their attempts to define themselves.

In response to current subjectivism and individualism, a free-for-all ethical pandemonium, many strands of Protestant Evangelicalism, true to their Calvinistic or Arminian roots, have pushed as never before strict rules for Christian living, sanctification via works, both among youth and for wider American society. Hence many Evangelicals either feed self-righteousness, their ability

---

[26] With respect to contemporary Epicureanism, see Benjamin Wiker, *Moral Darwinism: How We Became Hedonists* (Downers Grove: Intervarsity, 2002). With respect to Gnosticism, see Harold Bloom, *The American Religion: the Emergence of the Post-Christian Nation* (New York: Touchstone, 1992).

[27] See Jean-Paul Sartre, "Existentialism Is a Humanism," accessed January 5, 2018. https://www.marxists.org/reference/archive/sartre/works/exist/sartre.htm.

to fulfill the law, or find themselves trapped in horrendous self-loathing for their failures. Some Evangelicals eventually find a home in Lutheranism precisely because they are attracted to a faith tradition where Christ's cross and not the Torah scrolls are at the center of God's heart.

Given this antinomian flipside (no ultimate *telos*) of the secular nomianism (be all that you can be) prevalent in the secular West, some Lutherans give virtually a primary status to the third use of the law similar to many Reformed Christians. With the resurgence of a legalistic piety rampant among many Evangelicals, along with a Pietist heritage among North American Lutherans, other Lutherans insist that the attempt to seek guidance from the law for the Christian life betrays the power of the gospel to end law for the believer (Rom. 10:4). The insight from this school is that believers realize that when the law is at the center of their lives, and not Christ, they stay trapped within themselves. They discover that the law can never deliver them from the self's compulsion to improve itself. A law-centered life keeps them curved in on the self. The freedom that all legalists need is to be free of the self, with its self-centeredness, but the law feeds this monster and cannot deliver. Only Jesus Christ can do that.

That said, in today's world, many Christians who seek guidance or direction from the scriptures and the church do so in order to gain direction or insight for fulfilling their vocations. They should not be seen as legalists. They recognize that contemporary anomie, felt acutely by so many young people, the result of the loss of an objective *telos* to which all are accountable, is the wage of present-day consumeristic incurvation fed by the emptiness of various secular utopianisms. Nor do they think that the law can be domesticated, as if its accusation of sinners can be neutralized. It is not as if they are obsessed with charting the course of their sanctification or measuring their personal and visible holiness with respect to others, playing a game of spiritual one-upmanship. Jesus' merit is sufficient for them. They know that Christ is their wisdom, righteousness, *sanctification*, and redemption (1 Cor. 1:30). They know that in Christ they have all the righteousness that they will ever have because God's final verdict has already been rendered upon them in the words of absolution. But precisely for that very reason, they seek each day to grow into this identity given them in Christ. This is not for their own merit but in order to please God and to serve their neighbors.

So they are not seeking to feed the legalism of the old Adam but instead to provide a safe, wholesome environment in which to raise their families in the chaotic and unsupportive face of public schools, the media, and other public institutions that undermine those very health-giving standards that they seek to instill in their children. They wish to take seriously Luther's interpretation of the second petition of the Lord's Prayer ("thy kingdom come"):

> We ask here at the outset that all this may be realized in us and that his name may be praised through God's holy Word and Christian living. This we ask, both in order that we who have accepted it may remain faithful and *grow daily in it* and also in order that it may find approval and gain followers among other people and advance with power throughout the world.[28]

Now given the ethical chaos prevalent in society today, we must preach Christ to those afflicted with their own unrealistic and often sinful exploits developing from the quests for self-discovery and self-affirmation. But we must also establish some helpful parameters in congregations for wholesome behavior. To do that, we must affirm a robust approach to catechization for both youth and converts. Given that the wider public no longer supports a Christian ethos but

---

[28] Luther, "The Large Catechism," 447:52. Italics mine. See also 438:53: "Through it he gathers us, using it to teach and preach the Word. By it he creates and increases holiness, causing it daily to grow and become strong in the faith and in its fruits, which the Spirit produces." Elsewhere Luther speaks of justification: "These are the two parts of justification. The first is grace revealed through Christ, that through Christ we have a gracious God, so that sin can no longer accuse us, but our conscience has found peace through trust in the mercy of God. The second part is the conferring of the Holy Spirit with His gifts, who enlightens us against the defilements of spirit and flesh (2 Cor. 7:1). . . . Thus we are defended against the opinions with which the devil seduced the whole world. Thus the true knowledge of God grows daily, together with other gifts, like chastity, obedience, and patience." "Psalm 51" in LW 12:331.

in fact undermines it, congregations will need, as never before, to teach the faith—that is, God's Commands, the Creed, the gospel, the Lord's Prayer, and the efficacy of the sacraments.[29] In contrast to the Reformed tendency to wish to claim every inch of culture for Christ, this catechesis must be done whether or not it contributes to America as a "Christian nation." If current trends continue (and it is likely they will), the church's catechetical program will become more and more akin to that of the ancient church prior to its legalization in the Roman Empire.

With respect to the current debate over the third use of the law among Lutherans, I find Charles Arand's position helpful:

> In the final analysis, much of the debate about the third use of the law comes down to terminology. Both those who advocate for it and those who reject it advocate Christian instruction in ethics and the Christian life. Some call this the third use of the law, while others call it the first use of the law applied to Christians. The concern for those who reject a third use of the law is that the Christian life is not ultimately defined by the law. It does not begin with the law, nor does it end with the law as if the gospel were only a means to an end. Instead the gospel is the final word.[30]

The Power of Faith

For Luther, then, with respect to our relation to God, everything hinges on faith. Now faith is no inadequate approach to knowledge as Plato would have us think. Instead, it is a confident trust in God's promise, God's loyalty to us, in the face of everything that seems to challenge it, whether that be the accusations of the law or the apparent absence of God's care for us in creation or history. For no other postbiblical theologian whether Eastern or Western is the experience of faith so central or pivotal for life as it is to Luther. In his

---

[29] Here Jim Nestingen, along with Gerhard Forde, paved the way with the catechetical resource, *Free to Be.*

[30] Charles Arand, "Law and Gospel," in *The Oxford Encyclopedia of Martin Luther*, 98.

Lectures on Galatians (1531), Luther even goes so far as to claim that faith is the "creator of the Deity" (*fides est creatrix divinitatis*),[31] not of course with respect to God's own person but with respect to ourselves. Indeed, "it is the trust and faith of the heart alone that make both God and an idol."[32] Through faith, we "make God." As Oswald Bayer notes, the phrase "to make God" (*deum facere*) means to give or to attribute to God what is his.[33]

But as we have seen, there is no conflict-free relationship with God. Luther is cognizant that where we encounter God, a power struggle will always ensue. In his mind, we want to be our own gods. As sinners, our first impulse is to trust ourselves, and we resist putting our confidence in another or allow another to be there for us. In such an exchange between ourselves and God, a life-and-death struggle for mutual recognition, faith makes God. Faith acknowledges human impotency and need before God. In this way, as Jim Nestingen in his teaching so often put it, "we are being conformed to the image of the crucified."

The Receptive Life

Helpfully, Oswald Bayer notes that Luther avoids the Aristotelian alternatives of grounding theology in either *action* (*actio*) or contemplation (*contemplatio*). Instead, for Luther, in contrast to everything else, theology deserves to have its own unique name, the passive life or receptive life (*vita passiva*).[34] By this, Luther highlights the truth that God is the active subject and the Christian is the receptive object of God's action. God is the potter and we are the clay (Jer. 18:1–17). The Christian life therefore is passive in the sense that it suffers, it undergoes God's recreative work. Whatever we do in the world is shaped by God's ever-active work upon us. Thus the receptive life is connected with a particular struggle, one that we do not produce

---

[31] *Lectures on Galatians* (1535) in LW 26:227 (WA 40/I:360, 5f. [on Gal. 3:6]).

[32] Luther, "The Large Catechism," 386:2.

[33] Bayer, *Theology the Lutheran Way*, 20 (WA 40/I:360, 8f., 11; LW 26:227).

[34] Ibid., 22. See WA 5:165, 35f.

of ourselves but instead undergo as sinners who of necessity struggle with God for recognition. In Luther's own striking words, "It is by living—no, not living, but by dying and giving ourselves up to hell that we become theologians, not by understanding, reading, and speculating."[35]

How then are we sinners to be made right before God? It is God's forensic decree of acquittal for Jesus' sake that does this.[36] This forensic judgment is the vertical dimension to justification. But this vertical dimension carries with it a horizontal dimension as well, the whole of our lives as lived experience. Justification then is the fullness of life as it is granted to us by our creator. The "righteousness of faith" of which Luther speaks is wholly passive: day by day, we simply trust God to do his work in us. God is the craftsman who is ever shaping our lives, conforming us more and more to live in faith and so conformed to the image of Jesus Christ, trusting in God's promise. God is an artist, and we are God's artisanship. Faith, for Luther, is highly experiential, though experience is defined through the word and does not serve as a source of theological authority. I experience faith by trusting God to work it in me. The gospel promise is joyful and sweet. But the experience of the old Adam and Eve dying is painful indeed. For Luther, this is no mere picture language. But in contrast to all theologies of glory, it is honest and it gives life resiliency and buoyancy. It is refreshing that Luther gives a portrait of the Christian life as shaped by the cross and not as an illusory "pie in the sky bye and bye."

---

[35] *Operationes in Psalmos* (1519–21) in WA 5:163.23–29 (trans. Bayer, *Theology the Lutheran Way*, 23).

[36] See Mark Mattes, "Luther on Justification as Forensic and Effective," in *The Oxford Handbook of Martin Luther's Theology*, ed. Robert Kolb, Irene Dingel, and Ľubomír Batka (New York: Oxford University Press, 2014), 264–73; Mark Mattes, "Justification," in *Dictionary of Luther and the Lutheran Traditions*, ed. Timothy J. Wengert, et al. (Grand Rapids: Baker, 2017), 385–89; Mark Mattes, "Justification by Faith Alone," in *Encyclopedia of Martin Luther and the Reformation*, ed. Mark A. Lamport, vol. 1 (Lanham: Rowman & Littlefield), 392–94; and Mark Mattes, *The Role of Justification in Contemporary Theology* (Grand Rapids: Eerdmans, 2004).

Conclusion

Scripture exhorts us to "do the work of an evangelist" (2 Tim. 4:5).[37] It is sometimes thought that Lutherans are poor at evangelism. But that stance usually assumes that evangelism is equivalent to the revival tactics of the Second Great Awakening and thereafter. True, Lutherans are poor at manipulating sinners' alleged "free will" through either a "turn or burn" or a prosperity gospel tactic. The clue to evangelism is first of all to actually know the evangel. It is a gift-word, God's promise of forgiveness and mercy in Jesus Christ, that guides Lutheran pastors' hearts, giving them wisdom to discern law from gospel, empowering them to preach law by simply telling sinners the truth, and to preach the gospel with the liberating name of Jesus Christ ever on their tongue. May we who share in the office of the ministry seek to be true to this evangel, honor it by sharing it, and also raise up future generations of such evangelists.

---

[37] See Mark Mattes, "How to Cultivate Biblical, Confessional, Resilient, and Evangelistic Pastors," *Lutheran Forum* (Fall 2017): 38–46.

Luther's First Galatians Lectures (1516–17)

A Student's Experience

Dr. Hans Wiersma

Introduction

This essay attempts to peel back the layers of Luther's lifetime of reading, writing, and lecturing on the Apostle Paul's letter to the Galatians. The pinnacle of the reformer's work in "Pauline studies" is arguably the great *Commentary on Galatians*, first published in 1535. Of course, 1535 was not the first year that Luther worked on Galatians. The 1535 publication is itself based on lectures that Luther presented to his students in 1531–32. Those lectures were themselves a development of the interpretations found in Luther's first Galatians commentary, published in 1519. However, the 1519 publication drew heavily upon material that Luther had prepared for his students in lectures presented from late October 1516 to mid-March 1517. This essay, as the title indicates, is concerned about the content of Luther's original Galatians lectures. In addition, as the title also indicates, this essay is about the experience of one particular student who sat through those lectures and took notes.

This investigation, therefore, has at its center the extant physical copy of the lecture notes taken by one of the students present at Luther's first lectures on Galatians. I initially undertook this investigation to see if those notes might offer insight into how Luther was received by one of his earliest hearers.[1] At the beginning of this investigation, I confess that I was somewhat naively hopeful that I would find at least one noteworthy contradiction between what the student's notebook (*Kollegheft*, in German) says Luther said in 1516 or 1517 and what Luther himself eventually said in his polished and published Galatians commentaries of 1519 and of 1535. At the very least, I hoped that I might find something in the student's notebook that would further elucidate the present scholarly understanding around the development of Luther's so-called theological break-through. As it turned out, I discovered what previous investigators of the notebook also discovered: it does not contain any data that would overturn the present state of study of the early development of Luther's theology. On the other hand, in exploring the artifact itself—the notebook—I learned a thing or two about what it was like to be a student experiencing one of Luther's earliest lecture series. Most significantly, I discovered an odd detail that might explain why one anonymous student felt a need to distance himself ever so slightly from his famous teacher.[2]

---

[1] This essay is based in part on a paper I presented at the Sixteenth-Century Studies Conference, San Juan, Puerto Rico, on October 26, 2013. The subject of "Early Luther Reception"—namely, the ways in which Luther was received by his earliest hearer's and readers—was at the heart of my dissertation project and has been a focus of mine ever since. The title of my dissertation is "The Recantation, Restoration, and Reformation of Jacob Probst: An Early Luther 'Discipulus' from the Low Countries."

[2] It is a high honor to present this essay in thanksgiving for my teacher and friend Jim Nestingen. Jim served as my foremost mentor during my MDiv years and as my *Doktervater* (one of two) during my PhD years. Therefore, my indebtedness to Jim for his labor to turn me into a pastor and then a professor runs high. But even more significantly, Jim is the one I credit most for helping guide me to my higher vocations as husband and father. Words cannot express . . . so I won't even try.

The Development of Luther's Galatians Lectures: Existing Scholarship

In *Luthers Auslegungen des Galaterbriefs von 1519 und 1531: Ein Vergleich*, Karin Bornkamm offers a thorough comparison of Luther's two primary "takes" on Galatians.[3] In this 1963 publication, Bornkamm locates key patterns of development in the twelve years between Luther's major commentaries. Bornkamm identifies a number of theological frameworks implemented by Luther, including Luther's insistence on the all-sufficient revelation of Christ in word and sacrament and his high view of the preaching office. While the 1531 version might favor the phrase "the article of justification" rather than 1519's straightforward "justification," Bornkamm concludes that "the differences in Luther's [two] Galatians exegeses remain within the characteristic parameters, the inner structure of his theological pronouncements remained the same."[4] Bornkamm's upshot, in other words, is that while there are distinctions in formulations and emphases when comparing Luther's 1519 and 1531 Galatians treatments, there is no significant theological change of mind. For Luther scholars who understand that there is no significant difference in theological orientation between the "young Luther" and the "mature Luther," Bornkamm's conclusion should come as no surprise.

However, there are two items worthy of note when considering Bornkamm's comparison. First is the fact that she chose to compare the *amended and published* version of Luther's 1519 Galatians commentary with the unamended and initially unpublished notes of 1531—notes taken by Luther's faithful transcriber, Georg Rörer. While it is true that Rörer recorded Luther's 1531 Galatians lectures with an eye toward their eventual publication, it is also true that Luther himself amended Rörer's recordings in preparation for

---

[3] Karin Bornkamm, *Luthers Auslegungen des Galaterbriefs von 1519 und 1531: Ein Vergleich*, Arbeiten zur Kirchengeschichte 35 (Berlin: de Gruyter, 1963). Yes, the author is the daughter of the well-known Luther scholar Heinrich Bornkamm (1901–1977).

[4] Ibid., 387. My translation.

the 1535 publication.[5] The difference between Rörer's notes and Luther's own editing of them are plain to see, thanks to the Weimar Ausgabe's presentation of the two versions side by side (or rather top by bottom).[6]

In other words, Bornkamm's work compares Luther's own 1519 reworking of the 1516/17 Galatians lectures with the unreworked notes, taken by another, of the 1531 Galatians lectures. Bornkamm clearly had a good reason to proceed this way: she likely understood that Rörer's notes, presuming their relative accuracy, captured Luther's original verbiage better than did Luther's own reworking of Rörer's notes a few years later.[7]

This observation leads to a second item worth noting—namely, Bornkamm's dismissal of the lecture notes provided by a recorder of Luther's pre–Ninety-Five Theses lectures on Galatians. Indeed, just as the 1535 published commentary can be compared to Rörer's extant notes taken during the original presentation of those lectures in 1531, so also can the 1519 published commentary be compared to extant notes taken during the original presentation of those lectures in late 1516 and early 1517. Yet here, from her preface, is Bornkamm's only mention of those original notes: "I have left aside the lecture of 1516/1517, a comparison with which might have yielded an interesting special topic regarding the development of the young Luther. However, regarding the inquiry at hand, such a comparison would not deliver anything of significance, since, in my opinion, those lectures are, in all, so near to the 1519 commentary."[8]

It appears that Bornkamm was not aware that (1) the only contemporary record of Luther's 1516/17 Galatians lectures is in the form of an anonymous student's notes (the aforementioned *Kollegheft*) or that (2) there are in fact key differences between the 1516/17 version and the 1519 publication. If she was aware of either of these factors, she did not think them worthy of mention. When

---

[5] CITE introduction in the AE.

[6] CITE WA.

[7] Bornkamm's footnotes indicate her preference for Rörer's text, which she quotes almost exclusively.

[8] Bornkamm, *Luthers Auslegungen*, VIII.

one considers that Luther dated his theological "ah-ha moment" to a time after he had, in his words, "lectured in the university on St. Paul's epistles to the Romans, to the Galatians, and the one to the Hebrews,"[9] Bornkamm's neglect of the 1516/17 source comes as a slight surprise. True, the time lapse between the end of Luther's first Galatians lectures (March 13, 1517) and the start of his work on the publication of those lectures was a mere two years.[10] But these were by all accounts an eventful two years! The timing of Luther's "theological breakthrough"—as early as 1513(?), as late as 1519(?)—has been the subject of a well-worn discussion.[11] Therefore, to indicate such low expectations of the 1516/17 lecture notes—as Bornkamm's work indicates—does not quite compute.

As a response to Bornkamm, then, let us consider a second scholarly comparison of Luther's Galatians lectures: *Luther's Approach to Scripture as Seen in His "Commentaries" on Galatians 1519–1538* by Kenneth Hagen.[12] Hagen's overriding project is to adjust the understanding of "commentary" as it might have been understood and implemented by Luther. Hagen argues that Luther's exegesis of a text can hardly be called a commentary by modern standards. Hagen claims that the term *enarratio* fits Luther's intention and understanding better; Hagen supports this claim by demonstrating Luther's various *enarrations* of Paul's Galatians. Hagen's work concludes, in part, by urging readers to understand that Luther is not so much a biblical commentator in the modern sense; instead, Luther is properly

---

[9] LW 34:336. Luther completed his lectures on Hebrews in March 1518.

[10] On March 13, 1519, Luther informed Spalatin, "I am now giving birth to Paul's Epistle to the Galatians." Quoted in LW 27:x (Introduction to Volume 27) but doesn't cite WA Br. DeWette, Briefe I: 239 has *Jam et Paulus ad Galatas parturio*. Locate these words in WA Br.

[11] A brief summary of this discussion (as it existed in 1960) can be found in LW 34:325. For a most recent and most comprehensive overview of the context of Luther's "breakthrough"—including a helpful discussion of the challenges of putting a date or even a year on it—see Berndt Hamm, *The Early Luther: Stages in a Reformation Reorientation*, trans. Martin Lohrmann (Grand Rapids: Eerdmans, 2014).

[12] Kenneth Hagan, *Luther's Approach to Scripture as Seen in His "Commentaries" on Galatians 1519–1538* (Tübingen: Mohr Siebeck, 1993).

understood as a biblical *enarrator,* and in the case of the Galatians letter, Luther intentionally functions as an *enarrator* of the Apostle Paul. More on this idea of *enarratio* follows.

Another of Hagen's conclusions concerns the question of Luther's development. Although Hagen has his own critique of Bornkamm's work, Hagen nevertheless expresses interest in Bornkamm's central question. Hagen puts the question simply: "Did Luther change his mind over the years . . . ?"[13] Hagen's response to this question is unique. Instead of answering "Yes" or "No," Hagen questions the validity of the question, criticizing it as a modern rather than a medieval concern. Engagingly and convincingly, Hagen reorients Luther's (in)famous 1545 account of his circa 1519 ah-ha moment, asserting that the tale is rhetorical rather than historical.[14] Still, Hagen cannot resist answering the original question: "It is not true that Luther changed his mind on central theological matters such as the principal subjects of the Christian gospel, faith, and righteousness, or God, Aristotle, active and passive grammar, Old and New Testament, *humana* and *divina*"[15]—and certainly not as these subjects are encountered in Luther's *enarratio* of the Galatians letter, beginning in 1516. In short, as far as Luther's Galatians work is concerned, Hagen's conclusion matches Bornkamm's: there is no "breakthrough" when comparing the early and later versions of the commentaries, only development.

Finally, in regard to Hagen's work, is the question of the place of the 1516/17 version of the commentary. Despite the fact that the title of his book refers to Luther's Galatians commentaries from *1519* to *1538* (so, five in all), Hagen also frequently consulted the 1516/17 student's notebook, *das Kollegheft.* Hagen treats the student's notes as faithful recordings of Luther's original lecture, and for good reason, as we shall see. Unlike Bornkamm, Hagen does not neglect the

---

[13] Ibid., IX. For Hagen's critiques of Bornkamm, see 13, 19.

[14] Luther's best-known "long version" of the tale of his breakthrough moment is found in the Preface to Luther's Latin Works (CITE). One of the short versions has been dubbed Luther's "tower experience." This recollection, recorded by a student, is in CITE.

[15] Ibid., 123.

1516/17 lectures; instead, he freely cites the student's record of what Luther said in 1516/17, especially in regard to material that does not match up with the 1519 publication.[16] For instance, Hagen points out Luther's sharp criticism of Jerome on display in the 1516/17 lectures and notes that Luther softened his rebuke of Jerome for the 1519 publication.[17]

The Lecture Notes of 1516/17

At last we arrive at the matter of the material subject—namely, the 1516/17 notebook itself, the *Kollegheft*. What is it? Whose is it? What might it yet reveal? Is it possible that the *Kollegheft* reveals something about its creator, that University of Wittenberg student who, over a period of four and a half months, occupied a seat in the aula, listening to Luther lecture, dutifully transferring word to page?

Let us consider the first question: What is it? It is a volume of twenty large-format sheets of paper (or forty pages front to back) bound in a pigskin cover, at the time of this writing on display in the Melanchthonhaus museum in Bretten, Germany. Twenty of the pages are printed with Jerome's Latin text of the Galatians letter. Twenty additional pages were originally blank or mostly blank. These pages were originally ordered by Luther and printed by Johannes Grunenberg.[18] In the document at hand, all pages, including the title page, are filled with densely packed, handwritten notes.

---

[16] One may ask, Why then is Hagen's book titled *Luther's Approach to Scripture as Seen in His "Commentaries" on Galatians 1519–1538* rather than *1516–1538*? This question is easily answered. Hagen writes that his study "is based on the original prints of Luther's Commentaries on Galatians of 1519, 1523, 1525 (German), 1534, 1535, and 1538." He then clarifies that "Luther's lectures on Galatians of 1516–1517 have also been compared." Ibid., VII. In other words, because the anonymous student's 1516/17 *Kollegheft* was not published during Luther's lifetime, it was included in Hagen's title. Nevertheless, the *Kollegheft* is an important part of Hagen's analysis.

[17] Ibid., 46f.

[18] According to the description of Johann Oldekop, a hearer of Luther's 1515–16 Roman's lectures, "Luther had requested that the printer, Johannes Grunenberg, reproduce Paul's epistle with the lines widely separated from one

The biblical text is printed in large format (see figure 2.3), with ample space in between the lines and in the margins. As was the practice, the student recorded the teacher's words more or less verbatim. As he had done with his earlier lectures on the Psalms and on Romans, Luther, over the course of a two-hour lecture period, first went through the Galatians text word by word, sentence by sentence. As he progressed, Luther would dictate material that elucidated and amplified key words and phrases. These dictations represent the interlinear *glossa*. Then after a verse or section of verses was completed, Luther would offer additional exegesis, often citing ancient church authorities. These are the additional *glossa* recorded by the student in the margin areas. Finally, after a longer section had been completed, Luther offered more general explication, called *scholia*. When it came time to record *scholia*, the student would turn to one of the blank pages. Each new lecture would yield additional *scholia*, which the student would append to scholia previously recorded. (Our student's concluding column of *scholia* can be seen in figure 2.9.)

Save for one compelling clue, little is known concerning the whereabouts of the *Kollegheft* after Luther's first Galatians lectures were completed. But after more than three hundred years, the student's *Kollegheft* surfaced again in 1877 in an antique shop in Köln. By 1912, the notebook had landed in Melanchthon's birthplace, Bretten,

---

another, in order to allow the glossa, because that is where Luther would provide much commentary upon the collected writings of the old Catholic doctors." Johann Oldekop, *Chronik des Johan Oldecop*, ed. Karl Euling (Tübingen: Laupp, 1889), 45. My translation. Oldekop provides some additional reminiscences of his days as a young man studying in Wittenberg. On certain minor feast days, the students would organize parties, where they would "drink, make merry, and ask the villagers' daughters to dance." Worse, "the guys would put on the girls' caps; the maidens' would return the favor and put on the students' berets." Against these shenanigans, "Luther preached so sharply and firmly that the parents kept their unmarried daughters in their homes." Consequently, "Luther received support, praise, honor, and reward from the most distinguished citizens." Ibid., 45–46.

where it was studied by experts, including Hans von Schubert, who edited, transposed, and published the text in 1918.[19]

The editor of the Weimar Ausgabe's 1939 publication of the *Kollegheft* wondered (as we might), "Is it possible, via a comparison of [this student's notes] and Luther's published 1519 version, to be able to approach a reconstruction of Luther's own original lecture notes, now lost?" The editor, Karl August Meissinger, deemed this question "the most important of all questions concerning" the student's record.[20]

Alas, the problem of comparison presents itself almost immediately. Comparing Luther's published 1519 commentary on the first two words of Galatians—*Paulus Apostolus* ("Paul, an apostle")—with the student's notes on the same words already reveals differences. For instance, Luther's published 1519 commentary includes this passage: "But the one who proffers either his own laws or human laws, decrees, or dogmas of the philosophers, surely you will not say that he is an apostle." This sentence is missing in the 1516 *glossa* of the *Kollegheft*. Meissinger, however, takes this as a clue. If one removes all of Luther's antipope, antidecretals, antischolastic rhetoric from the 1519 lectures, almost all of which is missing in the 1516/17 *glossa* and *scholia*, and then synthesizes what remains with what the 1519 lectures have in common with the student's notes, then one has come closer to Luther's own original lecture notes.[21]

Perhaps. But in fact, if one were to read the text of the student's notes straight through in one sitting, one would be done with it in half a day. Clearly, the student could not and did not record everything that Luther said. There was in the medieval lecture hall, much as today, space for clarification, for elaboration, for digression, for off-the-cuff remarks, and even for discussion. Moreover, as Meissinger

---

[19] Hans von Schubert, *Luthers Vorlesung über den Galaterbrief 1516/17*, Abhandlungen der Heidelberger Akademie der Wissenschaften, Philosophisch Historische Klasse 5 (Heidelberg: Carl Winters, 1918).

[20] WA 57:XI. My translation.

[21] Ibid., XIII–XV.

himself acknowledges, Luther did not dictate everything that he had written in his own *glossa* and *scholia*.[22]

Alas, subtracting the surplus of negativity toward Rome so apparent in the 1519 lectures will not provide scholars with a "net outcome" that yields Luther's original version of the 1516/17 lectures any more than will taking our anonymous student's notes as a comprehensive, verbatim record of all that was originally spoken by Luther during dozens upon dozens of hours lecturing on Galatians in 1516 and 1517. However, even if it were possible to reconstruct Luther's original from the *Kollegheft*, "Can we reconstruct Luther's own original version of the first Galatians lecture?" is not the only or even "the most important question" that can be asked of the student's note-taking efforts.

The Student

We can ask another question. Perhaps it is not the most important question, but it is at least as important as wondering about reconstructing long-lost originals. The question we can ask is, What about the student? The student did his best, we can presume, to record what he was taught to record—namely, Luther's *glossa* and *scholia*. As the editor of the Weimar Ausgabe's presentation of Luther's 1515 Romans lectures observed,

> More frequently than is commonly known, student notebooks are extant from the time of the transition from the Middle Ages to the Reformation. Sometimes they are the witness of the lectures held by Luther, at other times, as in the case of the lectures on Romans, they are the indispensable complement to the Reformer's own elaboration and the concrete echo in which the university professor's work for the interpretation of Holy Scriptures and for the instruction of his students can be perceived in its immediate effect.[23]

---

[22] Von Schubert, *Luthers Vorlesung*, XI.

[23] LW 25:xiii (Introduction to Volume 25), quoting Ficker's Romans Lectures introduction in WA 47.

It is possible, therefore, that just as with extant students' notes of Luther's 1515 Romans lectures, the student's notes on Luther's 1516/17 Galatians lectures contain clues regarding the early reception of Luther and his teachings—clues pertaining to Luther's "immediate effect."

In fact, Luther's Romans lectures present a luxury of sources: both Luther's original *glossa* and *scholia* as well as several sections of students' notes are extant. The Weimar's presentation of Luther's 1515 Romans lectures includes references to some of these students' notes, especially where there are noteworthy differences or additions. In other words, for Luther's Romans lectures, historians have both the "professor's work for the interpretation of Holy Scriptures" *and* a record of the echo, the interpretation's "immediate effect" upon students. For the Galatians lectures of 1516/17, however, Luther's original lecture notes are lost. All that we have, in the form of the *Kollegheft*, is a record of the "immediate effect."

Or, to return to Ken Hagen's conclusions about Luther's career exegeting Galatians, what the student's notes represent are an early, enfleshed recording of Luther's *enarratio* of Paul and the "echo" of that *enarration* on our student. "Luther clung tenaciously throughout his life to the basic doctrines found in Galatians," Hagen explains. "Paul put forth his theology in public, and that is why Luther did the same. The genre of Paul's and Luther's work is an *enarratio*."[24]

Hagan suggests a variety of ways to understand *enarratio*, but my Latin dictionary offers adequate options: to *enarrate* means to recount, to set forth.

In his first lectures on Galatians, Luther sought to recount and set forth Paul's arguments in Galatians for the benefit of his students. Luther, according to Hagen, attempted to reflect Paul's speech to the Galatians, his turns of phrase, amplifying Paul's rhetoric in such a way that his students would not only understand it but also experience it as Luther himself did.

---

[24] Hagen, *Luther's Approach*, 120, 121f.

Reading between the Lines

When I first read about the nineteenth-century discovery of the *Kollegheft* and learned that it represented the only on-site record of Luther's first Galatians lectures, I figured that the document would offer insight into Luther's early apprehension of Paul's arguments regarding justification by faith apart from works. Which it does, as the original German redactors and, later, Ken Hagen discovered. But I also hoped the notes would reveal something about the notetaker himself, our student, as an in-the-flesh example of one of the earliest hearers of Luther's reflections on Galatians, the epistle Luther famously likened to his wife, "Kathe, my rib."

It's not that I imagined that I would find the student's doodles in the *glossa* or long personal reflections upon what he heard Luther say—that is, Luther's "immediate effect." But our student could not even manage a textual aside such as, "Wow, Luther is really going after Jerome here" or some such remark. The Weimar editor does point out some of the student's idiosyncrasies: the student often makes errors in grammar, a word is misheard here, another word is misspelled there. Our student sometimes uses shorthand and doesn't always fully quote verses cited from other books of the Bible. One idiosyncrasy that I wondered about was the student's odd practice of sometimes doubling the letter *f* when it appeared at the beginning of some key words. The Weimar editor described this as *Spielerei* (playing around) and did not include the double *f*s in the edited text. The Weimar editor offered no conjecture regarding what might be playful about doubling up on the *f*. However, when I said these words with two *f*s aloud—ffidelium, fforte, fferunt—it made me wonder if the student might not have been attempting to mimic the way Luther might have pronounced or emphasized words that began a new thought or idea.[25]

Otherwise, however and alas, the practice of the day—transcribing the professor's words verbatim—did not lend itself to students adding their own *glossa* or *scholia*. For the most part,

---

[25] Von Schubert, *Luthers Vorlesung*, XIV–XV, citing pp. 1335, 1931, and 2121 in his edition of the lecture notes.

therefore, the student remains hidden behind his more-or-less faithful replication of Luther's earliest *enarrations* of the Galatians letter.

However, at the very end of the 1516/17 *Kollegenheft*, there is something interesting, perhaps also haunting, if only because it may in fact give that hoped-for glimpse into the student's own "lived experience," as it might be called today.

After recording Luther's final *scholia*, the student entered these concluding words (barely distinguishable in figure 2.9):

Finis Pauli altera die
post georgi pape a doctore
martino   collectum
in vniuersate Wittembergensi

The End of Paul, the next day
after [the feast of] Pope Gregory [the Great], by Doctor
Martin [Luther], assembled
at the University of Wittenberg

The words concerning the feast of "Pope George"—the student misspelled or misconstrued "Gregory"—indicate March 12, the day after which Luther concluded his first lectures on Galatians.[26] The words *finis Pauli*—"the End of Paul"—represent a curious, perhaps even clever, shorthand. *Pauli* is also, after all, Latin for "a little bit." The End of a Little Bit? An example of sixteenth-century student irony? In any case, the student simply declares "The end of Paul" as delivered "by doctor Martin." Perhaps this sign-off can be interpreted as validation of Ken Hagen's contention that through the enarrations of Doctor Martin, the student heard and experienced the Apostle Paul.

Finally, there is the curious matter of the word "Luther." It has been carefully erased. That is, there is a lacuna, a gap, in the third line of the final block of text—a space between the word "Martino" and the word "collectum" (see figure 2.9). Apparently, close inspection of the original, physical page yields an impression of the original

---

[26] After Vatican II, the Feast of St. Gregory I was moved from March 12 to September 3.

word: *luder* or *ludero*. At some point in the *Kollegheft*'s history, likely earlier than later, someone excised the name of the lecturer, Luther. This excision could be the work of a later possessor of the notes—someone who, for whatever reason, did not want the document so easily recognized as a record of Luther's teaching.

Or the removal of Luther's name might have been the work of our student himself, perhaps out of fear of the consequences for possessing and propagating the teachings of Luther.

Here is what is known. Wittenberg University drew students from all over Northern Europe, including Scandinavia and the Low Countries. Even before Luther's ascendance with the publication and spread of the Ninety-Five Theses and subsequent works, Wittenberg attracted students from beyond Saxony. Between 1517 and 1521, Luther and Wittenberg found themselves increasingly at odds with the ecclesial and imperial authorities. Then came Luther's appearance at the Worms' Diet and, in May 1521, the resultant Worms' Edict. The judgments and punishments prescribed by the edict were aimed not only at Luther but at all "accomplices receiving or favoring Luther and his works in any way."[27]

While the Edict of Worms was barely published and mostly ignored in German lands, the same was not true of other areas, especially the Low Countries. Beginning in December 1521, Augustinians sympathetic to Luther in the Low Countries—some of whom had studied in Wittenberg—were warned, condemned, arrested, tried, and convicted. One—Jacob Probst—was forced to recant. Two others—Johann van Esschen and Hendrik Voes—were burned at the stake in Brussels on July 1, 1523.

Alas, we do not know where in Northern Europe our student—the creator of the *Kollegheft*—came from or returned to. But it is possible that at some point, our student—the recorder of the first Galatians lectures—had reason to be worried about being caught with a lecture containing some of Luther's earliest ideas about justification by faith alone. And so, in a meager attempt to conceal the evidence, he erased "Luther."

---

[27] CITE.

The following images are taken from Luther, Martin. *Luther's Vorlesung über den Galaterbrief 1516/17*. Edited by Hans von Schubert. Heidelberg, Germany: Carl Winters Universitätsbuchhandlung, 1918.

Bl. 1ᵃ

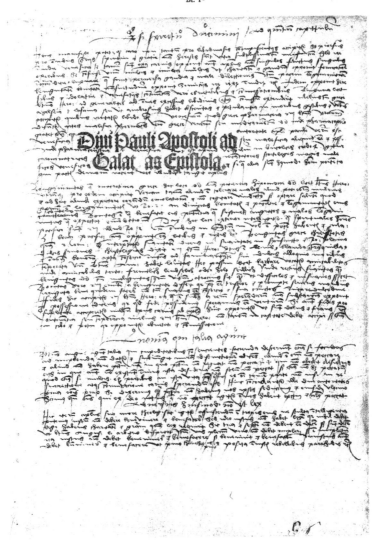

Figure 2.1: This is the cover page of the notebook. The Latin in large print translates as "Saint Paul, Apostle, Letter to the Galatians." The handwriting is the student's record of Luther's expanded comments on Galatians 5:19ff.

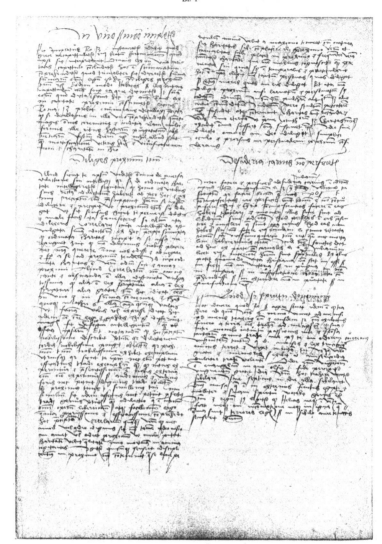

Figure 2.2: This is the inside of the cover page. The student chose this originally blank page to record Luther's expanded comments on Galatians 5:14–16.

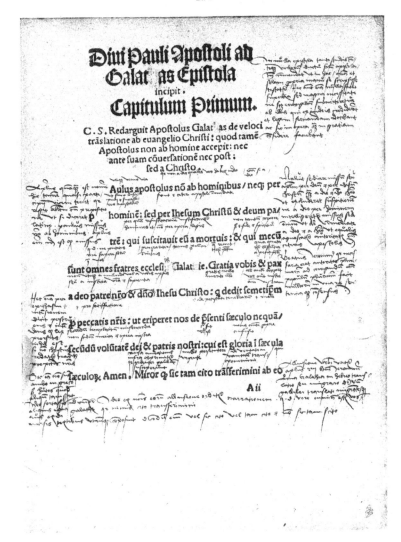

Figure 2.3: This is the first page that contains the printed Vulgate text of Galatians (a brief summary—by Luther—followed by 1:1–5a). In the spaces, the student has recorded his hearing of Luther's glossa. In the margins is the student's record of Luther's scholia.

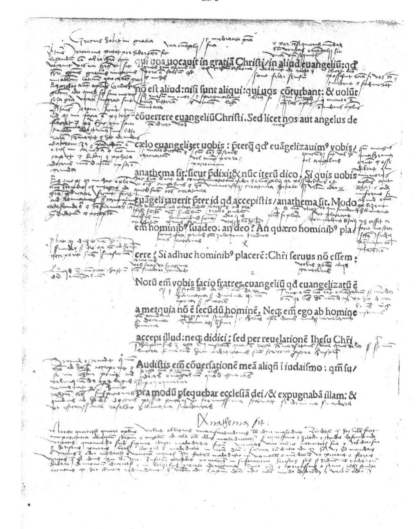

Figure 2.4: Text of Galatians 1:5b–13, plus the student's record of glossa and scholia. At the end of the third line of this page, you see the printed Latin that reads, *Sed licet nos aut Angelus . . .* This is the verse that goes, "But even if an angel from heaven had preached to you a gospel other than the one we have preached to you . . ." (Gal. 1:6).

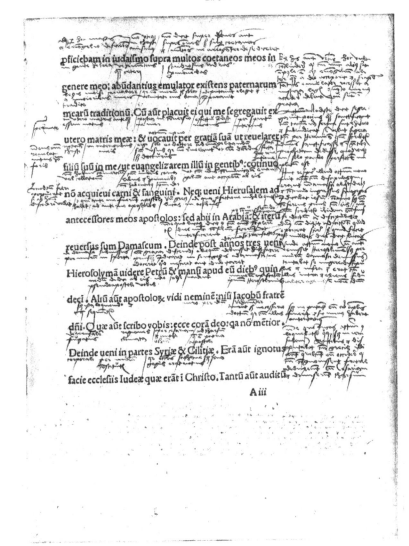

pficiebam in iudaifmo fupra multos coetaneos meos in

genere meo: abũdantius emulator exiftens paternarum

mearũ traditionũ. Cũ aũt placuit ei qui me fegregauit ex

utero matris meæ: & uocauit per gratiã fuã ut reuelaret

filiũ fuũ in me/ut euangelizarem illũ in gentib°: cõtinuo

nõ acquieui carni & fanguini . Neq; ueni Hierufalem ad

anteceffores meos apoftolos: fed abii in Arabia:& iterũ

reuerfus fum Damafcum . Deinde poft annos tres ueni

Hierofolymã uidere Petrũ & mãfi apud eũ dieb° quin

deci . Aliũ aũt apoftolox vidi neminẽ:nifi Iacobũ fratrẽ

dñi . Quæ aũt fcribo vobis: ecce corã deo: qa nõ mẽtior

Deinde ueni in partes Syriæ & Cilitiæ . Erã aũt ignotus

facie ecclefiis Iudeæ quæ erãt i Chrifto. Tantũ aũt auditũ

A iii

Figure 2.5: Text of Galatians 1:14–23, plus the student's record of glossa and scholia.

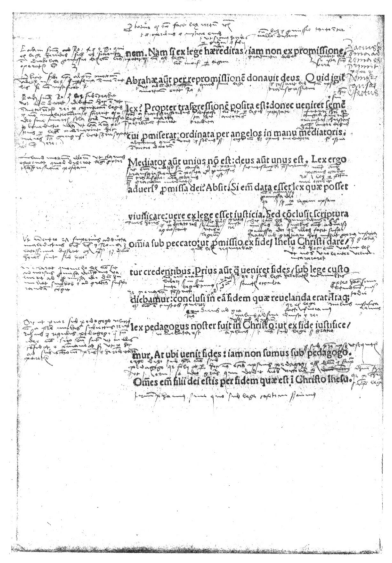

nem. Nam ſi ex lege hæreditas / iam non ex promiſſione,

Abrahæ aũt per repromiſſionē donauit deus. Quid igit

lex? Propter traſgreſſionē poſita eſt: donec ueniret ſemē

cui pmiſerat: ordinata per angelos in manu mediatoris.

Mediator aũt unius nõ eſt: deus aũt unus eſt. Lex ergo

aduerſ⁹ pmiſſa dei? Abſit. Si em data eſſet lex quæ poſſet

viuiſicare: uere ex lege eſſet iuſticia. Sed cõcluſit ſcriptura

omnia ſub peccato: ut pmiſſio ex fideſ Iheſu Chriſti dare

tur credentibus. Prius aũt q ueniret fides / ſub lege cuſto

diebamur: concluſi in eã fidem quæ reuelanda erat. Itaq;

lex pedagogus noſter fuit in Chriſto: ut ex fide iuſtifice /

mur. At ubi uenit fides : iam non ſumus ſub pedagogo.

Omes em filii dei eſtis per fidem quæ eſt i Chriſto Iheſu.

Figure 2.6: Text of Galatians 3:18–3:26, plus the student's record of glossa and scholia. At the start of the third line from the bottom, you see the printed Latin that reads, *lex pedegogus*. This is the verse in which Paul describes the law's function as an instructor/disiplinarian/guardian (Gal. 3:24).

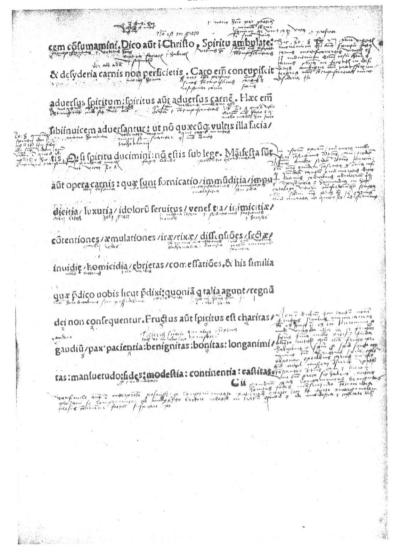

Figure 2.7: Text of Galatians 5:15–23, plus the student's record of glossa and scholia. The last 2.5 lines on this page contain the printed text of the Vulgate's version of the Fruit of the Spirit: *Fructus autem spiritus est caritas, gaudium, pax: patientia: benignitas: bonitas: longanimitas, mansuetudo: fides: modestia: continentia: castita*. However, if you count these up, there are eleven fruits, whereas we know only nine. Look carefully and you'll see that the student has crossed out *modestia* (temperance) and *castita* (sexual abstinence). This is because Luther told his students to cross these out, as these were later additions (by Jerome) and are not supported in the original Greek manuscripts. In the large block of student scribbling that surrounds these two verses (Gal. 5:22–23), you'll see the student's record of Luther's explanation of the difference between Jerome's text and the Greek original. This is a very cool example of Luther doing a bit of textual criticism based on his access to Erasmus's newly issued Greek New Testament. (I geek out on this stuff.)

Figure 2.8: Here begins the second half of the notebook, the half that originally contained all blank pages. Here is where students would record the professor's expanded commentary on sections of the biblical text. The printer has printed his specifics at the top, translated as "Printed at Wittenberg by Johannes Grunenberg, anno Domini 1516, at the place of [apud] the Augustinians." The student's notes on this page cover his record of Luther's expanded commentary on Galatians 5:25, 6:2, and 6:3. So you can see how the student took a kind of haphazard approach in organizing his notes of Luther's expanded commentary.

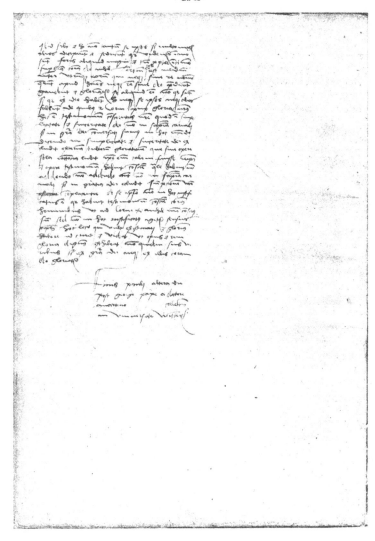

Figure 2.9: This page is near the middle of the notebook, but it represents the last page (and last day) that the student made a record of Luther's expanded commentary. His notes here are a continuation of the notes of Luther's comments on Galatians 6:3 begun on the previous page. At the very end, you see the odd sign-off and the gap between *Martino* and *collectum*. The gap represents the place where, upon close inspection of the original, it can be seen that the word *Luder* or *Ludero* has been carefully erased.

Ego Tamen Baptizatus Sum

Radical Lutheranism and the Life God Engenders

Rev. Prof. Thomas Aadland

In 1976, when James Arne Nestingen was summoned from his doctoral work in St. Michael's College at the University of Toronto to
teach at Luther Theological Seminary in St. Paul, Minnesota, he was
called to join a faculty dedicated to searching out the proper answer
to the question of Lutheran identity not as a description of a denomination but as a true confession of the gospel. He would join such
lights as Roy A. Harrisville Jr., Gerhard O. Forde, and Marc Kolden.
He would soon establish himself as premier catechist on the North
American continent. A generation of students was richly blessed and
stimulated to think anew on God's deed in Christ, having Nestingen
and Forde team up to teach them the Lutheran Confessions.[1]

When, following the death of Theodore G. Tappert in 1977 and
after a hiatus of ten years, Oliver K. Olson and others inaugurated the
new series of *Lutheran Quarterly* in 1987, Forde wrote the keynote

---

[1] The two taught from a concord of profound conviction. Unfortunately, I
was concluding my studies at Luther Theological Seminary just as Professor
Nestingen was arriving. I had known by then of his collaboration with Forde
in the catechetical instruction book *Free to Be*, the great merit of which is to
teach the justification of the ungodly in its most radical terms as death and life
and with its proper, eschatological horizon in a new creation.

article that remains the journal's charter, "Radical Lutheranism."[2] I shall be more deliberately in conversation here with his elder colleague, God bless his memory among us, than with our jubilarian himself. As we seek to appropriate critically what he taught us, we want to identify four ways by which witness to the gospel today by those seeking to be in accord with its Lutheran confession will be radical.

"A radical Lutheranism," Forde stated, "would be one which regains the courage and the nerve to preach the gospel unconditionally; simply let the bird of the Spirit fly!"[3] The epithet was deliberate— not "conservative" or "liberal" or any of a host of other modifiers, but "radical," driving to the *radix*, the root of that which has given us our birth, the gospel in all its unqualified splendor as sheer gift. The root of the current identity crisis among Lutherans, he continued, is the attempt to combine this radical message of God's justification of the ungodly with a humanist anthropology with which it cannot fit. That anthropology ever assumes the notion of the continuously existing subject. But such a notion is already ruled out by what justification entails—namely, death and resurrection with Christ. Nothing less than this is done unto a person in Holy Baptism.

Since we are innately hard of hearing the displacing and astonishing things written in God's Word, the task of catechesis continually remains. With Luther, God's children return again and again

---

[2] This essay, though not intended as fully programmatic, is yet full of promise and fresh energy, written just prior to the formation of the ELCA. Sadly, it did not get a proper hearing, received by some perhaps, and wrongly, as warrant for antinomianism, though that, said Forde, is just what happens when the Gospel is not preached precisely as the death of "the old Adam/Eve." Nevertheless, Forde's legacy continues also elsewhere, including the NALC. A number of his books have been required reading in LCMS seminaries—*Theology Is for Preaching, On Being a Theologian of the Cross, The Preached God*, and *The Captivation of the Will*.

[3] "Radical Lutheranism," in *Lutheran Quarterly*, n. s., 1/1 (1987), 13, also included in the *Lutheran Quarterly* book published jointly with Eerdmans, *A More Radical Gospel* (2004), and reprinted as the lead essay in *Justification Is for Preaching: Essays by Oswald Bayer, Gerhard O. Forde, and Others*, ed. Virgil Thompson (Eugene, OR: Pickwick Publications, 2012), 15–28.

to the simple but profound truths taught them in the catechism. Dr. Nestingen once remarked, "For a long time now I've been trying to get to the bottom of the Lord's Prayer; but after 30 years, I still can't get my hands under it."[4] I want to honor that spirit and humility in what follows.

1

> The decrees of natural theology and its correlate, natural law, suffice to hold the whole world accountable—all that is Adam—as guilty before the eternal God. Herein lies the radical diagnosis of the human condition (Psalm 19:1–4; Isaiah 45:18; Acts 14:17, 17:24–27; Romans 1:18–2:16; Hebrews 3:4).

The Apostle Paul's argument for God's justification of the ungodly is premised on this assertion: "His invisible attributes, namely, his eternal power and divine nature, have been clearly perceived, ever since the creation of the world, in the things that have been made. So they are without excuse" (Rom. 1:20), thus granting legitimacy to natural theology within this limit, that the creature must acknowledge the Creator by due thanksgiving and praise. The ungodly are so constituted by virtue of their denial of God's deity displayed incontrovertibly in the tapestry of creation. The evidence warrants but one conclusion—the eternal God exists, and only inexcusably may one fail to live up to the implications of that conclusion.[5]

---

[4] My best recollection of a remark made during the presentation of the Kolb-Wengert edition of *The Book of Concord* at Luther Seminary in St. Paul in 2000.

[5] Immanuel Kant (1724–1804) argued in his *Critique of Pure Reason* (1781) that the project of demonstrating God's existence through the natural order is utterly hopeless, since it depends on categories such as causation supplied by the perceiving subject. He then founded the three classic Enlightenment ideas of God, immortality, and human freedom on their practical necessity. The son of East Prussian Lutheran pietists, Kant's doctrine was the very opposite of what Lutherans confess; thus, "true religion is to consist not in the knowing or in the considering of what God does or has done for our salvation but in what

The more we investigate this universe and attend to what it is telling us, increasing the range of our observation both macroscopically and microscopically, the larger becomes the font in which Paul's "without excuse!" is written across the objects of our study. Recent discoveries indicate that after dominating Western imagination for nearly a century and a half, Darwinism is tottering to collapse. The intricacies of the human genome; the information-bearing properties of DNA,[6] writing three billion characters mapped into a

---

we must do to become worthy of it." And again, "The right course is not to go from grace to virtue, but rather to progress from virtue to pardoning grace." When shall we be pardoned? Cf. *Religion within the Limits of Reason Alone* (1793), trans. Theodore M. Greene and Hoyt H. Hudson (New York: Harper and Row, 1960), 123, 190. Though much influenced by the skepticism of David Hume (1711–1776), the first European of note to die an avowed atheist, Kant himself became the first to intuit the structure of the Milky Way as a great disk of stars. Order asserts itself. But there is a level of order beyond mere structure. We are not simply observing a universe of mass and energy and inferred causation. We are witness to intelligence. Specification of objective pattern plus improbability of occurrence equals information, and information implies intelligence. Design is the signature of a designer. To say this is not "dogmatic slumber" but wakeful reception of the thing-in-itself (*Ding an sich*).

Karl Barth (1886–1968), possibly confusing natural theology with natural religion, especially the neopaganism he foresaw arising in Germany, retorted "No!" to Emil Brunner's *Nature and Grace* (1934). Both essays are reprinted in *Natural Theology* (Eugene, OR: Wipf & Stock, 2002). Natural theology has happily survived both Kantian critique and Barthian "Nein!" and enjoys a rebirth of interest today. Cf. *The Blackwell Companion to Natural Theology*, ed. William Lane Craig and James Porter Moreland (Oxford: Blackwell's, 2009). Such a chastened natural theology must not be abused, as though apologetics itself gives life to faith. That would, of course, be a *theologia gloriae*.

[6] Mathematician William A. Dembski examines the nature of information in *The Design Inference: Eliminating Chance through Small Probabilities—Cambridge Studies in Probability, Induction, and Decision Theory* (Cambridge: Cambridge University Press, 1999). If the logic of the SETI Project (the search for extraterrestrial intelligence) is valid—namely, that the detection of an information-bearing signal, as a radio wave propagated from distant space at frequencies marking sequential prime numbers, would infer the search is over—then likewise the inference of intelligent design through information disclosed in the natural order itself is over. See also Michael J.

mind-numbing catalog of precise code, an exact molecular language that instructs the assembly of amino acids into specified proteins; the irreducible complexity and synergism of RNA and micromachinery within the cell nucleus;[7] the sudden appearance of fully differenti-ated phyla densely populating Cambrian strata without precursors in the geological record;[8] the statistically improbable coincidence of conditions exceedingly rare in the cosmos for life on this planet[9] all

---

Behe, William A. Dembski, and Stephen C. Meyer, *Science and Evidence for Design in the Universe* (Ft. Collins, CO: Ignatius, 2000).

[7] Stunningly illustrated by computer-generated graphics in the DVD *Unlocking the Mystery of Life*, Illustra Media, 2002. Available at http://www .illustramedia.com. Some would more precisely label Darwinism as materi-alistic naturalism. Not considerable is theistic evolution, and to posit such a notion is to run after a flight that has already pulled away from the gate. "God doesn't roll dice" (Albert Einstein).

[8] As documented in the DVD *Darwin's Dilemma*, Illustra Media, 2009. Also available at http://www.illustramedia.com.

[9] A partial list of conditions for sustainable life includes the following: a terrestrial planet, of correct mass, in a nearly circular orbit, with proper pro-portion of rocky crust to molten interior, enabling circulation of an iron-nickel core productive of a protective magnetic field to shield harmful radiation, with life-renewing plate tectonics, orbiting a spectral G2 dwarf main sequence star, protected from comets by outer gas giant planets, within the circumstellar habitable zone, a planet abundant in liquid water for assimilation and trans-port of nutrients, with a proper ratio of seas and continents to provide a com-plex biosphere, and seas of sufficient depth that a planetary moon produces in them tides and currents providing a kind of circulatory system to the bio-sphere, with an oxygen-rich atmosphere, yet one predominantly composed of nitrogen, with moderate rate of rotation, and moderate tilt for seasons, orbited by a relatively large moon to stabilize this tilt, belonging to a solar system that lies within a stable, flattened ("pinwheel") disk galaxy, a star system located midway between the bulging core and the outer rim where heavy elements are not to be found, nowhere close to the highly energetic galactic center and potential black hole, but within the habitable galactic zone, yet between and not within the spiral arms themselves with their active star-forming regions, nebulae and supernovae, inimical to life, and within a galaxy not gravitation-ally compromised by colliding neighbors. The list is growing as the science of astrobiology matures. The population of stars in our average-sized galaxy is recently estimated at one hundred billion; likewise, the number of galaxies

speak eloquently of an astonishing Providence elegantly defined in the words of the prophet Isaiah: "[The LORD] formed the earth and made it (he established it; he did not create it empty, he formed it to be inhabited!)" (Isa. 45:18). In such a world, atheism is an illegitimate, albeit perduring, intellectual enterprise.[10]

Today, visually stunning documentation shows that human conception and birth also bear witness to the majesty of God in his creation. Alexander Tsiaras, who wrote the algorithms for virtual surgery so that astronauts could be operated on in robotics pods in deep space flights, has now produced, using new scanning technology, striking images of structures in the human body on a wide scale.[11] As he concentrated his study on collagen—that rope-like

---

in the observable universe at one hundred billion. Generously assigning each condition as representing a value of one in ten, the possibility of life is a multiplication of all these together; but, conceding just one more such prerequisite for life, as an abundance of carbon, let us grant the possibility of a habitable planet as ten in twenty-two. The number of stars as candidates to be considered is already liberally given as 1,022 (one hundred billion times one hundred billion), though not every star, from the smallest red dwarf to the supermassive R136a1 (discovered by the European Space Agency in 2010), nearly three hundred solar masses and ten million times brighter than our sun, can be host to planets. Nevertheless, multiplying total candidates (1,022) by necessary conditions (ten in twenty-two) yields the number one. Even doubling prior estimates of average number of stars per galaxy and total galaxies in the observed universe still yields only four. Naturally, no hard claim is made here that the Earth is absolutely the only habitable planet in the universe. Yet these considerations suggest that the answer to the question whether habitable planets are common or rare in the universe must be decidedly weighted in favor of the latter, even more so as further requirements for life are discovered. Cf. Guillermo Gonzalez and Jay W. Richards, *The Privileged Planet: How Our Place in the Cosmos Is Designed for Discovery* (Washington, DC: Regnery, 2004).

[10] For a self-confessed secular Jewish perspective and a witty, sophisticated polemic against atheism written from within the scientific community, see David Berlinski, *The Devil's Delusion: Atheism and Its Scientific Pretensions* (New York: Basic Books, 2009).

[11] http://www.youtube.com/watch_popup?v=fKyljukBE70 (accessed 16 March 2012) gives a popular link to his presentation at the INK Conference on the occasion of the annual TED award presented to him in December 2010.

material in the human body that typically swirls and twirls but forms into a grid and is thus transparent only in the cornea of the eye—he saw it as "so perfectly organized, it was hard not to attribute divinity to it." He used these noninvasive techniques *in utero* for his video presentation, *From Conception to Birth*. The results have left him in awe. "The magic of the mechanisms inside each genetic structure saying exactly where that nerve cell should go—the complexity of these mathematical models is beyond human comprehension. Even though I am a mathematician, I look at this with marvel: How do these instruction sets not make these mistakes as they build what is us? It's a mystery. It's magic. It's divinity."

The moment with greater metaphysical significance is, of course, not birth but conception, in which a new being with a distinct genetic identity is begun. Yet the presence of miracle is easily lost on us in our inexcusable blindness. The developed nations of the Earth seem to have little difficulty forsaking their responsibility to protect the life of the most vulnerable and defenseless—unborn children. The previous president of the United States is unrivalled as a champion of "abortion rights," having once even issued an executive mandate via Health and Human Services to church bodies, their hospitals, schools, universities, and charities to provide free contraceptives, sterilization, and abortifacient drugs through their health plans, never mind the voice of conscience.[12] Apparently, no one within earshot of the president was asking the obvious philosophical question: if the notion of right implies, as Thomas Jefferson believed, transcendent origin—and with him anyone who has ever taken the nation's charter and *Declaration of Independence* to heart—how is it possible that one putative right may nullify another? Compounding the crisis, we are now dangerously close to the old Soviet notion of constitutional law, placing virtually unlimited demands on what government must provide its citizens while implying that rights are due either to the militant demands by a segment of the populace or

---

Cf. http://www.TED.com. For this work, Tsiaras has been hailed as a "digital-age Leonardo da Vinci."

[12] Final Rule, 77 FR 8725 http://www.regulations.gov/#!documentDetail;D=HHS_FRDOC_0001-0443, p. 8727.

to the generosity of an omnicompetent state rather than to the magnanimity of God, in whose image we are created.

The capacity to distinguish between what is and what ought to be is a remnant feature of the *imago Dei*. Moral utterances are inherent to being human. Across the gulfs of geography and history, cultures show a broad consensus that certain conditions exist only through fulfillment of which is civilization possible—filial piety and regard for nurturing and limiting authority, respect for the life of one's neighbor and his or her marriage, property, and reputation.[13] Righteousness by whatever name, whether Chinese *li* or Roman *iustitia*, is the intended content of such utterance; to speak of the *lex naturalis* is to recognize such conditions and a common morality that people share, operative in the conscience.[14] The Apostle Paul was simply acknowledging public fact when he stated this (Rom. 2:14–16).

However suppressed the sense of guilt may be in a given individual, violations of these conditions, whether lesser or greater in scope and public impact, reveal an underlying lack of fear of, love for, and trust in God. Sin is constituted as sin by virtue of this attendant status. Thus David's criminal behavior against Bathsheba, against Uriah, and against the people of Israel is sin only as it is realized as a certain violence against the moral fabric of his creation before God (Ps. 51:4). *Coram Deo*, all engendered of Adam are sinners. The witness of conscience stands together with the witness of the created order to the God of holy love before whom all manner of unrighteousness is inexcusable. Sin dehumanizes. The glory of God, says Irenaeus, is a man fully alive. The Apostle Paul asserts that all have fallen short of this glory (Rom. 3:23).[15]

---

[13] Cf. C. S. Lewis, "Appendix—'Illustrations of the Tao,'" in *The Abolition of Man* (New York: Macmillan, 1970), 95–121.

[14] Long overdue, *Natural Law: A Lutheran Reappraisal* (St. Louis: Concordia, 2011) is an explication and assessment of this theme by sixteen Lutheran scholars, teachers, and pastors in the wake of the Barthian obfuscation of the Law-Gospel distinction and dynamic.

[15] To the extent to which the first article and its concerns are marginalized, so too will the Gospel be seen as without divine authorization and as irrelevant

2

> The human will is bound upon itself and cannot change
> of its own accord, so that we remain Adam and spiritu-
> ally impotent. The radical prognosis for humanity is that
> it has absolutely no potential to overcome its most desper-
> ate destitution (Isaiah 40:6–8; Jeremiah 13:23; John 3:6a;
> Romans 3:22b–23).

The really disturbing thing for someone who has been caught by the opening blows of Paul's *Epistle to the Romans* is that God does indeed exist. This God gives no evidence that He is about to relinquish his Godhood. He will be God, for He alone is our highest good. His holy love is this: that He will not cease from being God. But what kind of God will He be?[16] That is now the real question. And it is a terrifying one. That is why Luther says that one who remains only with the evidence of what he sees, the evidence of natural theology, is not yet deserving properly to be called a theologian.[17] One who claims

---

to human concerns, as some strange erratic boulder on the terrain of human discourse.

[16] Cf. Jonathan F. Grothe, *The Justification of the Ungodly: An Interpretation of Romans* (self-pub., 2005), volume I, p. 56, n. 18: "Thus the critical matter is not whether God is faithful and righteous, but *what kind of God* he is—a God of Law or a God of Gospel. One could, theoretically, know the orthodox formulae about the Triune God but, failing to hear that God is 'for us' (*pro nobis*), believe nonetheless that the Holy Trinity is a God of Law, an exacting taskmaster, and that Jesus will return on the Last Day to be a harsh judge only" (emphasis original).

[17] The Latin Vulgate rendition of Romans 1:20 is referenced in Luther's Thesis No. 19 in his Heidelberg Disputation (*invisibilia enim ipsius a creatura mundi per ea quae facta sunt intellecta conspiciuntur sempiterna quoque eius virtus et divinitas ut sint inexcusabiles*), viz., "That person does not deserve to be called a theologian who claims to be able to see the invisible things of God *through those things which have been made.*" Luther asserts that natural theology is not theology proper. Only God's alien work, not his proper work, can be accessed there—Law, not Gospel. But theology proper, that preparation for proclamation of God's proper work, is precisely a reflection on the radical Gospel of new creation for Jesus' sake, through death and resurrection with him. In his excellent commentary, Gerhard Forde acknowledges the discussion over these

to see into the invisible attributes of God misuses them in the most horrible way as goals for his own achieving. Precisely this is what it means to play God. And yet, when one does this, the player is always looking over his shoulder to see if anyone is watching!

Human beings have an inborn prejudice against God. Luther put it in characteristically uncompromising terms: "A man is not able naturally to want God to be God. Indeed, he wants himself to be God, and God not to be God."[18] It would be difficult to locate a more succinct dogmatic definition of original sin. But the trouble with Luther, with Paul, with anything so uncompromising, for that matter, is that it leaves none of us any wiggle room. It is not just those who fail to defend the right to life of the unborn child—as important as that issue remains for the life of the nation; it is all of us who fail to render God due thanks and praise—all, that is, who fall under the demanding, threatening, accusing, terrifying, damning, and killing voice of God's law—who are born into this life under the wrath of God. As a corollary, we who want ourselves to be God and God not to be God are bound to be who we are, doomed to have our own way without radical life-saving intervention. No self-reformation project, no protest of human freedom to change that condition for the better, no brilliance of thought, no sincerity of intention, no ecstasy of invented religious emotion will do.[19] A sinner cannot choose not to be a sinner.

---

words, whether they refer to knowledge of God by analogy from creation or to that of divine attributes as goals for imitation by human works, as Thesis 22 indicates. In natural piety, the one leads quickly to the other. Cf. *On Being a Theologian of the Cross: Reflections on Luther's Heidelberg Disputation, 1518* (Grand Rapids: Eerdmans, 1997), 72, fn. 3.

[18] Martin Luther, "Disputation against Scholastic Theology," Thesis 17. *Non potest homo naturaliter velle deum esse deum, Immo vellet se esse deum et deum non esse deum. Luthers Werke*, Weimar Ausgabe, I, 225 (AE 31:10).

[19] In one of the great ironies in the history of ideas, Immanuel Kant, perhaps one of the most brilliant minds of the last three hundred years, at the apex of the rationalist Enlightenment hastened to its conclusion by his critical philosophy, accepted nevertheless the reality of "radical evil"—original sin. He had exclaimed on the last page of his *Critique of Practical Reason* (1788): "Two things fill the mind with ever new and increasing admiration and awe, the

The human creature tells himself a myth. The individual operates as the center of a universe in which he is determined to decide
for himself what is advantageous or disadvantageous, to possess
the knowledge of good and evil; yet the outcome of such a project
is always in doubt.[20] His world thus becomes structured by a legal
scheme of approval and disapproval but one in which he feels himself adequate to make appropriate adjustment to achieve the good.[21]
Against such presumption, the prophet Jeremiah levies the sarcastic
and damning indictment: "Can the Ethiopian change his skin or the
leopard his spots? Then also you can do good who are accustomed to
do evil" (Jer. 13:23).

It is the doing of good that, despite any history of failure, appears
to be precisely the thing that is always within our reach, for which

---

oftener and more steadily we reflect on them: the starry heavens above me and
the moral law within me"—but not apparently the Incarnation and the Cross.
At once more pessimistic and more optimistic than St. Paul, his "starry heavens above me" could not convince him of God's existence, yet his "moral law
within me" postulated both God and human freedom and also sufficed with
some help of the church to "overcome" radical evil in human nature. While
not denying revelation, he held that it was not strictly necessary to achieve this
end. The good citizens of Königsberg could set their clocks by his daily walk,
but there is no report his feet ever took him to Divine Service. For Kant, the
"ought" of moral law implied the "can" of human freedom. It's an old song,
of course—one that Luther had already silenced in his debate with Erasmus.
In effect, by his skepticism Kant denied Romans 1 and by his meliorism read
Romans 2 in an unspeakably shallow manner. Yet both created order and natural law imply an inexcusable human condition that is inescapable and irresolv-
able (ἀναπολόγητος; so Rom. 1:20 and 2:1). The last gasp of *homo religiosus* is
his defiant declaration that he is yet free to save himself.

[20] While not accepting any existentialist reduction of the meaning of the
biblical text, I do believe Dietrich Bonhoeffer to have been essentially correct
and profound in his reading of Genesis 1–3 and view of the "tree of the knowledge of good and evil." Cf. *Creation and Fall* (New York: Macmillan, 1959),
especially "The Middle of the Earth," 48–59.

[21] Cf. Oswald Bayer, *Living by Faith: Justification and Sanctification* (Grand
Rapids: Eerdmans, 2003), for a penetrating analysis of the way humanity is
inescapably bound to the language of approbation by which its world is structured and which, apart from faith, binds it to self-justification.

we have at least some potential. Plato's early Socratic dialogues show the philosopher ruminating over such questions as "What is virtue?" "What is justice?" The assumption is that knowing the good is the real difficulty and that, once known, it can be done.[22] Jeremiah warns of the immovable roadblock between any such speculation about the good, about ethics, about God's ways with the world on the one hand and deliverance from the human condition on the other, which is the will held captive by its own assertion of adequacy and godhood. A will in such captivity cannot free itself.[23]

Only when the diagnosis of the human condition is sufficiently radical will its prognosis and prospects for self-salvation be seen to be equally dismal. Sin is not something superficial but is of bottomless depth. We are sinners not because we sin, but we sin because we are sinners. The child of Adam is marked by a radical distortion, a being-curved-in-upon-oneself (*incurvatus a se*, as Luther, following the medieval tradition, put it). The biblical word for this is iniquity (עָוֹן)—literally, twistedness (Ps. 32:1). We are the heirs of a misbegotten project, the attempt to be our own god. The children of Adam are perversely self-begotten. A creature with an inborn penchant to regard itself as the center of the universe and the sole determinant of its value is not only quite bent out of shape; it has no capacity to transcend this posture, to undo the distortion in the heart of its being.[24]

---

[22] Cf. Frederick Copleston, S.J., *A History of Philosophy: Volume I, Greece and Rome Part I* (Garden City, NY: Doubleday, 1962), 129: "According to Socrates, knowledge and virtue are one, in the sense that the wise man, he who *knows* what is right, will also *do* what is right."

[23] The two great debates in the West, that between Augustine and Pelagius in the fifth century and that between Luther and Erasmus in the sixteenth, were about the human will. Neither these debates nor their outcomes held the attention of Eastern Orthodoxy. So notes John Meyendorff, "The Significance of the Reformation in the History of Christendom," in *Catholicity and the Church* (Crestwood, NY: St. Vladimir's Press, 1983), 65–82. But is the East stronger or weaker for that? The human will and its obduracy is a major theme in Sacred Scripture. *"How often I would . . . , but you would not"* (Matt. 23:37).

[24] Not surprising, therefore, was the outcome some few decades ago, of the sectarian television evangelist, who would habitually denounce a particular transgression ("It's sin, and God says it's got to stop!") and who was later found

None are exempt. The unity of the human race lies not only in its special creation as an image of God but also in its rebellion. The dogmatic definition of the spread of this rebellion was famously put by Augustine: *non imitatio sed propagatio*, not by imitation but by propagation, certainly a hard pill to swallow!

Though the human will cannot change its perversity by its own power, it can be changed if God wills it so. But how shall that be done? It cannot be done by means that would leave the presumption and usurpation of godhood by the self, the child of Adam, intact. It cannot be done, that is, by means of wisdom or strength. Such things for the assessment and enjoyment by the self as are immediately perceptible to the senses only serve to leave the myth in place. Only by means of death and resurrection can a new self be brought forth, a creature who will let God be God, a new being, that is, who lives by faith alone in what God bestows.

The radical intervention that is necessary to displace the usurpation and restore the creature must come from without the created order. And yet it must happen within it in such a manner as not to destroy it altogether. That is to say, law already structures the created order. Law impacts the presumptive self with a voice that can only demand, threaten, accuse, terrify, damn, and kill. The highest truth that is available from this voice, from within the created order itself, is the trivial and monotonous observation, "It is good to be good, and bad to be bad." The intervention will thus come as something radically new. Though scandalous for not being some generally accessible truth, something particular must be done. In particular, the voice of the law must be stilled, not by way of contravention or annulment but by first fulfilling it and disarming it at the same time.

Christ is the end of the law (Rom. 10:4), in the sense not only that He has silenced its demanding, threatening, accusing, terrifying,

---

to be himself held in the grip of this very addiction. When sin is treated superficially, as though one can be rid of it by a mere act of the will, the Gospel is not heard in its saving depth and power. True preaching of the law leads to despair in one's own ability to live by it and leads only then to the timely delivery of the word of the Cross—the Holy Proclamation, the Holy Absolution, Holy Baptism, and the Holy Supper. Cf. Martin Luther, *Heidelberg Disputation*, Thesis No. 18, *Luther's Work*, vol. 31 (Philadelphia: Fortress, 1957), 51–52.

damning, and killing voice but that He has first perfectly embodied the love that is eternally its holy content.[25] Christ's love is actively engaged not only in acts of mercy toward those ravaged by sin nor simply in a word of forgiveness as such but also in what is traditionally called His passive righteousness, for He actively willed His passion, set His face like a flint to undertake it, and, of His own accord, gave His blood for it.

Christ indeed does this by way of substitution and exchange.[26] Such language seems strange and difficult to grasp not because its

---

[25] Cf. *Solus Decalogus est Aeternus: Martin Luther's Complete Antinomian Theses and Disputations*, ed. and trans. Holger Sonntag (Minneapolis: Lutheran Press, 2008), 127, 129. "The Decalogue, however, is greater and better [than the law of circumcision] because it is written in the minds and hearts of all and will remain with us even in the coming life. Yet not so circumcision, as baptism also will not remain, but only the Decalogue is eternal—as such, that is, not as law—because in the coming life things will be like what the Decalogue has been demanding here." An intriguing footnote in Gerhard Forde's published doctoral dissertation invites the question whether he had thought through this statement with its distinction between *voice* of law to the sinner and *content* of law as "holy and righteous and good" (Rom. 7:12). "The writings of Luther against the Antinomians represent an important and relatively untapped source for Luther's view of the law. Ebeling has apparently recognized this and has promised a study of the disputes (*Wort und Glaube*, note 64, p. 65, also p. 68), but to my knowledge it has not yet appeared." *The Law-Gospel Debate: An Interpretation of Its Historical Development* (Minneapolis: Augsburg, 1969), 178, fn. 9.

[26] Admittedly, this essay differs from Gerhard Forde in its view of the atonement. More than one voice finds a variance between Forde and the Lutheran Confessions in his view of divine law, atonement, and justification. Cf. Jack Kilcrease, "Gerhard Forde's Theology of Atonement and Justification: A Confessional Lutheran Response," in *Concordia Theological Quarterly* 76, no. 3–4 (July/October 2012): 269–93; and Jordan Cooper, *Lex Aeterna: A Defense of the Orthodox Lutheran Doctrine of God's Law and Critique of Gerhard Forde* (Eugene, OR: Wipf & Stock, 2017). The proper statement of Christian doctrine exhibits coherence and beauty. This is seen in the pattern of meaning among all the articles, including those dealing with creation and law, atonement, justification, and eternal glory. But where one article is amiss, the whole suffers. In the previous footnote, Luther sees a clear distinction between the voice of law and the eternal will of God for the good of his creation, the *lex aeterna*. When

reality is remote from us but because it is ever present, close at hand. In our very conception and bearing, a woman receives from her man, substituting her life for his in a way appropriate for her own, just as he must give himself for her and exchange his life for hers. So in our everyday economic life, we are continually doing what is put into our hands, that which others do not do just then and there, that we might also receive from them the fruits of their labors in exchange.

In his 1535 commentary on the epistle to the Galatians, Luther speaks pointedly, even shockingly, of this atonement as substitutionary, especially as he interprets these words in 3:13: "Christ redeemed us from the curse of the law by becoming a curse for us." Luther writes,

> And all the prophets saw this, that Christ was to become the greatest thief, murderer, adulterer, robber, desecrator, blasphemer, etc., there has ever been anywhere in the world. He is not acting in His own Person now. Now He is not the Son of God, born of the Virgin. But He is a sinner, who has and bears the sin of Paul, the former blasphemer, persecutor, and assaulter; of Peter, who denied Christ; of David, who was an adulterer and a murder, and who caused the Gentiles to blaspheme the name of the Lord (Rom. 2:24). In short, He has and bears all the sins of all men in His body—not in the sense that He has committed them but in the sense that He took these sins, committed by us, upon His own body, in order to make satisfaction for them with His own blood.[27]

So the law attacks Christ and damns and kills Him. But if our sins be on Christ, they are not on us. Instead, placed on us

---

this distinction is maintained, one will readily affirm the confessional view of the law's third use, the abiding love of God that never condones what is evil and perverse, and the substitutionary atonement by Christ Scripture reveals. We hold with David P. Scaer that the atonement proceeds from eternity as something objective, independent of its human reception through faith. Cf. "The Nature and Extent of Atonement: In Lutheran Theology." *Bulletin of the Evangelical Theological Society* 10, no. 4 (Fall 1967): 179–87.

[27] Martin Luther, *Luther's Works, Vol. 26: Lectures on Galatians 1535, Chapters 1–4* (St. Louis: Concordia, 1963), 277.

is Christ's righteousness, life, and salvation. This marvelous duel (*mirabile duellum*)—between the righteous and blessed Christ on the one hand and law, sin, death, devil, and damnation on the other—eventuates in what Luther called the wondrous exchange (*fröliche Wechsel*). The atonement is accomplished.[28] The deliverance Christ achieved on Golgotha for all the world must be delivered to the individual. This God the Holy Spirit does through the means of grace that God the Son has provided.

3

> It has pleased God to save members of a lost and con-
> demned humanity through His own radical cure, the
> washing of regeneration and renewal by the Holy Spirit
> (Holy Baptism), bestowing upon them that which was
> purchased and won for them by the blood of Christ—
> forgiveness of sin, deliverance from death and devil, and
> everlasting salvation. In Holy Baptism the voice of the
> Holy Trinity speaks God's children into life, for therein a

---

[28] τετέλεσται (John 19:30). The radical proclamation of the unconditional Gospel has its correlate in objective justification—that the Lamb of God has taken and borne away the sin of the world (John 1:29; cf. 1 John 2:2). Without this there would be nothing to proclaim. What else could one preach on the basis of a double predestination, a limited atonement, and an election to damnation but "be of good cheer—Jesus may have died for your sins!"? Thus it is objective justification—that is, the atonement—on which subjective justification is founded. "For *all* have sinned and fall short of the glory of God, and *are justified* by his grace as a gift through the redemption that is in Christ Jesus, whom God put forward to be a propitiation by his blood, to be received by faith" (Rom. 3:23–25). The word for "propitiation" here (ἱλαστήριον) is that used by the Septuagint for the Mercy Seat (Exod. 25:17), the lid over the Ark of the Covenant, between the two cherubim, prefiguring the angels attendant at the Empty Tomb, seen by Mary Magdalene, "in white, sitting where the body of Jesus had lain, one at the head and one at the feet" (John 20:12). The *hilastērion* is the place where the blood of a spotless Lamb is poured. There is no Atonement, no forgiveness of sins without the shedding of blood (Heb. 9:22). But for the Atonement, there could be no proclamation of the Gospel *propter Christum*.

new being is engendered, one with a radically new genetic identity, an identity not of Adam, but of God (Matthew 28:18–20; Mark 16:16; John 1:12–13, 3:5–7; Acts 2:38; Romans 6:2–4; Galatians 3:27; Ephesians 4:5; Titus 3:5–7; James 1:18, 2:7; 1 Peter 1:3, 23, 3:21; 1 John 5:7).

The marvel of human conception and birth still has proximate cause within the created order and so must to that extent give place in comparison with God's act of new creation. Human gestation normally spans nine months, the interval between conception and delivery. With God, however, there is no lapse between engendering and birth for those He brings forth as His children. And yet He does honor His creation by utilizing its most elemental substance, water. That event, defined in radical terms by the New Testament, is Holy Baptism.

As Jesus was conceived by the Holy Spirit *ex Maria Vigine* when the Archangel Gabriel spoke the Word of God into her ear, so God's children are begotten of water and the Word in its most compact form. Paganism is the presumptuous attempt to give a name to God. With the water of Holy Baptism, God graciously bestows His own true and proper name upon us: "The name of the Father and of the Son and of the Holy Spirit." Accordingly, Holy Baptism is justification, the acknowledgment by the Triune God of the one made His child (Titus 3:5–7). God cannot deny His own name or His own children.

Just as the awe and mystery of physical birth can be diminished in thought and action, so can one's estimation of the nature of new creation. The statement of the gospel is compromised by a diminished regard of the scripture as Word of God that norms it. Likewise, our reception of the sacred gift of Holy Baptism can be lessened by a mistranslation of the biblical text.

The sacred gifts of Christ are properly received as their bestowal is normed by the words of the Giver. There is no reason to believe this will happen where regard for the inspired text of Holy Scripture is lost. One German exegete calls the words of the dominical institution of Holy Baptism into question and their formulation in St. Matthew's Gospel "late," despite Matthew's continuity with the early Jerusalem church and that earliest writing of the New Testament, the epistle of Bishop James, who references the sacrament and its form (cf.

James 1:18) and "the honorable name by which you were called" (τὸ καλὸν ὄνομα τὸ ἐπικληθὲν ἐφ ᾽ ὑμᾶς, James 2:7).[29]

The word *sacred* means "Hands off! This is not to be manipulated!" Yet even that most proper Name of God itself has been doubted by those whose view of sacred things has become profaned. Four years prior to the formation of the Evangelical Lutheran Church in America in 1988, a discussion took place within the seventy-member commission for a New Lutheran Church regarding the statement of faith to be placed at the beginning of the new constitution. Objections were raised against the "exclusive" nature of the traditional language used to confess faith in "God the Father, the Son, and the Holy Spirit." The Triune God, whose praise shall endure for the ages of ages, world without end, was, in the discussion's end, "elected" by a slim margin of thirty-three to thirty.[30] Did the holy angels rejoice or did they weep?

Beyond dispute, a deeper regard for Holy Scripture as God's words sent from heaven in the minds and hearts of delegates to the 2009 ELCA Church Wide Assembly would have averted the disaster of August 21, whereby the door was opened to the ordination of those in homosexual bondage and the blessing of same-sex unions. Ironically, by this act alone, the ELCA, pledged to an ecumenical

---

[29] Walter Schmithals, *The Theology of the First Christians*, trans. O. C. Dean Jr. (Louisville, KY: Westminster John Knox Press, 1997), 214.

[30] "The document's introductory sentence, which concludes with the words '. . . we confess our faith in the one God, Father, Son, and Holy Spirit,' provoked prolonged debate. Ewald (Elwyn Ewald, AELC representative from St. Louis), voicing a concern for inclusive language, proposed ending the sentence with '. . . one Triune God,' dropping references to 'Father, Son, and Holy Spirit.' Dr. H. George Anderson of Decorah, Iowa, opposed the change, stating that the church's language is in a time of transition and that the terminology is taken directly from the Scriptures, creeds and Lutheran confessions. Similarly Dr. Fred Meuser of Columbus, Ohio, said it 'would be fatal' to drop the words. He pleaded for more careful study of inclusive language issues. Others, like Nilssen (June Nilssen, a campus clergy person at the UW-Milwaukee) and Lois Quam, currently a Rhodes scholar at Oxford, England, said the male characterization of God is found to be exclusive by many people. Ewald's amendment eventually lost, 30–33." The American Lutheran Church, Office of Communication, news release, February 27, 1984.

agenda, cut itself off from the one holy catholic and apostolic church, gave itself over to a church-dividing mentality, and exchanged its prophetic voice for a mere echo of the pagan world.[31]

No practice of Holy Baptism is self-norming. The *verba* of its dominical institution are essential just as are the *verba* of the Lord's Supper. But there is no administration of water along with the vocables of the Divine Name where the gospel is denied by public doctrine (as among Mormons) that can be regarded as Holy Baptism. Nor is the gospel in any of its forms self-norming.[32] As a practical matter, without constant return to the Holy Scripture and a reading of it in a manner commensurate with its depth and power, one will lose the specific contours of God's act and will, to that extent, fail to honor it.[33]

---

[31] Already, in Rome on November 7, 2005, Pope Benedict XVI warned then–LWF president and ELCA presiding bishop Mark S. Hanson of "a general climate of uncertainty regarding Christian truths and ethical principles which formerly went unquestioned." http://www.vatican.va/holy-father/benedict_xvi/speeches/2005/November/documents/hf_ben_xvi_spe_20051107_lutheran-federation_en.html. Accessed 25 April 2012. Although Rome has a different formulation of the formal principle (expressed that day as follows by Benedict XVI: "The mission of the Church is to *witness* to the truth of Jesus Christ, the Word made flesh. Word and witness go together: the Word calls forth and gives form to the witness; the witness derives its authenticity from total fidelity to the Word, as expressed and lived in the apostolic community of faith under the guidance of the Holy Spirit"), clearly the need for such was indicated in his address to the LWF delegation.

[32] Cf. *Gospel & Scripture: The Interrelationship of Material and Formal Principles in Lutheran Theology* (A Report of the Commission on Theology and Church Relations, The Lutheran Church—Missouri Synod, November 1972).

[33] It is so with the Holy Absolution. Contemporary liturgies in their General Order for Public Confession often lapse into a mere public recital of 1 John 1:8–9, in gnomic fashion, rather than actually performing the Office of the Keys. Christ wants his own to enjoy precisely the same certitude and joy of release as he granted to the paralytic at Capernaum. As much as the pastor acts in the stead of Christ in Holy Baptism, so he is to be a *shaliach*, a commissioned emissary of the Risen Lord, and actually forgive sins on the spot in the name of the Blessed Trinity. What else is the Divine Service?

Curiously, current translations of the Bible, even aids to students of New Testament Greek, reveal a discernible tendentiousness
that fails to honor the radical nature of God's gift bestowed in Holy
Baptism.[34] We might be shocked anew by the import of our Lord's
words to Nicodemus were we to understand them as indicating not
simply a new birth but a new conception or engendering.

To be "born anew" is not just a starting over but being granted a
radically new beginning to a life that is different in kind, of different
lineage. In John 1:12 and 3:5–6, ἐκ indicates origin. To be engendered
"of Adam" is a being-toward-death. To be engendered "of God" is a
being-toward-life.

Our Lord's words to Nicodemus in John 3:3 (ἐὰν μή τις γεννηθῇ
ἄνωθεν) are such that his mistaking them was possible. Though
γεννάω may mean either "to beget" or "to give birth," since other
words have the latter meaning as their particular referent, as τεκνόω,
"to bring forth children," or τίκτω, "to deliver," it is at least reasonable
to ask whether a given author does not in fact have "to beget" or "to
engender" in mind when he uses it.[35] The context must decide. But

---

[34] For example, *The UBS Greek New Testament: A Reader's Edition* (Stuttgart:
Deutsche Bibelgesellschaft, 2007), is printed with a running Greek-English
dictionary, edited by Barclay M. Newman. Despite remonstrance from the
author, which he kindly received, that symbology inhabits a realm of mentality, while Deluge and Baptism are real events, no change in subsequent edi-
tions has been made to the definition of ἀντίτυπος in 1 Peter 3:21, given as
"serving as a symbol."

[35] The meaning of these three words overlaps considerably, even during the
classical period. According to the Liddell-Scott lexicon, Xenophon uses οἱ
γεννήσαντες for "the parents" and Plato γέννημα for "that which is produced"
or "progeny," yet rarely in Aeschylus is the verb used of the mother for "bring
forth." The ambiguity seems to derive from the word's origin in antiquity as
the causal of γίγνομαι (the older form of γίνομαι). Since the root is ΓΕΝ*,
it would seem the basic meaning of γεννάω is "engender." The emphasis of
τεκνόω is on giving birth to children (τὰ τέκνα) and the passive simply means
"to be furnished with children." In Sophocles's *Oedipus Rex*, γάμον τεκνοῦντα
καὶ τεκνούμενον identifies the tragic marriage wherein son and husband
are one and the same, "bringing forth and having been brought forth." And
τέκνωσις can mean either "begetting" or "bearing." Whereas τεκνοποιός can
mean either child-bearing (of the wife) or child-begetting (of the husband) in

in the New Testament, where the new creation is referenced, the only agent is God the Father, and the voice is commonly passive. Since Greek adverbs ending in -θεν indicate "place from which," ἄνωθεν cannot be taken as simply equivalent to πάλιν, though that is just what Nicodemus hears. Later, in John 3:31, the adverb is clearly used to mean "from above," Jesus' true origin.

As is typical of the pattern in John's Gospel, our Lord's meaning in 3:3 drives toward a specification in 3:5, which can only mean Holy Baptism, a means of grace already anticipated in 1:12–13. The phrase "born again" has become a greasy coin with little dependable currency. Given the synergistic tendency of many of its users, now meaning a certain class of citizens, even a subdivision among supposed Christians counted by Gallup polls during an election cycle, the phrase should be dropped altogether. The adverb points heavenward. God bestows a radically new genetic identity in Holy Baptism.

The proper translation of γεννάω has to do with the act of fatherhood—begetting. As the eternal relation between Father and Son in the essential Trinity is properly named as "begetting" and "only begotten," so the apostles and evangelists name that event by which a new life is created by the Holy Trinity as a being-begotten-from-above.

Yet the precise nature of that life that God gives to His children cannot be discerned by scientific method. It is apprehended only through faith, and faith has no way to live except by the Word of God, divine promise, ultimately grounded in the sacred scripture itself. The order, design, and evident intelligence behind this universe all may be detected by the senses, but not this proper work of God.

Holy Baptism saves apart from what can be seen and judged by human understanding. Its significance is taught in sacred scripture, which gives us right regard for it. The means of grace participate in the same lowliness of Christ who gives them. Radical Lutheranism is

---

Euripides, τεκνοσπορία is clearly simply "a begetting of children." The same range of meaning is found for τίκτω. In Aeschylus, the substantive ὁ τεκών is "the father" and ἡ τεκοῦσα is "the mother." So a distinction naturally remains in the use of these words, though one cannot say roughly that γεννεῖν is a father's work, while τέκτειν belongs to a mother.

the desire to confess the pure Gospel that gives life to faith—in short, to let God be God.

4

> The child of Adam lives by self-justification. The child of God lives by faith. Faith delights in the perfect tense and the passive voice and finds its security there. This is so because faith glories in that which lets God be God. The redeemed take comfort in the God who has made them his own, "the God who is most at home when he is justifying the ungodly and giving life to the dead."[36] In this manner, they confidently express and live by the radical and stubborn "nevertheless," the *tamen*, of faith (Job 13:15–16; 19:25–27; Psalm 66:12; 73:23; 118:17; Habakkuk 3:17–18; John 19:30; 2 Corinthians 6:8–10).[37]

Faith is purely passive (*pure passiva*). For that reason, its strength and tenacity derive not from itself but from the certainty of the promise and the utter truthfulness of the One who bestows it.

The notion of the unity of experience is fractured by the reality that a person is constituted as he is addressed. But there is a fundamental distinction, a great divide, between how he is addressed in law and in gospel. A person is reconstituted, created anew, as he is addressed by the God who justifies the ungodly, who creates something out of nothing, and who gives life to the dead. In a certain but restricted sense, this new being, begotten of the creative love of God, is discontinuous with the old, which is marked by demand unfulfilled and is hounded by wrath unending. The new being clings to

---

[36] The concluding phrase from a sermon by our jubilarian.

[37] One hears this same "Nevertheless!" in Arvo Pärt's remarkable *Credo*. After hell has unleashed its fury, heard in the harshly dissonant deconstruction of J. S. Bach's *Prelude in C Major* (*The Well-Tempered Clavier*, Book 1, No. 1, BWV 846), and in the teeth of the *lex talionis* sung in the background by the choir, faith remains because Christ remains faithful.

Christ, who alone is the end of wrath because he is the end of law's condemning voice.[38]

Faith does not properly say, "I was baptized" but rather confesses, "I *am* baptized." Faith is anchored by such perfect passives that indicate a past event with ongoing significance: "It is written" (Rom. 1:17); "It is finished" (John 19:30); "Jesus of Nazareth, who was crucified" (Mark 16:6), our Lord's title for all eternity.

In the Divine Service, where the justification of the ungodly by the bestowal of the passive righteousness in Christ is witnessed, bodily gestures, posture, and movement will express its reverent reception: kneeling, adoration, bowing, making the sign of the Cross, as often as we are being forgiven, being washed, and being fed with a food beyond our comprehension and by a love that surpasses understanding. The sense of awe before the astonishing wonders of the created order is closely related to and yet surpassed by the sense of reverence before the mysteries of the Divine Service. Certainly, the blind are made to see and the deaf to hear in being welcomed by the God who restores through Word and Sacrament. Yet these remain things of faith, not of sight.

How shall we regard our baptism? Luther in the Large Catechism teaches us,

> We must think this way about Baptism and make it profitable for ourselves. So when our sins and conscience oppress us, we strengthen ourselves and take comfort and say, "Nevertheless, I am baptized. [*Ego tamen baptizatus sum.*] And if I am baptized, it is promised to me that I shall be saved and have eternal life, both in soul and body." For that is why these two things are done in Baptism: the body—which can grasp nothing but the water—is sprinkled and, in addition,

---

[38] The theme of personhood as constituted by address has a further implication. In a fundamental way, we *are* not except as we are in communion with others, as argued by the Metropolitan of Pergamon, John D. Zizioulas. Cf. his *Being as Communion: Studies in Personhood and the Church* (Crestwood, NY: St. Vladimir's Press, 1985). Though, strictly speaking, there is no direct analogy, psychological or social, between creature and Triune Creator, one may see in light of the divine economy "patches of Godlight in the woods of our experience" (C. S. Lewis).

the Word is spoken for the soul to grasp. Now, since both, the water and the Word, make one Baptism, therefore, body and soul must be saved and live forever (1 Corinthians 15:53). The soul lives through the Word, which it believes, but the body lives because it is united with the soul and also holds on through Baptism as it is able to grasp it. We have, therefore, no greater jewel in body and soul. For by Baptism we are made holy and are saved (1 Corinthians 6:11). No other kind of life, no work upon earth, can do this.[39]

Faith holds tenaciously onto God's promise.

When faith is most passive in receiving the gift of righteousness, which is Christ Himself, it becomes for that very reason most active in showing mercy to the neighbor.[40] "Freely have you received, freely give." This is so simply because He is such a Savior, who wills to give Himself totally to the other. "My life for yours" is thus the motto of His fair city, that most excellent Zion.

Conclusion

We said we wanted to identify four ways by which true confession of the Gospel is radical. While not limiting the Gospel's verity and power to its presence in the scripture, we have held that Gospel proclamation must always be normed by the scriptures that cannot be broken. First, the scriptures lead us to be radical in making the diagnosis of human need. Second, they prompt us to be radical in our assessment and bleak prognosis for human potential. Third, they beckon us to appreciate the radically new nature of the life given us in Holy Baptism. Fourth, the scriptures witness the radical tenacity of faith that is purely passive in receiving Christ.

A great man leaves behind those who are enabled to stand on his shoulders. Gerhard Forde has left a legacy of enduring published material and also generations of former students and colleagues who are contending for a radical Lutheranism—not for Lutheranism for

---

[39] Large Catechism, IV:44–46.

[40] I suspect this is the meaning of Luther's "In faith Christ himself is present [*In fide Christus ipsius adest*]."

its own sake but for the daring confession of the unconditioned, law-free gospel. We have suggested that a task remains for those who are a part of this legacy and who wish to preserve what is good and faithful and strong in it. Four topics need to be addressed as further parts of this task; first, the role of the formal principle—more specifically, the interrelationship between gospel and scripture; second, the doctrine of creation as the ground for natural law; and third, how the proclamation of an unconditioned gospel is to be safeguarded from antinomianism by a consistent specification that it is the theological use of the law, the legal scheme, that finds its end in Christ, for Christ alone silences its demanding, threatening, accusing, terrifying, damning, and killing voice just as he silences the demons. It is this legal scheme as such that is ended and not the eternal character of God as embodied in holy love. And finally, the nature of the atonement. While he may not agree with my assessment or with everything I have written in this brief catechetical comment, James Arne Nestingen continues to be a clear, bold, and principal voice among those sharing in this legacy.

About the Bible

Dr. Roy A. Harrisville

The invitation to contribute to this volume in honor of James Arne Nestingen has been most welcome. As student, colleague, and son of a seminary schoolmate, we have been friends for more than fifty years. By way of this article, I express the hope that his continuance in enunciating Reformation theology may persist 'til he joins the choir immortal to which, God grant, we will all belong.

Contemporary biblical scholarship has been characterized as having little or no concern for the Christian community. When, a few years ago, a distinguished scholar published a piece on biblical criticism in which he insisted that it must take into account the faith and confession of the Christian community as reflected in its creeds and symbols, there was no resounding "Yeah" and "Amen" heard from the American sector. Some regard the New Testament as an interesting pan-Hellenistic document that deserves investigation and research but give no attention to its function as a norm for inclusion in the Christian community. Others negotiate a transfer from the divinity school to the university "yard," exempting themselves from the preparation of clergy. Still others flatly refuse to engage in theological discourse, and more than one has seconded the statement once made by a Chicago Divinity School professor who did not "give a damn" what the Church thought since John D. Rockefeller paid his salary.

To some this lack of concern on the part of the "guild" is of little moment, for the reason that the academic community has seldom exercised any real influence on the general public. From this perspective, biblical research is scarcely calculated to have any influence on the Christian community. Christians will proceed to an encounter with the living God through the testimony of the scriptures, the demurral of the academic to the contrary notwithstanding. The thought may be comforting, but it is suspect. In the last century, we witnessed the collapse of a regime whose record of cruelty and suffering far exceeded that of Hitler's Germany. The monstrosity of that regime is such that reflection on it leads to either stupor or silence. In the words of one Russologist:

> Because Communism is so clearly the handiwork of intellectuals; because its ideology appears, like its language, so complex; because it ruled so much of the earth—it is difficult to dismiss it as one would, say, a quack medicine.[1]

The halls and seminar rooms where the elite meet are occupied by the clergy of tomorrow, certain to wield influence with their communities. The influence may be largely negative, perhaps in the nature of "fallout" from an encounter with criticism. Exposed to a congeries of methods harnessed to a congeries of presuppositions to the point of total confusion that not even pursuit of a doctorate can cure, contemporary preaching—the event that all this exposition and interpretation and methodology and hermeneutic was designed to serve—is marked more by free association occasioned by the biblical text than by the struggle to translate it. Preaching is at a low, not for lack of time spent in the pulpit, though some lean on the hymnal to save them from having anything to say (who knows whether current preoccupation with liturgy and the accoutrements of worship is twin to the malaise?), nor for lack of words but for lack of attention given the biblical text.

Once upon a time, something remarkable happened in theology. A fire was set that for many of my generation has never been put out. One epoch in biblical interpretation was dying, being done to death, really, and another was coming to birth. That tired old epoch

---

[1] Brian Moynahan, *The Russian Century* (New York: Random House, 1995), 107.

was marked by what John Alexander Mackay of Princeton years ago called "the balcony-view," the assumption that the Bible could be read objectively, loosed from presuppositions, from a posture or stance or commitment for or against it. In his second attempt at a commentary on Romans, a young Swiss pastor described that period:

> Recent commentaries contain no more than a reconstruction of the text, a rendering of the Greek words and phrases by their precise equivalents, a number of additional notes in which archaeological and philological material is gathered together, and a more or less plausible arrangement of the subject-matter in such a manner that it may be made historically and psychologically intelligible from the standpoint of pure pragmatism.

Then he asked,

> Can scientific investigation ever really triumph so long as men are content to engage themselves with amazing energy upon the work of interpretation with the most superficial understanding of what interpretation really is?. . . . Do they not perceive that there are documents, such as the books of the New Testament, which compel men to speak at whatever cost, because they find in them that which urgently and finally concerns the very marrow of human civilization?[2]

The new epoch, the new period, would be marked by the conviction that where the biblical text was concerned, there could be no neutral ground, no "objectivity," which, in the words of one Iowan who arguably emerged as one of this country's greatest historiographers, was the "best substitute for ideas yet invented." The three names most attached to this movement were those of Adolf Schlatter, Karl Barth, and Rudolf Bultmann. The differences between them were mammoth, but at certain points they converged.

---

[2] Karl Barth, *The Epistle to the Romans*, trans. E. C. Hoskyns, author's preface to the second edition (Oxford: Oxford University Press, 1933), 6, 8–9.

First, all three were struggling to get free of an intellectual tradition, a struggle echoed in Schlatter's word to his students at Tübingen in 1931:

> I admonish every student that he hold fast to evangelical rejection of infallibility in every situation, toward himself and every teacher, every book, every school, every party.[3]

For all three, that tradition comprised unequal parts of Orthodoxy, Rationalism, Pietism, of religion construed in terms of "feeling," of Positivism, and the advocacy of a "religious a priori." Each allegiance came under attack, though Schlatter reserved his bitterest attack for orthodoxy of the Lutheran variety:

> We could not saunter back into the old Tübingen, where everyone had the true, pure faith, and where a violent man sat in the chief official's house, and a thief in the house of the lower city—both, however, indubitably orthodox and Lutheran.[4]

Second, all three were adamant in the conviction that if revelation is a reality within human existence, then the word about that reality, the biblical word, is more than the report of an available fact of world history. Then it is the disclosure of our existence.

In a piece entitled "Atheistic Methods in Theology," Schlatter responded to an article by a well-known Freiburg pastor who had urged that theology should work only with the method recognized in the university, which being interpreted meant that God had to be bracketed out of historical study. Only such a method, argued the famous pulpiteer, could be represented as scientific. Theology was thus to be carried on as the science of religion. (Incidentally, I understand that Harvard has altered the name of its divinity school to read "Non-Sectarian School of Theology and Religious Studies.")

---

[3] Adolf Schlatter, "Zur Theologie des Naune Testaments und zur Dogmatik," *Theologische Bücherei* 41, 259.

[4] Adolf Schlatter, *Erlebtes* (Berlin: Furche Verlag, 1924), 76.

Schlatter replied that historical research did not put faith in question but rather uncovered its effectiveness. In other words, the act of thinking followed living, for which reason one's own life situation had to be incorporated into the historical putting of the question. As far as Schlatter was concerned, that life situation was given him beforehand, in the context of the effects of the history of Jesus Christ. The historical task, as he saw it, was to understand his existence in that context.[5]

Theology, wrote Bultmann, requires a mode appropriate to its object, the mode we call faith. It cannot be carried on "out of curiosity" or for the purpose of earning a living but as a "venture, in which we ourselves are at risk." He continued: If God is the object of faith and accessible only to faith, then a science apart from or merely alongside faith sees neither God nor the mode of access appropriate to its object.[6]

Years later, one of the principal thinkers of the Western world, and a baptized Catholic, would write,

> The gospel does not exist in order to be understood as a merely historical document, but to be taken in such a way that it exercises its saving effect. This implies that the text, whether law or gospel, if it is to be understood properly—i.e., according to the claim it makes—must be understood at every moment, in every concrete situation, in a new and different way. Understanding here is always application.[7]

Later still, one of the most provocative thinkers since the 1960s—and a circumcised Jew—would write,

> There can, as Rudolf Bultmann has shown in his study of the Gospels, be no "presuppositionless readings" of the past. To all past events,

---

[5] Cf. Luck's introduction to Schlatter, "Zur Theologie des Neuen Testaments und zur Dogmatik," 13, 17–19, 24–25.

[6] Rudolf Bultmann, *What Is Theology*, trans. Roy A. Harrisville (Minneapolis: Augsburg Fortress, 1997), 20, 22, 84, 102, 155, 160.

[7] Hans-Georg Gadamer, *Truth and Method*, trans. Joel Weinsheimer and Donald G. Marshall (London: Sheed and Ward, 1989), 309.

as to all present intake, the observer brings a specific mental set . . . there are no non-temporal truths. The articulation now of a supposed past fact involves an elaborate, mainly subconscious network of conventions. . . . None of these contentions is susceptible of final logical analysis.[8]

Third, as far as Schlatter and Bultmann were concerned, biblical research and faith, that mode appropriate to doing theology, were not at odds. Schlatter wrote,

> For me, faith and criticism never divided into opposites, so that at one time I would have thought in a Bible-believing way, and at another critically. Rather, I thought in critical fashion because I believed in the Bible, and believed in it because I read it critically.[9]

In Württemberg, where Schlatter spent most of his teaching life, theologians had once bludgeoned each other over the question of the degree to which Christians should be occupied with worldly learning and science (the so-called Pietist Controversy of 1840).

In a review of Barth's commentary on the Romans, Bultmann wrote,

> When in exegeting Romans I detect tensions and contradictions, places high and low; when I take pains to show how Paul is dependent on Jewish theology or popular Christianity . . . I am not just carrying on historical-philological criticism. I am doing it from the viewpoint of showing where and how the subject matter is expressed, in order to lay hold of the subject matter which is greater even than Paul.[10]

---

[8] George Steiner, *After Babel* (Oxford: Oxford University Press, 1998), 143–44.

[9] Adolf Schlatter, *Rückblick auf seine Lebensarbeit, Beiträge zur Forderung christlichen Theologie*, Sonderheft (Gütersloh: C. Bertelsmann, 1952), 83.

[10] Rudolf Bultmann, *Anfänge der dialektischen Theologie*, ed. Jürgen Moltmann, *Theologische Bücherei*, vol. 17 (Munich: C. Kaiser, 1962–63), 141–42.

It is symptomatic that the guild has ignored most if not all of Schlatter's work and concentrated on Barth's distaste for critical method and on Bultmann's link to phenomenological analysis, thus ignoring the passion that they shared. Schlatter, when understood— and he was not always understood, not even by Germans—seemed naïve, biblicistic. For all his commitment to the critical method, he was damned as a pietist whose faith in the Bible rendered him unfit for scientific work. Barth, with his shattering of every religious state- ment on the idea that God is inaccessibly distant (Schlatter's word), seemed to leave no room for the act of thinking, while Bultmann appeared to do quite the opposite, to reduce the biblical text to one long, elongated, and pendulous disquisition on self-understanding to the point where he was unable to speak of God in objectifying fashion. As far as I am able to tell, "Process Theology," with its prom- ise to do precisely that, had its start with those who had fallen out of love with Bultmann or Barth. And the logical birthplace was the University of Chicago, where, according to legend, the faculty had once read Alfred North Whitehead's *Religion in the Making* and invited the process empiricist Henry Nelson Wieman to the chair in philosophy so that he could explain it.

Here it is important to note that there was no causal connec- tion between the passion Schlatter, Barth, and Bultmann shared and the vehicles they used to express it. As noted, Barth was miles from Bultmann, and Schlatter was miles from both. But they had wit- nessed, experienced, perceived, intuited something quite apart from whatever systems they might later develop: exegesis, biblical inter- pretation apart from a stance toward the text is impossible, apart from what Schleiermacher—largely responsible for the damage done theology in the past—had called "sympathy," and what Barth came to call "spiritual exegesis" and Bultmann "decisions-understanding." And if it took Barth time to acknowledge that his "inaccessibly dis- tant" God had created a community, and if Bultmann would finally admit that ecclesiology had not stood at the center of his work, their insistence on faith as the mode appropriate to the Bible's interpre- tation and upon revelation as the origin of faith would move Barth to a "Church" and not simply a "Christian Dogmatics" and would move Bultmann to charter membership in the Confessing Church, to remain in Germany and risk his neck in public opposition to the Führer-Prinzip and its hellish anti-Semitism.

It would be an error to imagine that the passion that Schlatter, Barth, and Bultmann shared was limited to Europeans. It was not. If, after the pattern of Harnack, who argued that "the scientific theologian who begins with setting aflame and edifying brings strange fire to his altar," Harvard's[11] Henry Joel Cadbury would deny that "only in so far as we shared the New Testament belief ourselves can we understand the New Testament,"[12] there were others at Yale, Union, and Princeton who affirmed precisely that. In one way or another, Frank Chamberlain Porter of Yale, Frederick C. Grant, and Samuel Terrien of Union insisted that the Bible was to be interpreted by means of the response that it intended to invoke. Let my doctor father Otto Alfred Wilhelm Piper speak for them all. Writing that "the interpretation of a document consists of two different though closely related processes—exegesis and appropriation," he added that "a true interpretation must be both historical and spiritual." Piper thus commended Barth's commentary on Romans for insisting that the biblical books presented themselves as revelation and "demanded of the reader to accept them as divine truth." He likewise commended Bultmann, who taught that as divine truth, the Bible addresses itself "not merely to my intellect but primarily to my very self." According to Piper, the "openness" required of the interpreter presupposed recognition of the Bible as God's Word, as the divine Word of truth to be held in supreme authority. Such a recognition, Piper argued, was not an attitude or posture to be assumed but occurred only through faith. As he put it,

> The claim of the Biblical books to contain a divine message of supreme importance for all men cannot be appreciated except by faith.[13]

---

[11] Cf. Karl Barth, *Der Römerbrief, Erste Fassung* (1919), in *Gesamtausgabe* (Zürich: Theologischer Verlag, 1985), II, 643.

[12] Henry Joel Cadbury, "Current Issues in New Testament Studies," *Harvard Divinity School Bulletin* 51 (1954): 61.

[13] Cf. Otto A. Piper, "Principles of New Testament Interpretation," *Theology Today* 3 (1946): 193, 202–3; "Biblical Theology and Systematic Theology,"

According to Piper, this "openness," interpreted as a "search for the present Christ who speaks to us through the Bible," had hardly begun in Protestantism.[14] In my opinion, with us this "openness" died stillborn. Biblical research in the United States is being attempted as if that earthquake of my youth had never occurred. Still, there is no need to consign what concerned Schlatter, Barth, and Bultmann to the archives. What we believe, teach, and confess urges us in a contrary direction. For our confession is that scripture, the Bible, is a self-effervescing source that does not take its credibility from its interpretation, in or outside the Church.

Which reminds me: In my salad days, there were Lutherans who taught that the authority of scripture was guaranteed by the mode of its inspiration. They wrote not only that the Holy Spirit impelled its authors to write but that he furnished them with the fitting word and the fitting content (*impulsus ad scribendum, suggestio rerum, suggestio verbi*). Whatever contradictions were noted were only apparent, and one needed merely wait 'til they disappeared of themselves. This position superimposed a metaphysical principle upon the scriptures in an attempt to guarantee their inerrancy. But the authority and thus the inerrancy of scripture is of a radically different sort, for which reason there is always the possibility of its being denied. The authority of the Bible stems from its self-authentication in the heart and mind of the believer. The scriptures derive their authority as sole and final rule for faith and life from their power to evoke assent and trust, to wring a "yes" from deep inside us; such power as to cut us adrift from whatever allegiance we once may have had; to leave us without an ideology, without a metaphysic or political program, to suspend us between heaven and hell, risking everything on words whose truths resist establishing by human act or logic.

The parables of Jesus illustrate the point. In each parable, the material seems common and everyday: a sown seed, a lamp lit, bread baked, or a field worked (Mark 4), but in every instance everything is turned on its head. A woman loses a coin, finds it, and throws a party

---

Journal of Bible and Religion 25, no. 2 (1957): 109; and *Protestantism in an Ecumenical Age* (Philadelphia: Fortress, 1965), 191.

[14] Piper, *Protestantism*, 215.

costing who knows how many times more than the penny she lost. A father kills the fatted calf for a son who couldn't wait for him to die to get at his inheritance (Luke 15). The last hired to tend a vineyard are paid an amount equal to that earned by those who labored the entire day (Matt. 20). The activity is absurd. There is nothing in it that squares with common sense, nothing to induce us to say after hearing it, "Well, yes, that's exactly how things are." Belief that the parables of Jesus are ordinary, plain vanilla devices designed to add to our already bursting fund of information about God's kingdom is misplaced. Their subject is an absurdity. Nothing can be brought to them from the outside to help us understand. Our experience, our way of observing the world, it all takes us in precisely the opposite direction. There is only one possibility left for understanding, and that is involvement with the one who tells such tales that turn everything on its head, "letting him in." This is why Jesus says to his disciples, "To you has been given the secret of the kingdom of God, but for those outside, everything comes in [not 'parables,' but] riddles."

To return to our argument, scripture, independent, its integrity underived, is its own interpreter. *Scriptura sui interpres*. On its own, it yields understanding, for on its own it gives the Spirit through whom it can be understood, and on its own it possesses the quality of a certainty that neither feeling nor experience can equal. It was this confession that triggered the debate with the papal legate at Augsburg, that brought Cajetan hot and sweaty from Rome to Augsburg in 1518. To that "prince of the Church" in his red hat, Luther said,

> Ego non possum revocare, nisi meliora edoceor, nam a scriptura non possum discedere (I cannot recant unless instructed, for I cannot depart from scripture)[15]

For this reason, scripture does not require exposition because it is obscure. It is most often exposition, whether of the orthodox, liberal, structuralist, poststructuralist, or feminist variety that obscures the Bible. More, no exposition is equal to this self-effervescing

---

[15] Martin Luther, WTi 5; 5349.

source. To paraphrase Luther, our knowledge of scripture resembles a ball on a billiard table, touching the surface at only one spot and moved by the slightest nudge. At the end of a Christmas postil, the Reformer wrote,

> Here you see from all my palaver how immeasurably unlike every human word the word of God is, how with all his talk none can get at or explain one single word of God. It is an infinite word: it intends to be grasped and examined with a quiet spirit, as the . . . Psalm [85:9] reads: I will hear what God himself says to me.[16]

What gives to scripture this great power, this effervescence, this independence and nonderivability, is its witness to Jesus Christ. He is its content and rules the method of its understanding. My mentor at Princeton, Otto Piper, not at all a radical critic, nevertheless declared that the witness to Jesus Christ, God's Son, was not incompatible with addressing the disturbing historical questions. Ernst Käsemann, friend for over thirty years, wrote that the most radical criticism would not mar or endanger that witness. Bultmann's most gifted pupil but the one least influenced by his teacher's presuppositions, Käsemann could cavil at arguments over the empty tomb and assign to legend narratives and sayings of Jesus he believed were birthed by the later church but had this to say of what lay at the core of that witness:

> No one belongs to Christ who did not give him one's heart, and with it the disposition over one's will and life. The radicality of the first commandment may not be infringed, a commandment which forbids serving two masters and wanting to compromise with the forces laying claim to us.[17]

As to the method urged by that witness, he wrote,

---

[16] Martin Luther, W 10, I, 1; 728, 9–22.

[17] Ernst Käsemann, *Kirchliche Konflikte* (Göttingen: Vandenhoeck und Ruprecht, 1982), 78.

We should not begin with the creation or with the hope in resurrection, or with the enumerating of the mighty acts of God. This can occur on either side of Golgotha. . . . And we should not begin with the idealism of faith in human goodness, or with the cynicism of the conviction of human evil. There is an even division where Pilate, Herod, and Caiaphas, the incited mob, the two thieves, the complaining disciples, and the Roman captain are gathered in Jesus' passion. We must begin and end with the Crucified.[18]

When reflecting on a specific genre of the New Testament record, he had this to say,

The biblical miracle stories are misunderstood when we do not also see them in the perspective of the cross. For the God of Jesus Christ does not appear in order to make us supermen as the idols of the world promise. He reveals himself in the Nazarene in human fashion and effects (affects?) humanity. For the believer, the signature of the Crucified alone is the measure of life and promise for the world.[19]

He could just as well have said this of the historical narratives, the speech material, the apothegms, dominical sayings, and parables of the Gospels.

But if that revelation is in human fashion, then just as the flesh of Christ, it risks humiliation. "It is a worm," wrote Luther:

Not a book when matched against other books. It doesn't get the honor . . . other writings do. It is well off if it lies under the pew. Others tear it apart, crucify it, scourge and expose it to all kinds of martyrdom, till finally they do it to death, kill and bury it, to the point where it is shoved off the world and forgotten.[20]

Closer to home, the "Confession of Faith" in the Constitution of the Evangelical Lutheran Church in America, chapter 2, paragraph 3,

---

[18] Ibid., 94.

[19] Ibid., 203.

[20] Martin Luther, W 48; 31, 4–14.

reads, "This church accepts the canonical Scriptures of the Old and New Testaments as the inspired Word of God and the authoritative source of its proclamation, faith, and life." I take it to mean that whatever this body projects or performs shall conform to that collection of sixty-six books called the Old and New Testaments acknowledged to be "the inspired Word of God." Suppose that such is not occurring. Suppose that this body does not conform to that canon. Suppose it has erected this device, penned this statement, simply to maintain its tax-free status as a religious organization but does not actually shape its life to it. In my days as a boy scout, spent absolutely without distinction, we spent the first few minutes repeating the scout oath, then after our scoutmaster left we turned the lights out in the old Methodist church gym, had ourselves a knock-down, drag-out melee, and after an hour or so turned the lights on again to determine who had been wounded in the fray. The oath was purely for purposes of advertising; it had nothing to do with our behavior. Suppose a denomination with its bishops, pastors, lay leaders, all the while affirming "the canonical Scriptures of the Old and New Testaments as the inspired Word of God and the authoritative source of its proclamation, faith, and life" consciously, deliberately, with malice aforethought or without any thought at all, does not function according to that norm—that the norm is mere advertisement without relevance to that body's interior life.

The possibility that such should occur, that a church should confess one thing and do another, that it should affirm the Bible as the norm but proceed to function as if it were not, that possibility has always existed. In face of that eventuality, splinter groups have been created, pledging to keep free of such contradiction. The Lutheran Church in this country is punctuated with groups established to protect themselves against it. God bless all such, but there is nothing in the way of a confession, a doctrine, a discipline, a hierarchy, or a constitution that ultimately can prevent a church from failing to live by "the canonical Scriptures of the Old and New Testaments as the inspired Word of God." Just as the flesh of Christ, that revelation risks humiliation.

Still, there is no alternative to establishing biblical authority beyond opening oneself to it, body and soul. And the loss of *this* authority is worse, far worse than the loss of any external authority, any authority given it from the outside. For in this case, the Bible is lost to the Church in terms of its power to evoke the resolve to live or die by it. With respect to its inerrancy, the Bible is indeed inerrant *in respect finis*, as the old dogmaticians put it—inerrant with respect to its aim of evoking faith in Christ. Regarding *that* goal, the Bible is sure and certain, without error. The fear that once a datum appearing in the Bible is challenged or threatened the entire biblical witness is put in doubt rises from the notion that its authority can be guaranteed from the outside. And in the last analysis, what is *that* but the assumption that the Bible's integrity can be guaranteed by human means? Whatever support the paleologist or archaeologist may give to the biblical data is welcome, but the assumption that biblical integrity can be secured by human means is contrary to the Bible's purpose.

To sum up, to see this book for what it is it cannot simply be reproduced with the self, the "I" excluded. Faith alone yields understanding, penetrates behind that poor child in the crib to the Savior of the world. Luther never tired of saying that the word does not reach its goal until it becomes life and deed. "Es ist nicht lesewort . . . sondern eitel lebewort"; "It is not a word to be read, but a word for life, plain and simple."[21]

For this reason also, the word of scripture must take on the flesh and blood of its expositor. When in his *History of the Synoptic Tradition* Bultmann stated that scarcely a piece of the Jesus tradition had not undergone alteration prior to its assuming written form, in instances even taking to itself what was alien, this was but the reverse side of the recognition that the gospel must reincarnate itself in its interpreter so as to become a *viva vox*, a living voice. For his form-critical demonstration of that "Lutheran" idea, Bultmann was hereticized, though nowadays no one leaves church in a temper over sermons composed of heaps of anecdotes, personal references, and a thousand and one other devices forced on the Jesus tradition all in the name of preaching.

But if this book, this word, everlastingly endures crucifixion, just as often it rises from the dead to taunt the generation that mishandles it and beckons new generations to discover life in it. It has taunted this generation, but the next may discover life in it.

---

[21] Martin Luther, W 31, 1; 67, 3–14.

The Gospel for Those Broken by the Church

Dr. Rod Rosenbladt

A lecture delivered to an invited audience at Concordia University in Irvine, winter, 2004.

This evening, I want to address a particular problem: what a Christian might be able to say in conversation with people who see themselves as "alumni" of the Christian faith.

And of course, I am *not* referring to those who have been translated by death from what Christians call the "church militant" into the "church triumphant"! I mean people we meet or know who say that they once believed that Christ and His shed blood freely justified them before God, freely forgave their sin, freely gave them eternal life—but who add that they no longer believe these things.

It seems to me that in the four gospels (roughly, the biographies of Jesus authored by Matthew, Mark, Luke, and John), virtually every person who rejected Jesus' claims to be God and Messiah, the Savior of the world, went away either *sad* or *mad*.

First, I'm going to try to deal with today's "sad ones," the longing, the "having-given-up-on-Christianity" ones. **Second**, I want to talk a little about the gospel of Christ for today's "mad" ones, the angry ones.

I can't tell you how much it bugs me that there exists such a group as the one called "Fundamentalists Anonymous"! But there *is* such a "self-help group." If there is any kind of "Christian recovery group," I want it to be "Liberal Protestants Anonymous" or "Recovering Neo-Orthodox Protestants" or "Liberation Theology Advocates Anonymous" or "Open Theism Recovery Group." (You get the idea.) For all of its faults, American fundamentalism *at least is Christianity* of a sort. Still, to be perfectly honest, I really *can* understand why such a group as "Fundamentalists Anonymous" exists. Maybe you can, too. Many of these people about whom or to whom I am going to speak tonight are casualties of Bible-believing churches. Some seem to be able to remain in this form of Christianity for years and years. But certainly not all. For some reasons (reasons that, I think, are very specifiable), more people than we would like to think *leave* fundamentalist Christianity. I think the same dynamic is often the case with people who belong to what are called "the holiness bodies" (Wesleyan Christianity). Some are sad about it. Some are angry about it.

You might say, "Well, my church is certainly *not* 'fundamentalist.'" I think mine is part of what *Newsweek* and *Time* call "mainline churches." If that is the case, probably not much that I have to say tonight will be very helpful to you. I am not going to be talking much about "mainline Protestant" churches—liberal Lutheran, liberal Presbyterian, Episcopal—for the simple reason that for most of them, there isn't enough theology left to make people really "sad" or "mad," make them convinced that they have to leave or their hearts will break. Or makes them leave because if they don't, they fear they will "uncork" on some Shepherd or sheep and get arrested for it. The reason for this is, I think, a relatively simple one: there just isn't enough substantial theology in most "mainline" Protestant churches to upset anybody. There isn't much of *anything* left in mainline Protestant sermons or curricula—except maybe lessons in ethics and perhaps new opportunities for social service. As one wag put it, "The trouble with theology today is that there isn't any!"

Many of us have met and talked with the *sad alumni* of Christianity. And many of us have also met and talked with some of the *mad alumni* of Christianity. The venue may vary, but most of us know or have met men and women who tell us that Christianity was a part of their life in years past but that they no longer consciously identify with Jesus Christ in His claim to be God and Savior.

They perhaps earlier identified themselves with some form of Christianity, but no longer. Every pastor runs into these people. So do lay people. It seems to "go with the territory" these days. You and I know them, meet them. You might be one of them. I have run into it in decades of working on the college campus—first with the Inter-Varsity Christian Fellowship, later as a professor. In these roles, it has been (for whatever reasons) easier for students to tell me the truth. I think they have said things to me that they were afraid to tell their pastors or priests. It is perhaps easier to tell a professor that you once believed that Jesus was your sin-bearing Savior but that you no longer believe that. Or that you *wish* you could still believe in Jesus but you just can't. If you are a Christian pastor or layman, you have probably more than once heard the same thing from friends or acquaintances. In our day, there are so many of these people that it is hard *not* to come into contact with them. There are thousands of them.

First, a Few Words about the "Sad" Alumni of Christianity

Many of these people were *broken by the church*. I know that sounds harsh. As Christians, it's bothersome to hear words like that. But for many people, this is how they really see what has happened to them.

Now almost certainly, many of us have also had contact with people who have struggled for their whole lives with being deeply upset psychologically. The church, for whatever reasons, draws people who the professionals recognize as "bipolar" or wrestling against what they call "clinical depression." Or whose guilt is so great that they are inwardly immobilized, people who are so frightened that just coping day by day is truly heroic. But it is *not* about any of these people that I will be speaking tonight. I am not competent to do so. It seems to me that such people deserve all of the care and empathy that we can muster. But again, it is *not* about such people that I am speaking tonight.

By the "sad alumni" of the Christian faith, I mean the hundreds and hundreds whose acquaintance with the Christian church was often one in which they were helped to move from unbelief (or from a suffocating moralism) into real saving faith in Jesus Christ. They heard the preaching of God's law and then heard the announcement of Christ's work on their behalf on the cross—Jesus as the God-man who met the law's demands for them and died for their sin, died to save them, died to give them eternal life. They heard the wonderful message of God's grace in the cross and death of Jesus Christ. They heard the astonishing news that God in Jesus Christ died for them, died so that they can be—and are!—freely forgiven based solely on that atoning death. They heard that Christ's blood redeems sinners, buys us out of our self-chosen enslavement. They came to believe that Christianity is not so much about what is in *our* hearts as much as it is about what is in *God's* heart—and this proven by Christ's vicarious and atoning death for them, for their sin. They came to believe that the cross of Christ was their salvation. For free. And forever.

But something happened after that, something that broke them. And in general, I think what happened is nameable. (At least in many cases.)

In my Lutheran church—Missouri Synod—we would speak of it as the confusion of Law and Gospel. Dr. Charles Manske, the founding president of Christ College Irvine, used to teach a course in Christianity for freshmen. In that course, he characterized the various churches of Christendom this way:

- Rome: Law
- Lutheran: Law–Gospel
- Wesleyan evangelical: Law–Gospel–Law

I think Dr. Manske was definitely "on to something" here, and I think it is that third point that results in a lot of "sad alumni" of Christianity.

Now if you are Lutheran or Reformed, we too have a category that, if not done carefully and well, will turn out just as destructive as any Wesleyan, Pentecostal, or Nazarene preaching. I am referring, of course, to "the third use of the law." (In Lutheran theology, the content of this "third use" of the law is spelled out in a section of our *Book of Concord*—specifically in what we call the Formula of Concord.) If you are Reformed, you will recognize this category immediately, recognize it as tracing back to John Calvin himself. Too, if I am correct, in what Calvinist Christians call the "Three Forms of Unity": the Canons of the Synod of Dort, the Belgic Confession, and the Heidelberg Catechism? If I am wrong on this one (not being "Reformed"), I apologize for an inaccurate characterization of your position.

What do we Reformation folk mean by "the third use of the law?" It claims to be primarily informative, informative for the Christian. And something that fleshes out "What is the will of God for me as a Christian day-by-day?" (What about the law thundering to us that we are deeply fallen, unable to fix our problem? That we are guilty before a holy God and His holy law, that unless God does something one-sidedly to rescue us, we are without hope and certainly condemned? That we from the Reformation call "the second use" of the law, the "pedagogical use." Luther thought this was the major function of the law in the Bible, designed to drive us to despair of our character, our works, our anything! And to drive us to Jesus Christ as the atoning, dying Lamb/substitute for our sin—mine and yours, too.)

At any rate, if we Reformation folk do the "third use of the law" badly, we get very close to the infamous "application section" of the sermon so common in Wesleyan and evangelical preaching. And if we do it badly, the sensitive Christian believer can be driven to a slavery as bad as any slavery done to them by a totalitarian dictator. If the Ten Commandments were not impossible enough, the preaching of Christian behavior, of Christian ethics, of Christian living, can drive a Christian into despairing unbelief. Not happy unbelief. Tragic, despairing, sad unbelief. (It is not unlike the [unhappy] Christian equivalent of "Jack Mormons"—those who finally admit to themselves and others that they can't live up to the demands of this non-Christian cult's laws and excuse themselves from the whole shebang.) A diet of this stuff from pulpit, from curriculum, from a Christian reading list, can do a work on a Christian that is (at least over the long haul) "faith destroying." You might be in just this position this evening. Many of us have a friend whose story is not a far cry from this. We all regularly rub shoulders with such "alumni of the Christian faith"—sad that the gospel of Christ didn't (for them, at least) "deliver the goods," didn't "work."

In a Christian context, the mechanism of this can be, I think, a very simple one:

1. You come to believe that you have been justified freely because of Christ's shed blood.
2. Freely, for the sake of Jesus' innocent sufferings and death, God has forgiven your sin, adopted you as a son or daughter, reconciled you to Himself, given you the Holy Spirit, and so on. Scripture promises these things.
3. Verses like "Be ye perfect as your Heavenly Father is perfect" seem now—at first read—to finally be possible, now that you are equipped for it. Or you hear St. Paul as he writes, "I can do all things through Christ who strengthens me." Same thing.
4. You realize that you might have had some excuse for failure when you were a pagan. But that's over. Now you have been made a part of God's family, have become the recipient of a thousand of His free gifts.
5. And then, the unexpected. Sin continues to be a part of my life, stubbornly won't allow me to eliminate it the way I expected.
6. Continuing sin on my part seems to be just evidence that I'm not really a believer at all. If I were really a believer, this thing would "work"!

We start to imagine that we need to be "born again *again*." (And often the counsel from non-Reformation churches is that this intuition of ours is *true*.) Try going again to some evangelistic meeting, accept Christ again, surrender your will to His will again, sign the card, and when the pastor gives the "altar call," walk the aisle again. Maybe it didn't "take" the first time, but will it the second time? And so forth.

How do I know this one "from the inside"? (You might be able to tell that I don't have to search for words. And you're right.) I was brought up in a pietistic Norwegian Lutheran church. For those of you who haven't heard the term *pietism*, it began with certain Lutherans (Arndt, Spener, and others) who wanted a more "living Christianity" than seemed to be taught and encouraged in their Lutheran parishes in Germany. But it was as close as Lutherans in Germany, Norway, Sweden, Denmark, and America ever came to being just like Teutonic or Scandinavian outposts of Biola or Wheaton College! The Reformation emphasis on Christ outside of us, dying for us, and on the justification of sinners "gratis" was de-emphasized. Baptism and the Lord's Supper were de-emphasized. Instead, the emphasis shifted to the individual's experience of conversion and to the victorious life of the true Christian day by day.[1]

My church's pietism made me an agnostic by the time I was a senior in high school. The "evangelical" parish of your youth might have had the same result in your case. How so? Well, imagine a Sunday School curriculum filled with Bible stories designed to teach a moral point with every lesson. Beware Sunday School curricula! That stuff is dangerous to children! One of the happiest days of my life was the morning when, standing in the church narthex, my wonderful father delivered me out of Sunday School!

One Sunday morning, I came from Sunday School to meet my folks. My dad (I still remember where each of us was standing in the narthex, remember which sport coat he was wearing that day!) asked me, "How was Sunday school?" I answered, "OK, I guess." He saw written on my face how it was going, and he asked, "How would you like to quit going?" I immediately answered, "Dad, I'd love to quit Sunday school!" He said, "Well, why don't you? Come in and sit with me in the adult class." (I didn't understand a tenth of what they were talking about, but I was ecstatic to just sit next to him during that hour each Sunday.)

My father had—with a single stroke!—delivered me out of the hands of gray-haired women trying to make me more moral and using Bible stories to do it! It was like escape from prison! He had again made my life happier (it was not the last time, by any measure, either!) But it really wasn't the fault of those gray-haired Sunday

---

[1] See the *Christian History* issue on "Pietism" for a more positive presentation of it than I would give. See also *The Pieper Lectures*, vol. 3: *Pietism and Lutheranism*, ed. John A. Maxfield (St. Louis: Concordia Historical Institute [and] The Luther Academy, 1999). Dr. Ronald Feuerhahn's essay is, I think, much more realistic about the problems pietism inevitably causes the believer.

School teachers either. It was the theology they were assigned to teach. It was the curriculum, the content of the lessons they were assigned to teach us kids. Such Sunday School materials should have never been allowed to make it into our parish.

Now even though I am not Reformed, and don't speak "Reformed" very well, let me see if I can use a couple of categories from the Heidelberg Catechism to guess how you might have the same dynamic and its problems (at least when executed badly)?

Think of the paradigm of "Guilt—Grace—Gratitude." Don't you have the same sort of problem that we Lutherans had with pietism (at least when the paradigm is executed badly)? If I am elect and regenerate, why is it that my gratitude is so small, so lacking on a daily basis? "The hurrier I go, the behinder I get!" Or, "If I really were elect, my life would certainly reflect that fact more than it does." "Maybe I'm just fooling myself. Maybe I'm not really elect—because the peace, the joy, the confidence Paul says the Christian is to have (and that other Reformed believers seem to talk about) I don't have. I'd be lying if I said I did. Maybe I never was part of the elect, and I'm still not?"

And for those of you who are Wesleyans, you are in this mess "up to your eyeballs." Wesley's charge to his pastors was very clear. They were called to (1) evangelize pagans (something for which Wesley gets an "A" in my book!) and to (2) urge their parishioners on to Christian perfection (something for which Wesley deserved an "F"—at least in the way he executed it, preached it to Christian believers!) Sunday after Sunday of exhortation (i.e., law). If it's of any comfort to you Wesleyans, you can blame us Lutherans for a lot for this stuff! (We Lutherans try to blame the Strasbourg Reformed for Lutheran pietism, but I'm not so sure we didn't do it "all on our own steam.") Through Nicolas von Zinzendorf at Herrenhut and Peter Böhler, we Lutherans bequeathed a lot of this mess of ours to Wesley. I wish I could say that it all came from Wesley's reading of the church fathers, from reading William Law and others like Law, but I can't. In fact, it was we Lutherans who managed to corrupt all sorts of denominations with this junk—not just our own Lutheran churches but also the free churches, the brothers Wesley, Cotton Mather in the New World (about Jonathan Edwards, I don't know)—this stuff knew (and knows) almost no bounds! And almost all of it traces to

Lutheran Germany in an earlier century. If this stuff was done to you in some "Protestantish" church, I apologize to you. We Lutherans might just have been the ones who bequeathed it to your denomination, to your pastor's seminary profs. At any rate, if I'm right here, I'm sorry.

For our purposes this evening, *the upshot is always the same: broken, sad ex-Christians who finally despaired of ever being able to live the Christian life as the Bible describes it.* So they did what is really a sane thing to do: they left! The way it looks to them is that "the message of Christianity has broken them on the rack." To put it bluntly, it feels better to have some earthly happiness as a pagan and then be damned than it feels to be trying every day as a Christian to do something that is one continuous failure—and *then* be damned anyway. Trust me on this one. This is how things look.

It seems to me that the key question here is a very basic one: Can the cross and blood of Christ save a Christian (failing as he or she is in living the Christian life) or no?

I hope that most of us would say that the shed blood of Christ is sufficient to save a sinner. All by itself, just Christ's blood, "nude faith" in it, "*sola fide*," "faith without works," "a righteousness from God apart from law," a cross by which "God justifies wicked people," and so on. So far, so good, right?

But is the blood of Christ enough to save a still-sinful Christian? Or isn't it? Does the gospel still apply, even if you are a Christian? Or doesn't it? It seems to me (1) that the category "sinner" still applies to me, (2) that the category "sinner" still applies to you, and (3) that the category "sinner" still applies to all Christians. (If you are a Wesleyan and have reached perfection, what I have to say here doesn't, of course, apply to you.) But for the rest of us, it seems that what Luther said of the Christian being "simultaneously sinful and yet justified before the holy God" is critical. Is what Luther said biblical? Or isn't it? Is it biblical to say that a Christian is "*simul justus et peccator*" or no? Are we Christians saved the same way we were when we were baptized into Christ or when we came to acknowledge Christ's shed blood and His righteousness as all we had in the face of God's holy law? That all of our supposed "virtue"—Christian or pagan—is just like so many old menstrual garments (to use the Bible phrase)? But that God imputes to those who trust Christ's cross the true righteousness of Christ

Himself? We are pretty sure that unbelievers who come to believe this are instantly justified in God's sight, declared as if innocent, adopted as sons or daughters, forgiven of all sin, given eternal life, and so on. But are *Christians* still saved that freely? Or are we not? We are pretty clear that imputed righteousness saves sinners. But can the imputed righteousness of Christ save a Christian? And can it save him or her all by itself? Or no? I think the way we answer this question determines whether we have anything at all to say to the "sad alumni" of Christianity.

We Lutheran pastors haven't done a great job of getting across the central nature of righteousness by imputation alone. I hope you've done a better job at it than we have!

Decades ago, a gigantic survey of our clergy and laity showed that we Lutheran pastors hadn't even convinced our own members of the sufficiency of Christ's cross and blood and death for them! (And I mean Lutheran members who might never have sneaked out to attend some evangelical revival, might never have spent five minutes watching the crazy Trinity Broadcasting Network.) Proof: *A Study of Generations* (results: 75 percent gave perfect Roman Catholic answers!).

- "When you die, are you sure you will enter heaven?" ("I hope so.")
- "I was president, tithed, sang in the choir, taught Sunday School," and so on.
- *Perfect Roman Catholic answers!* And this survey was done decades ago!

What the "sad alumni" need to hear (perhaps for the first time) is that Christian failures are going to walk into heaven, be welcomed into heaven, leap into heaven like a calf leaping out of its stall, laughing and laughing, as if it's all too good to be true.

It isn't just *that* we failures will get in. It's that we will probably get in *like that!* We failures-in-living-the-Christian-life-as-described-in-the-Bible will probably say something like, "You mean it was that simple?!" "Just Christ's cross and blood?! Just His righteousness imputed to my account as if mine? You gotta be kidding!"

"And all of heaven is ours just because of what was done by Jesus *outside of me*, on the cross—not because of what Christ did *in* me—in my heart, in my Christian living, in my behavior?!" "Well, I'll be damned!" But of course, that's the point, isn't it? As a believer in Jesus as your Substitute, you *won't* be damned! No believer in Jesus will be. Not a single one!

As C. S. Lewis put it, "There are going to be a lot of surprises" at the eschaton. There are going to be people there that we just don't imagine will be there (think of the non-Israelite that C. S. Lewis purposely put in heaven at the end [*The Last Battle*])! Boy, did that ever "get the goat" of some Christians! But read what Aslan said to him: "I suppose you're wondering why you're here?" And then tells him why. There are going to be in heaven believers in Jesus who never darkened the door of a church. (That's no encouragement not to attend, not to be baptized, not to receive the Lord's Supper. It is just saying that faith in Jesus saves—saves all by itself, "nude," "apart from works.") There are going to be scads of Roman Catholics, people who never listened—not really—to the theology preached by their priests, but just believed in the sufficiency of Jesus' blood—no matter what their priest was preaching. People of all sorts who just believed in Jesus and His blood shed for them for complete payment for their sin. There are going to be call girls, there are going to be drug dealers, maybe even a couple of lawyers! There are going to be members of the cults who never really "got" what the cult leaders taught but just trusted that Jesus' blood and cross were for their sin and for their hatred of God, for their wickedness. Surprises, lots of surprises. It bugs me to say it, but there might even be a couple of IRS employees, maybe a congressman or congresswoman. (Everyone has some class of people they really don't want to die as believers in Jesus! Those are mine!)

But to put it closer to home, there might even be a theologian or two who believed in Jesus, "bet the blue chips" on the blood of Jesus and nothing else other than, or in addition to, that blood. There might even be a despicable leftist socialist college professor or two! Academics who daily sold out the wonderful American Constitution and instead filled their students' heads with statist drivel and mush. In heaven we will meet cowards, scum, "bottom-of-the-barrel" reprehensibles, jerks, deadbeat dads, murderers, all sorts of rabble. And they died believing in Jesus and His blood as their only hope.

Ask yourself: Is sola fide *true or is* sola fide *not true in the case of failing Christians?*

Is Paul's letter to the Galatians true or no? And if Galatians *is* true (and it most certainly is, but an *apologia* for that is not our subject tonight!), can a failing Christian be saved simply by the cross and blood of Christ? Or can he or she *not* be so saved just by Christ's shed blood alone? If you answer, "Yes, he or she can," well, that's the message that's gotten lost on most "jack Christians"—at least the ones I've met.

Many times the law has already done its work on them.

Boy, has it ever done its work on them! They need more law like they need a hole in the head. The law was (is?) killing them. True, Paul says, the law kills. He writes as if that is what the law is for. The law is designed to crush, to crush human pride and supposed self-sufficiency toward God. It is intended to kill, designed to kill. The biblical connection is law/sin. What gives sin its power is the law. And more so, the law is designed to make the problem worse! It is to be gasoline on an already blazing fire! (Want to have sin run out of control? Go to a church in which the law is preached, then the law is preached again and more stringently and deeply, and then the law is preached even more!)

Think of John Lithgow's portrayal years ago of a law-preaching pastor in the film *Footloose*. Didn't you just cringe? I mean, even if you're a Southern Baptist, you had to cringe at that character. Drawing the Christian "line in the sand" at the possibility of a high school dance? Lithgow could not listen to his daughter even if hearing her would have instantly resulted in world peace! Man, was he righteous! In *Footloose*, Lithgow's wife should have been the pastor!

(Don't quote me! I could be thrown out of the Missouri Synod for even joking about such a thing! You Missouri Lutherans, that's a joke! Chill out! Or, as Phil Hendry says in his radio ad, "It wouldn't hurt you to laugh!" You non-Lutherans, all of this is an "inside joke." Ask your Lutheran friends later why that's a joke in our circles.)

My point is that the whole film *Footloose* was "Jesusless"—no cross, no atonement, nothing of Christianity, really. Same as *Chariots of Fire*—completely Christless, completely gospel-less!

Back to the point: for many of the "jack Christians" we've met, the law is all their ears ever heard! For them, the gospel often got lost in a whole bunch of "Christian life preaching." And it "did them in." So they left. And down deep there is a sadness in such people that defies description. If you and I don't understand that, we should! They were crestfallen. So great their hopes, so devastating the failure.

C. F. W. Walther said that as soon as the law has done its crushing work, the gospel is to be instantly preached or said to such a man or woman—instantly!

Walther said that in the very moment that the pastor senses that the law has done its killing work, he is to placard Christ and His cross and blood to the trembling, the despairing, the broken.

- "Be of good cheer, my son. Your sins are forgiven."
- "The Son of Man came not to be served, but to serve, and to give His life a ransom for many."
- "Fear not, little flock. It is your Father's good pleasure to give you the kingdom."
- "Come to Me, all you who are heavy laden. Take My yoke upon you, for My yoke is easy and My burden is light."
- "And He, when He comes, will neither break the bruised reed, nor quench the smoldering wick."
- "When You return, remember me." "I tell you, this day you shall be with Me in paradise."
- "It is finished!"
- "Christ redeemed us from the curse of the law by becoming a curse for us."
- "He Himself bore our sins in His body on the tree."
- "God made Him to be sin who Himself knew no sin."
- "For in Christ Jesus you are all sons of God, through faith. For as many of you as were baptized into Christ have put on Christ."
- "For by grace you are saved, through faith, and that [faith in Jesus is] not of yourselves, but it is a gift of God, lest any man should boast."
- "And to the man who does not work but trusts the One who justifies the wicked, his faith is counted as if it were righteousness."

- "For we maintain that a man is justified by faith, apart from works of the law."
- "Knowing a man is not justified by works of the law but through faith in Jesus Christ."
- "But now a righteousness of God has been manifested apart from the law, . . . the righteousness of God through faith in Jesus Christ for all who believe."
- "Therefore, since we have been justified by faith, we have peace with God through our Lord Jesus Christ."
- "There is now, therefore, no condemnation for those who are in Christ Jesus."

Second, Let's Talk about Those Alumni of Christianity Who Are Not Sad but "Mad"

It is not all that uncommon. I find that these "angry ones" have usually not switched from Christianity to another religion. Nor have I found that they have switched from one Christian denomination to another. Instead, I find that they are angry at any and all religions and anyone who represents any religious position—but especially Christianity. And that is natural. After all, it was Christianity, as they see it, that "used them up and threw them away." I suppose the most visible examples would be men like the late comedian Sam Kinison and ex–Roman Catholic George Carlin. You may (and probably do) know better contemporary examples than I know. All of us are in the vicinity of people like this at one time or another, maybe know a few of them as friends, or have at least met one or two in passing. Why do I say that? Because such people are, as I said, not all that uncommon these days.

Now I certainly can't this evening exhaust the dynamic involved in such people (again, I'm no clinical psychologist). But I still think a lot of the "mad alumni" also often have a nameable history just as the "sad alumni" have one.

People like this often speak as if Christianity "baited and switched" them—just like a used car salesman "baits and switches" a young couple at a car lot.

Christians promised them a new life in Christ in such a way that it was going to be a life of victory, God's designed route to earthly happiness, a new, divine power that would solve the problems so obsessing them. Then when the promises didn't seem to work the way they were supposed to, the church put it back on these believers that they were somehow "not doing it right."

- They weren't reading their Bible enough.
- They weren't praying enough or praying right.
- They weren't attending enough church meetings.
- They weren't making right use of the fellowship.
- You name the prescription, you "fill in the blanks" any way you want to.
- Some pastor or layman told them that Christianity was failing them because "they weren't doing it right."
- And often, these believers took that counsel to heart and set themselves to trying to "do it better" or "do it right" so that "it would work."

But again, Christianity seemed "not to deliver on its promises." It "didn't work." As they see it, they "gave it every shot" and Christianity "failed to deliver." And then, to boot, they were called guilty "for not doing it right!" These people feel not just disappointed; they feel betrayed, "conned." And they are deeply angry about it.

Or take another example: those who heard much of Christ and His saving blood and cross in an evangelistic meeting became Christians and then heard very little of that wonderful message in the week-by-week pulpit ministry of their congregation. Instead, they heard recipes as to how to conquer sin—over and over and over. These people also often "give up on Christianity." And they are angry about it! Really angry. And I don't blame them, really. Nor should you. The church has an obligation to preach the gospel to these people on a weekly basis. And deep down, they somehow know that. But if that isn't what happens, they react. I would, too! After all, what does the church have for a man, a woman, a child other than Christ and His work on their behalf? Not much! Not compared to the gospel of Christ preached as crucified for them and for their sin, Christ risen from the dead for their justification. Not compared to being absolved, not compared to eating the body of Christ given into death for their sin and drinking the blood of Christ shed for their sin.

Is there anything we can do that is of genuine help to such angry "alumni" of Christianity?

I think so. And the answer I'm about to give you comes right from a guy close to one of those angry ones. From whom? From Sam Kinison's brother, Bill! How so?

One night I happened to be watching a 60 Minutes *interview with Bill Kinison.*

After Sam was in an auto accident on a lonely highway near Las Vegas, he lay dying. Bill was cradling Sam's head in his arms as Sam died. Sometime later, the interviewer asked Bill about Sam's hatred of Christianity. And Bill looked at the interviewer and said, "What? You think Sam was not a Christian believer? You're wrong! Sam died as a believer in Jesus Christ. You'll definitely see Sam in heaven! Sam never was angry with Jesus. He was angry at the church!" And I jumped out of my chair and yelled, "That's it! There it is! There is the answer—and from Sam Kinison's brother!"

What did I mean, "That's it!"?

We can respond to the angry and say something like, "Oh, oh, oh, I see! You're not angry at Jesus Christ. You're angry at the church!" "Boy oh boy, join the club! So am I! And so are a whole bunch of other Christians!" (Here, if we had time, I would digress on how Christians angry with Christ will be saved by His cross, too. But this is not the time for that.)

Now this response takes more than a few minutes of thought on our part.

That is, "Am I ready to say such a thing?" And that's not an easy question. For many of us—especially for us clergy—this question can be really difficult. Why? Because there is a predictable psychological profile of the clergy, including our closer relationship with our mothers, but *not* with our fathers. For most of us pastors, the link between Jesus and the church (a mother symbol) is so tight, so identical, that to be angry with mother church is the same as rejecting Jesus! It is not. But I'm recommending, at least in conversation with "the angry," that we—all of us—identify with the anger of these people at the church, that we say, "Well, of course you are angry!

With what it did to you? It would be insane *not* to be angry at it! I just misunderstood. I thought you had dismissed Christ, were rejecting His death for your sin. Thanks for clarifying."

Again, I know that this is tough stuff. It raises questions in us that are not easy ones—particularly for us pastors who were closer to mom than to dad (and, unfortunately, that is most of us pastors). But I recommend that "we take the hit." It's not unlike the case with something like the Crusades or the Inquisition. I think most of us don't want to defend everything the church has done in the past—at least I hope we don't. And believe me, the "angry" alumni are listening closely to see whether we are going to defend the church as much as we defend the gospel. I recommend that we do *not* defend the church as much as we defend the gospel! I recommend that we immediately "cop to" horrendous things done by the church. (And for those of you who are Lutheran, this is *not* the time to try to catechize this guy into the finer points of Luther's "Two Kingdoms" theory!)

Let me illustrate with a couple of particularly embarrassing examples in my own church's history.

(Believe me, you've got some parallels in your church, too—no matter which church you belong to.) Two of the lowest points in Lutheran church history have to do with both the Peasants' Revolt and our persecution of the Anabaptists in the sixteenth century. The Peasants' Revolt deeply frightened Luther (Luther very much feared anarchy as the worst of possibilities). In a letter to the German princes, Luther ordered them to use the sword and to slash and slay anyone who was out on the streets behaving like a revolutionary. (He quickly wrote a letter that appealed to the princes to ignore his first letter, but it was too late!) The peasants, thinking that Luther was backing them, were astounded when they learned that Luther had ordered the princes to "cut, slash, and kill them." They felt totally betrayed. A real dark chapter in my church's history.

In a similar way, to the degree to which Anabaptist Christians represented any sort of "Spirit-given" ecclesiastical anarchy, one that had no place for church order, Luther unleashed on them, too. Lutherans took part in baptizing such people by immersion for about ten minutes (Reformed and Roman Catholics went along with us in this, but I'm just speaking about my own church here).

Reprehensible? You bet! Do I want to defend such executions to one of those "angry" at the church? Not a chance! Hate it as I might, I need to agree with the person with whom I am speaking. Same with some of the anti-Semitic things Luther himself wrote in his later life.

I said that I recommend that we "cop to" some of the evil things the church has done. We might be tempted to start by trying to balance the charges, viz., mention the wonderful things the church has sometimes done. I recommend against that, too—at least in an evangelistic/apologetic conversation. Later on, we might speak about a book like Al Schmidt's *Under the Influence: How Christianity Transformed Civilization* (Concordia) that catalogs just how our western world's every corner was affected to the good by historic Christianity. Not now, however.

But since hearing Sam Kinison's brother, I *don't* want to leave the matter there. I hope you don't either. You and I "copping to" the evil done by the church still leaves the "angry one" satisfied, justified in his anti-Christic state, and still miles from the gospel. If the law has done its work on him, I want next to talk to this guy about the gospel. I want to talk about Jesus' claims—and if I can, particularly about Jesus' claims regarding what He was going to do for sinners (including me and including him!) on the cross.

Now you Lutheran pastors, don't talk to me at this point about the Scriptural truths he would learn in your Pastor's Inquirers class about the sacraments! This kind of a guy *isn't going to come* to your Inquirers' class to learn about the sacraments—or to learn about anything else! He's too angry! Same for you Reformed pastors. This is not the time to start talking to this guy about the Scriptural truths he would learn in your Pastors Inquirers' class about the finer points of predestination! This kind of a guy *isn't going to come* to your Inquirers' class to learn about election—or to learn about anything else! He's too angry.

So what am I going to do?

I'm going to talk about the gospel *as if it can be believed in totally apart from the church!* You say to me, "Rosenbladt, that isn't how Scripture presents the church!" I answer, "I know. But first things first! This guy needs Christ, Christ as priest, Christ as having bled for his sin, Christ as giving eternal life to sinners for free." And in his mind, *the church is what is keeping him or her away* from

Jesus Christ! If he comes to trust Christ and Christ's sin-bearing death, the guy might *later on* deal with passages about "not forsaking the assembling of yourselves together." But not now. To this guy, the church and its behavior *is* the "scandal"! (The real *scandalon*, according to Paul, is that we are sinners under condemnation and cannot do anything to make things right with the holy God. The true *scandalon* is that Someone Else is going to have to satisfy God's justice *for* us because we are unable—and unwilling—to do that.)

To put it another way, we sinners are in need of a divine Mediator. And without a divine Mediator, we are doomed. Scripture says, "There is one God and one Mediator between God and men, the man Christ Jesus." At the judgment, the law of God will justly declare us condemned. And the gospel is that God the Son freely agreed to die our death *for us*, to suffer our deserved condemnation and doom in our place. And He didn't just agree from eternity to do that. He actually did it. On the cross. For free! And for each one of us (Rom. 5:8).

If your friend can see for just a moment that the truth of the gospel does not turn on Christ's church, but only on Christ's resurrection from the dead, it might be the first time he has ever thought such a thought. Will he bend the knee to Christ as His Lamb and Substitute? Who knows? But you will have done him or her a great service. Would that *all* people who are angry agnostics or atheists were clear that their animosity toward the church for giving them nothing but morality as soon as they became Christians is really understandable. That we would have that same reaction. Believe it or not, that's progress. I've sometimes said to people who reject Christ and His death as for their sin, "Well, you are one of the few I've met who has really rejected the Christian gospel for the right reasons. Congratulations for that! But I recommend that you keep thinking about it." And keep asking the question, "Was Jesus really raised from the dead, or was He not?" Because if Jesus Christ *was* raised the third day, that is the best reason in the world to believe that He can make good on His claim that His death was a death for your and my sin and that His cross and blood will be enough for anyone who dies still a sinner. Me. You.

Lastly, we might be surprised to find that this guy is a Christian. He's just vowed never to let a church do to him ever again what was done to him earlier. Do you know a church that *won't*? (Don't answer too quickly. There are not a lot of these—no matter what the "label" on the door.) Most of today's churches will just reinflame his anger, giving him "law-gospel-law." Find one for him instead that will speak to him of Christ—after he is a believer. If you don't know one, tell him that. At least it's honest.

Batter My Heart:
Demanding of God in Christ

John Donne's "Holy Sonnet 14"

Dr. Scott L. Keith

Introduction

Is it ever appropriate to demand of God? When God, the Almighty Creator of all things, has chosen to act, who is the creature to demand that He act differently? Within the Christian religion, it is generally accepted that the created ought not attempt to coerce the Creator. Yet this is what the priest-poet John Donne (1572–1631) seems to do in his "Holy Sonnet 14":

> Batter my heart, three-person'd God; for you
> As yet but knock; breathe, shine, and seek to mend;
> That I may rise, and stand, o'erthrow me, and bend
> Your force, to break, blow, burn, and make me new.
> I, like an usurp'd town, to another due,
> Labour to admit you, but O, to no end.
> Reason, your viceroy in me, me should defend,
> But is captived, and proves weak or untrue.
> Yet dearly I love you, and would be loved fain,
> But am betroth'd unto your enemy;
> Divorce me, untie, or break that knot again,
> Take me to you, imprison me, for I,

Except you enthrall me, never shall be free,
Nor ever chaste, except you ravish me.[1]

Background

Also known by its first line as "Batter My Heart," this sonnet is one of
a set of nineteen written by Donne and commonly referred to as *The
Divine Meditations*, or *The Holy Sonnets*. Not published until 1633,
two years after Donne's death, the numbering scheme nevertheless
derives from the 1620 *Westmoreland Manuscript*, a compilation of all
nineteen sonnets assembled by Donne's friend Rowland Woodward.
The dates of composition are uncertain, but the scholarly consensus
seems to be somewhere between 1609 and 1611, with an obvious
exception or two (e.g., "Holy Sonnet 17," on the death of his wife
Anne, must have been written after August 1617).[2]

Along with "Holy Sonnet 10" ("Death Be Not Proud"), the four-
teenth is probably the most well known and well regarded. It was first
brought to my attention while I was studying with Dr. Nestingen, as
it is his favorite. Since I was (and remain) almost completely unfa-
miliar with poetry, it took me some time to digest the meaning of
this work. And though I cannot dissect its value poetically, theologically I do read in it the perennial human conflict between love of the
old Adam (or sin) and love of God in Christ.

If we accept the consensus dating, it is likely Donne wrote
"Holy Sonnet 14" in the final years of an intense decade of personal
turmoil that included a secret, unendorsed marriage, the loss of his
position as chief secretary to the Lord Keeper of the Great Seal, the
end of his diplomatic career, a prison term, and a forced retirement,
all while struggling through a conversion to Anglicanism from the

---

[1] John Donne, *Poems of John Donne*, ed. E. K. Chambers, vol. 1 (London:
Lawrence & Bullen, 1896), 165.

[2] William L. Stull, "Why Are Not 'Sonnets' Made of Thee? A New Context
for the 'Holy Sonnets' of Donne, Herbert, and Milton," in *Modern Philology*
80, no. 2 (Nov. 1982): 129–35. See also Gary A. Stringer, *The Variorum Edition
of the Poetry of John Donne*, vol. 7, part 1 (Bloomington: Indiana University
Press, 2005), ix–x, 5–27.

Roman Catholicism of his youth. And even though, by 1611, he had mostly reestablished himself, he would never again be part of the royal court. So King James (yes, that King James) urged the reluctant Donne to take holy orders,[3] and in 1615, he was ordained priest in the Church of England.[4]

Despite his reluctance, for Donne, like many of us, it seems the more theological education he received, the more he became engrossed in the search for a deeper understanding of God. In particular, "Batter My Heart" can be viewed as an eloquent portrayal of the conflict between his sinful, self-absorbed life and his new life in Christ. All his efforts to make himself right with God—to self-justify—fail time and again. Thus he asks God to come and take him, literally to "ravish" him. Using Luther's terminology, we might even say that after all attempts at living a successful theology of glory had failed, Donne here in "Holy Sonnet 14" succumbs to a life lived under the theology of the cross.

Setting the Stage

Donne begins by asking the Triune God (the Father, Son, and Holy Ghost; Donne's "*three-person'd God*") to attack his heart as if it were the fortified gate of a well-defended city. He entreats God to invade his heart forcefully, directly, and violently, instead of subtly, gently, and through means. Next, in line five, Donne explicitly draws a comparison between himself and a town overthrown by invaders: "*I, like an usurp'd town . . .*" He wants to let God enter, but he wavers, hanging on to what his natural reason would tell him: "*To another due, Labour to admit you, but O, to no end.*" Just like a city under attack, his will fights back, not wanting to be overtaken by this invading authority.

---

[3] Stanley Kunitz and Howard Haycraft, eds., *British Authors before 1800: A Biographical Dictionary* (New York: Wilson, 1952), 156–58.

[4] Will Durant and Ariel Durant, *The Age of Reason Begins: A History of European Civilization in the Period of Shakespeare, Bacon, Montaigne, Rembrandt, Galileo, and Descartes: 1558–1648* (New York: Simon and Schuster, 1961), 154.

At the "turn"[5] of the poem, Donne admits that he loves God and that he wants to be loved in return by God, but alas, he is *"betroth'd unto [God's] enemy."* This enemy goes unnamed, but images of Satan swirl in a jumble with subtle inferences that it is Donne's own natural reason with which God wars. Donne pleads for God to break the ties that bind him to this enemy and for God to force Himself upon him, not letting him go free. He then explains why he wants this, reasoning with double meanings: he can't really be free unless God enslaves and excites him, and he can't turn to God in true conversion unless God turns him, shocks his soul, and ravishes him.

Analysis

Many types of analysis may be brought to bear on this type of literature. In this essay, two will be examined: (1) Donne's rhetorical style of argumentation and (2) his theological propositions. As the former cannot rightly be separated from the latter, the analysis of each concept will, at points, intertwine. Beyond all question, however, Donne's keen intellect grasps the significance of the "New Philosophy" and expresses his theologically unique concepts in terms of the humanist philological skill.[6]

The particular rhetorical description of "conversion" used here by Donne was a common means of communicating the *ordo salutis* in late sixteenth-century humanism.[7] Known as "rhetorical invention,"

---

[5] The structure of a sonnet of the time included two parts that together make up a compact form of argument. First is the octave, which forms the proposition and describes a problem or question. Second is the sestet (two tercets), which proposes a resolution. Typically, the ninth line initiates what is called the "turn," or "volta," and signals the move from proposition to resolution. Even in sonnets that don't strictly follow the problem/resolution structure, the ninth line still often marks a "turn" with a change in the tone, mood, or stance of the poem (https://en.wikipedia.org/wiki/Sonnet, accessed 19 May 2018).

[6] Beatrice Johnson, "Classical Allusions in the Poetry of Donne," in *PMLA* 43, no. 4 (Dec. 1928): 1098–1109.

[7] See Philip Melanchthon and his three (really four) causes of conversion as first explained in the 1535 *Loci Communes*, wherein Melanchthon describes

it is a systematic investigation by argumentation whereby reason—
guided by the places (*loci* or *topoi*) of arguments—could rapidly
organize all the matters for which each word or thing argues. For
example, to form concepts of man, one may consider that his efficient cause is God; his material cause is his body, his formal cause is
his soul, his final cause is God's glory, his effects are his actions, and
so on.[8] Man argues all these, and all these are part of his true relationships within a known and knowable order.[9]

In "Holy Sonnet 14," the reader may thus see Donne using the
following rhetorical invention:

1. God is the efficient cause as the mover.
2. The material cause is Donne himself desiring change but
   unable to effect it.
3. The formal cause is Donne's rebellious will (the thing in
   need of "ravishing").
4. Finally, the *telos* (end goal) of the entire experience is the love
   of God toward Donne and his love toward God in return.

Said more commonly, Donne's greatest theological poems (or
sequences of "holy" poems), though various in tone and topic, man-
ifest a common developmental pattern:

1. A confident (or at least decisive) opening.
2. A move from initial certainties to new perceptions, evolving finally to an assured conclusion.

---

the need for the will to assent (*material cause*) by the work of the Holy Spirit
(*final cause*) taking the heart captive by the Word (*efficient cause*).

   [8] For a discussion of ancient and Renaissance definitions of "'rhetoric,'"
see Donald Lemen Clark, *Rhetoric and Poetry in the Renaissance* (New York:
Columbia University Press, 1922), 23–31, 43–55. One of the clearest discus-
sions of the modern meaning of "rhetoric" is Donald C. Bryant's "Rhetoric:
Its Functions and Its Scope," *QJS* 39 (1953): 401–24. In this case, see Abraham
Fraunce, *The Lawiers Logike*, vol. 8 (London, 1588), fol. 86r.

   [9] Thomas O. Sloan, "John Donne," *Studies in English Literature 1500–1900*
3, no. 1, *The English Renaissance* (Winter 1963): 31–44.

3. Certain discoveries concerning himself that neither he
nor his readers have fully anticipated.
4. Though always involved in an inward crisis, a self-
examination in relation to God.[10]

Any poetry review of "Holy Sonnet 14" must surely mention
Donne's obsession with the idea of faithfulness (i.e., lack of it, concerning man, and ultimate faithfulness, concerning God), and how
he dealt with this concept both rhetorically and theologically. In
"Batter My Heart," some readers will intuitively sense echoes of primal, "Old-Adam" fears of separation anxiety and rejection in Donne's
dealings with God, harkening back to the fall (in the Garden) and
mankind's initial separation from God. Hence Donne asks his *three
person'd God* to literally attack and destroy his heart using forceful
verbs like "batter," "overthrow," "bend," "burn," "ravish," "divorce,"
and "break."

This arguably base language could be understood to imply the
intensity of (Godly) force required to turn Donne—a sinner who has
fallen so far from grace—back to God. That is, John Donne believes
God just hasn't tried hard enough to win back his black heart—a
heart that has refused to turn or believe on its own and has always
been as disloyal as a town that, after rising up against its own rulers,
finds itself under siege and, when all hope is finally lost, halfheart-
edly pledges its allegiance to another master.

"Holy Sonnet 14" also reflects the more Protestant idea that faith
comes but from God alone, by the ravishing of the heart. In theological terms, faith comes by the power of the Holy Spirit through the
hearing (means) of the preached Word. The texts of Scripture are
almost audible in Donne's demand for a changed heart: "You did not
choose me, but I chose you and appointed you that you should go
and bear fruit and that your fruit should abide,"[11] and, "Faith comes
from hearing, and hearing through the word of Christ,"[12] and, "For

---

[10] Carol Marks Sicherman, "The English Renaissance," in *Studies in English
Literature 1500–1900* 11, no. 1 (Winter 1971): 69–88.

[11] John 15:16.

[12] Romans 10:17.

the word of the cross is folly to those who are perishing, but to us who are being saved it is the power of God,"[13] and, "For I am not ashamed of the gospel, for it is the power of God for salvation to everyone who believes,"[14] and, "For by grace you have been saved through faith. And this is not your own doing; it is the gift of God,"[15] and finally, "That which is born of the flesh is flesh, and that which is born of the Spirit is spirit."[16]

Nor are the words of Luther and Calvin far behind. Donne liberally uses the theological concepts of the great reformers, forming the foundation of a building for which his sonnets are the building blocks. Says Luther, "But you ask: 'How must one begin to become pious, or what must one do to move God to begin to work in us?' Answer: Indeed! Do you not hear that in you there is no doing and no beginning toward becoming pious, just as increase and completion are not in your power? God alone begins, furthers, and completes the change. Whatever you begin is sin, no matter how pretty it may appear to be. You can do nothing but sin, no matter what you do."[17]

As well, Calvin can be heard in the same context and toward the same end: "Only damnable things come from man's corrupt nature. . . . Man is very clearly shown to be a miserable creature. . . . Man must be reborn [John 3:3], for he is 'flesh' [John 3:6]. Christ is not teaching a rebirth of the body. Now the soul is not reborn if merely a part of it is reformed, but only when it is wholly renewed. Whatever we have from our nature, therefore, is flesh."[18]

Donne, like Luther and Calvin, admits to being an unholy sinner in the sight of an ever-holy God. Further, he confesses that in

---

[13] 1 Corinthians 1:18.

[14] Romans 1:16.

[15] Ephesians 2:8.

[16] John 3:6.

[17] Johann Georg Walch, ed., *Dr. Martin Luthers saemmtliche Schriften*, vol. 11 (St. Louis: Concordia, 1880–1910), 8.

[18] John Calvin, *Institutes of the Christian Religion*, Library of Christian Classics 20–21, ed. John T. McNeill, trans. Ford Lewis Battles, vol. 1 (Philadelphia: Westminster, 1960), 289.

order for him to become a new person—to *"rise, and stand"* before the God of all love and wonder—his will (sinful nature) must first be overthrown—literally broken, or "ravished," by God's will. To "ravish," then, could be read as "to seize and take away as plunder or spoil; to seize upon (a thing) by force. The town, then, would be chastened, that is, subdued after being ravished."[19] Donne then continues his exposé, revealing that he is thoroughly buried in his own sinfulness, is essentially in a relationship with evil, and is utterly left on his own. He cannot change this situation.

Donne is demanding not only that God choose him but also that God thrust faith upon his heart. Why would he do this? For certainty, of course: if God is "running the verbs" (doing the doing), then Donne can be sure. "The doctrine of predestination, like all the major Protestant doctrines, was meant, in the words of the Church of England Articles of Religion, to be 'full of sweet, pleasant, and unspeakable comfort,' justification by faith was 'a most wholesome Doctrine, and very full of comfort.'[20] The sweetness of psychological 'comfort' was central to the theology. The key to this comfort is the doctrine—and the experience—of assurance."[21]

Much like Paul in Romans chapter 7, Donne states these things in order to show God that his earnest desire is for God alone, even though that desire is conflicted. Says Paul, "When I want to do right, evil lies close at hand. For I delight in the law of God, in my inner being, but I see in my members another law waging war against the law of my mind and making me captive to the law of sin that dwells in my members. Wretched man that I am! Who will deliver

---

[19] José Ángel, "John Donne: Holy Sonnet XIV or the Plenitude of Metaphor," in *Sederi* VII (Spain: Universitat De València, 1996), 147–52.

[20] Church of England, Articles of Religion, Article 17, in *The Faith of Christendom: A Sourcebook of Creeds and Confessions*, ed. B. A. Gerrish (Cleveland, 1963), 191; Article 11, 189.

[21] Richard Strier, "John Donne Awry and Squint: The 'Holy Sonnets,' 1608–1610," in *Modern Philology* 86, no. 4 (May, 1989): 357–84. See also Strier, *Love Known*, chaps. 3–5; and Gene Edward Veith, *Reformation Spirituality: The Religion of George Herbert* (Lewisburg, PA: 1985), chap. 4.

me from this body of death? Thanks be to God through Jesus Christ our Lord!"[22]

Also present in this poem is the language of separation—"divorce," "cut," "break," and "untie," as Donne labors in anguish against a bondage that keeps him from being the good and changed creature God has promised he will be. For Donne, his failure here—his lack of salvation—meant only one thing: utter loneliness as a result of separation from the God he loved and needed. Eternal damnation meant permanent exclusion from the warmth, security, and protection of God's love and from the changed body and soul promised in conversion.

The tortuous, pleading, and supplicant tone of the sonnet is understandable given Donne's intrinsic need for God to be the worker of salvation in him. Without this forced working of salvation through conversion, there would be no redemption for Donne. Donne conveys to the reader that this is the case not only for him but for all who encounter God as a beggar in need of release from the toil of their own self-inflicted poverty of reason.

Finally, since Donne recognizes that he is "married to sin," he pleads for God to write him a bill of divorce. This is reminiscent of Christ's teaching on divorce in the New Testament Gospels. Divorce is not something sanctioned by God but rather something God concedes because of our sin. "Because of your hardness of heart Moses allowed you to divorce your wives."[23] Divorce is never ideal, yet Donne understands that his sinful nature is not what God had intended and knows that it requires an intentional separation, or divorce. He needs this divorce so that he can be free from his "vows" to sin. He cries, "Break that knot again."

Once again, the structure of the rhetorical invention can be seen. Donne needs to be loved by God and to love God in return. This primal need he cannot meet of his own effort, merit, or accord; this is to be left for God alone to fulfill. Yet God appears to be pensive, not turning him as he needs to be turned. Donne demands that God act, that He be the turning agent (efficient cause) and make

---

[22] Romans 7:21–25.

[23] Matthew 19:8.

HANDING OVER THE GOODS

him new (material cause). Over and over again, biblical imagery is interlaced with popular (to Donne's time) rhetorical construal. "The sonnet as a whole is unified by a shifting viewpoint which produces the effect of God's boring from the outside into the very center of the human heart."[24]

Finally, Lynette McGrath's thoughtful analysis contends that persuasion was constantly at the forefront of his thought. That is, he saw poetry as a powerful medium for the Word preached and shared. "Donne's judgment of the power of poetry, and the persuasive purposes to which it might be turned, remained constant despite his alteration of habit from poet to preacher. In his prose we can find elements of an aesthetic that may first have influenced the poet's production, and later helped define the preacher's more disinterested attitude to poetry."[25] For Donne, then, poetry and preaching were always intertwined.

Answering the Question

This author recalls a lecture given by Professor Peter Groves at the University of Oxford, Christ Church. The lecture was on the theology of the English "Priest-Poets." Professor Groves exclaimed quite ardently that "Holy Sonnet 14" from Donne was "simply rubbish!" When asked why he would say such a thing of a timeless and well-regarded piece of English poetry, he retorted, "The poetry isn't rubbish, the theology is. You can find nowhere in all of Scripture where

---

[24] John E. Parish, "No. 14 of Donne's Holy Sonnets," in *College English* 24, no. 4 (Jan. 1963): 299–302.

[25] Lynette McGrath, "John Donne's Apology for Poetry," in *Studies in English Literature, 1500–1900* 20, no. 1, *The English Renaissance* (Winter 1980): 73–89. Says McGrath, "The sharp break we used to imagine between Donne's poetry and prose seems less plausible now in light of Helen Gardner's re-dating of Donne's work and the new critical readings of Donne." See *The Elegies and the Songs and Sonnets*, ed. Helen Gardner (Oxford: Clarendon Press, 1965), lviiff. Murray Roston, in *The Soul of Wit* (Oxford: Clarendon, 1974), acknowledging his debt to Gardner's dating, argues that "it would appear that [Donne's] secular and religious concerns were more intimately related than has generally been assumed" (8).

God is acting in one manner, the sinner demands a change, and God capitulates."

So this is the question: Is it "rubbish" to expect God to capitulate when we, the sinners, demand a change in the way He is doing things in our conversion or in the giving of peace? This author's answer to that question is a resounding "No!" It is not "rubbish" to expect such a thing. In fact, such a change is to be demanded of God, and we ought to expect His capitulation on this matter because He has promised it. While several Scriptural citations could be given to serve as *sedes doctrinae* (seat of doctrine)—including the obvious portions of Psalm 51 and Psalm 139[26]—for this theological formulation, two others will be examined: first, the account of the Canaanite woman in the Gospel of Matthew; and second, the account of "doubting" Thomas in John's Gospel.

In Matthew's Gospel (as well as in Mark's), the Canaanite woman simply appears, demanding a blessing for her sick daughter, a healing from Christ. Luther's sermon on this passage shows similarities to Donne's demanding explanation in "Holy Sonnet 14."[27]

---

[26] Psalm 51:1–12 (NIV): "*Have mercy on me, O God, according to your unfailing love; according to your great compassion blot out my transgressions. Wash away all my iniquity and cleanse me from my sin. For I know my transgressions, and my sin is always before me. Against you, you only, have I sinned and done what is evil in your sight, so that you are proved right when you speak and justified when you judge. Surely I was sinful at birth, sinful from the time my mother conceived me. Surely you desire truth in the inner parts you teach me wisdom in the inmost place. Cleanse me with hyssop, and I will be clean; wash me, and I will be whiter than snow. Let me hear joy and gladness; let the bones you have crushed rejoice. Hide your face from my sins and blot out all my iniquity. Create in me a pure heart, O God, and renew a steadfast spirit within me. Do not cast me from your presence or take your Holy Spirit from me. Restore to me the joy of your salvation and grant me a willing spirit, to sustain me.*" In verse 7, the Hebrew word translated here, as "cleanse" is תְּחַטְּאֵנִי, literally meaning to forcefully purify from wrongdoing or sin. Similar in tone to "*nor ever chaste, except you ravish me.*"

[27] Luther's sermon on the Matthew 15 account of the Syrophoenician woman can be found in Martin Luther, *Sermons of Martin Luther*, vol. 2 (Grand Rapids: Baker, 1983), 152–54. Also see Martin Luther, "Reminiscere," in *Dr. Martin Luther's House-Postil, or, Sermons on the Gospels for the Sundays and Principal*

First, though, the account from Matthew:

> And Jesus went away from there and withdrew to the district of Tyre
> and Sidon. And behold, a Canaanite woman from that region came
> out and was crying, "Have mercy on me, O Lord, Son of David; my
> daughter is severely oppressed by a demon." But he did not answer
> her a word. And his disciples came and begged him, saying, "Send her
> away, for she is crying out after us." He answered, "I was sent only to
> the lost sheep of the house of Israel." But she came and knelt before
> him, saying, "Lord, help me." And he answered, "It is not right to take
> the children's bread and throw it to the dogs." She said, "Yes, Lord, yet
> even the dogs eat the crumbs that fall from their masters' table." Then
> Jesus answered her, "O woman, great is your faith! Be it done for you
> as you desire." And her daughter was healed instantly.[28]

She had obviously heard about Jesus previously, maybe even
from offhanded comments or rumors. Her daughter was sick, so
she sought the gossiped-about Jesus as He was leaving for Tyre and
Sidon. Martin Luther comments of her that "the woman is not vexed
with doubts as to her privilege of coming to Christ: she does not
spend time in debating the question, whether she dare come or not;
she simply starts upon her way and comes."[29] Needless to say, she, in
all likelihood, had not prepared herself, given the apparently rude
way in which He treated her. Luther, however, surmises that rather
than putting her off, Christ was in fact pursuing faith in her like the
"hunter, driving up a pheasant in the field."

Luther's claim is that Christ, knowing her faith, is playing with
her, and He goes right for the kill spot, right for the jugular. He is
not polite; He ignores her and tells her that He literally has not come
for her. Yet she knows, because she has already heard the Word in
regard to Him, that without Him there is no hope. To our conven-
tional, human way of thinking, Christ should have demanded of her

---

Festivals of the Church Year, ed. Matthias Loy, vol. 1, 2nd ed. (Columbus, OH:
J. A. Schulze, 1884), 360–70.

[28] Matthew 15:21–28.

[29] Luther, "Reminiscere," 361.

a polite request, and she should have found any answer He gave sufficient. He is God, after all. But the Word has worked faith in her;
it explodes and demands results.[30] Says Luther, "Just here we notice
the beauty and excellence of this example; for we learn from it the
mighty strength of faith. Faith takes hold of Christ's words, even
when they sound harshly, and changes them into soothing expressions of consolation."[31]

This woman has been brought to faith on the basis of what she
has heard from gossip and mere rumors about Jesus, the Christ. She
literally has nothing more to go on. And what happens? She tries to
get His attention and gets nothing but rudeness as a reply.

Next, she begins to draw more attention to herself with the disciples and demands of them that Jesus—the God of all the universe—
listen to her, stop toying with her, and do what He has promised to
do: bring healing and peace. She pesters the disciples until finally
they are beyond annoyed with this demanding alien and heathen.
So they go to Jesus and say, "Send her away, for she keeps crying out
after us." Jesus says to her, "It is not right to take the children's bread
and toss it to their dogs."

Yet she knows who He is and what the rumors say He has done.
The Word, even by means of irreverent gossip, has begun to take hold
of her. "Yes, Lord, but even the dogs eat the crumbs that fall from
their masters' table." This is the faith that Donne demands. And on
the woman's demand that (1) He stop toying with her, (2) that faith
based on rumor ought not abide, and (3) that He do as He has promised, He responds, "Woman, you have great faith! Your request is
granted." The Christ does it; He capitulates to her insolent demands
of Him. She endured His harsh treatment of her and, just as Jacob
had done,[32] she wrestled the blessing right out of His hands, and
now He rejoices with her. This is the power that Donne is demanding from the Word in conversion. He believes that the Word—as
the means of grace for his "three person'd God"—has this power. The

---

[30] Romans 10:17.

[31] Luther, "Reminiscere," 365.

[32] The account of Jacob wrestling the blessing from God can be found in
Genesis 32:1–33.

Word has this power when it gets loose, and it ravishes until peace—the peace that surpasses all understanding—rests on the sinner.[33] As Luther himself concludes his sermon, "He will be merciful and ready to help us if we but come unto Him with our sorrows, and trust in Him with a believing heart."[34]

Finally, we come to the account of "doubting" Thomas in the Gospel of John, chapter 20. John records that after His resurrection, Jesus appears to Mary Magdalene, and then to the disciples who were hiding in the upper room. Christ, knowing their fear, first absolves them by saying, "Peace be with you." Then He commissions them to spread the "good news" of His resurrection. But Thomas was not among them. John records that Jesus then appears a second time, and this time Thomas is present:

> Now Thomas, one of the twelve, called the Twin, was not with them when Jesus came. So the other disciples told him, "We have seen the Lord." But he said to them, "Unless I see in his hands the mark of the nails, and place my finger into the mark of the nails, and place my hand into his side, I will never believe."
>
> Eight days later, his disciples were inside again, and Thomas was with them. Although the doors were locked, Jesus came and stood among them and said, "Peace be with you." Then he said to Thomas, "Put your finger here, and see my hands; and put out your hand, and place it in my side. Do not disbelieve, but believe." Thomas answered him, "My Lord and my God!" Jesus said to him, "Have you believed because you have seen me? Blessed are those who have not seen and yet have believed."[35]

---

[33] This analysis of Luther's sermon on the Syrophoenician (Canaanite) woman was first presented by Dr. James Arne Nestingen (professor emeritus, Luther Seminary, St. Paul, MN) at the Evangelical Lutheran Church in America's 2006 Word Alone Convention (Golden Valley, MN) and was first entitled "Handing Over the Goods." The analysis presented in this paper is wholly modeled after and dependent on that presentation and applied to the subject of Donne's demand for change in *Holy Sonnet 14.*

[34] Luther, "Reminiscere," 370.

[35] John 20:24–29.

This is probably the more apt example. From the resurrection onward, those who become Christian are converted on the basis of the disciples' eyewitness testimony.[36] This is true of us all, except for Thomas and perhaps Paul.

Jesus, in all of His resurrection glory, presents Himself to the disciples in the upper room and shows them that He lives. They, in turn, present their witness to Thomas who refuses to believe. Faith is the result of the message of the gospel preached and shared. It seems that God in Christ is making an attempt to convert Thomas to the truth of the resurrection based on this shared Word. Yet Thomas "doubts"—more accurately, Thomas rejects. He says, effectively, that unless God "ravish" him, he will not believe. He demands that his fingers be placed into the nail holes in Jesus' hands. Furthermore, he exclaims that his heart will not bend to belief unless he thrusts his hand into the chasm left in the side of Christ by the piercing of the spear. Can this be described as anything but a ravishing?

The lowly creature is demanding of the incarnate and risen God of the universe that He present Himself and physically turn Thomas from unbelief to belief. Should God capitulate to the demands of the insolent Thomas? Is it rubbish theology to expect that He will? "And I tell you, ask, and it will be given to you; seek, and you will find; knock, and it will be opened to you."[37] It seems we might have reason to expect it.

So what is the result? Christ fulfills the demands of Thomas and presents Himself to him so that Thomas may be ravished by the truth. Thomas's response is finally one of a converted and faithful believer, freed and chastened: "My Lord and my God!" All that Donne is demanding in "Holy Sonnet 14" is now given to Thomas: he is divorced from his enemy and unbelief, he is set free, he is ravished to the point of dropping to his knees, he is imprisoned by faith, and he receives a blessing and admonition.

This is not meant to be the normative pattern of how Christians are to react to the witness of the risen Christ given in the text of

---

[36] St. Paul was commissioned an apostle by Christ Himself after the resurrection (Acts 9:1–19) and the other apostles endorsed Paul (Gal 2:6).

[37] Luke 11:9.

scripture. But it is evidence of what Luther says in his Heidelberg Disputation, thesis 26: "The Law says 'do this,' and it is never done, grace says 'believe this,' and it is done already."[38] The law would demand that Thomas believe on account of the witness provided by the ten who were in the room. But grace, on account of Christ, presents itself in the person of the risen Christ and physically and forcefully creates that faith so that it is done immediately.

Conclusion

Is the forcefulness of Donne's prose sometimes difficult to read? Yes. Is it rubbish theology? No. Perhaps it is truly Lutheran theology or at least Reformational in character. Certainly, though, it is Scriptural theology. The following line-by-line textual correspondence should help show this to be the case:

> *Donne*: "Batter my heart, three-person'd God."
>
> *Answer*: "We destroy arguments and every lofty opinion raised against the knowledge of God, and take every thought captive to obey Christ" (2 Cor. 10:5)

> *Donne*: "For you as yet but knock; breathe, shine, and seek to mend."
>
> *Answer*: "Heal me, O LORD, and I shall be healed; save me, and I shall be saved, for you are my praise" (Jer. 17:14).

> *Donne*: "That I may rise, and stand, o'erthrow me, and bend."
>
> *Answer*: "For it is written, 'As I live, says the Lord, every knee shall bow to me, and every tongue shall confess to God'" (Rom. 14:11).

> *Donne*: "Your force, to break, blow, burn, and make me new."
>
> *Answer*: "Hide your face from my sins, and blot out all my iniquities. Create in me a clean heart, O God, and renew a right spirit within me. Cast me not away from your presence, and take not your Holy Spirit from me" (Ps. 51:9–11).

---

[38] Jaroslav Pelikan and Helmut T, Lehmann, eds., *Luther's Works*, American ed., vol. 31 (St. Louis: Concordia, 1955–86), 56.

Donne: "I, like an usurp'd town, to another due, Labour to admit you, but O, to no end."

Answer: "I will rise now and go about the city, in the streets and in the squares; I will seek him whom my soul loves. I sought him, but found him not" (Song of Sol. 3:2).

Donne: "Reason, your viceroy in me, me should defend, but is captived, and proves weak or untrue."

Answer: "For the sake of Christ, then, I am content with weaknesses, insults, hardships, persecutions, and calamities. For when I am weak, then I am strong" (2 Cor. 12:10).

Donne: "Yet dearly I love you, and would be loved fain, But am betroth'd unto your enemy."

Answer: "For I do not do the good I want, but the evil I do not want is what I keep on doing. . . . Wretched man that I am! Who will deliver me from this body of death? Thanks be to God through Jesus Christ our Lord!" (Rom. 7:19, 24–25).

Donne: "Divorce me, untie, or break that knot again, Take me to you, imprison me, for I, except you enthrall me, never shall be free."

Answer: "Jesus answered them, 'Truly, truly, I say to you, everyone who practices sin is a slave to sin. The slave does not remain in the house forever; the son remains forever. So if the Son sets you free, you will be free indeed'" (John 8:34–36).

Donne: "Nor ever chaste, except you ravish me."

Answer: "If then you have been raised with Christ, seek the things that are above, where Christ is, seated at the right hand of God. Set your minds on things that are above, not on things that are on earth. For you have died, and your life is hidden with Christ in God. When Christ who is your life appears, then you also will appear with him in glory" (Col. 3:1–4).

Appendix

Handing Over the Goods

Dr. James A. Nestingen

Word Alone Convention, 2006

Well, a funny thing happened to me when I was going on sabbatical, and it's taken me a while to come home. We're still living out in Oregon, me and Carolyn, my beloved. And we've got a house out there, and we are going to come back at the end of August. She's going back to work, and so I was very happy to accept this invitation— among other things, to get a chance to see so many of you who are old friends and former students and colleagues, friends of my dad and my brother. It has been an absolute joy to be here and buoyed me no end. So thanks so much for your hospitality. As they always say, sinners find one another sooner or later. I figured I tumbled into a bunch of them here.

As evident as it may be, there is something deeply mysterious about the gift of faith. Though sometimes disputed, the facts of the case, if we can call them that, are fairly well known. So Article V of the Augustana, the Augsburg Confession, when it speaks of handing over the goods, the transmission of the faith from one person, from one generation, from one culture to another, says this: "To obtain such faith God instituted the office of the ministry; that is, provided the Word and the sacraments. Through these, as through means, . . . he works faith." Thus biblically, and confessionally, we can say right from the start, "Faith is a product of God's work." The Word and faith belong together. It is out of God's speaking that we are brought to fear, love, and trust Him above anything else. With that, we can speak of the community that gathers, sustains, and holds us. As Luther once said, "With His word, God gives us the new birth, and places us on the belly of our mother, the church." So we can speak of the Word and the community, the calling and the gathering. Together they are the means, Word, and sacrament through which faith happens.

Yet Augustana Article V cannot finish without acknowledging the mystery that always hangs around the edges: "To obtain such faith, God has instituted the office of the ministry; that is, provided the Word and the sacrament. Through these, . . . he works faith when and where he pleases, in those who hear the Gospel." This when and where He pleases is, of course, the frustration of it all. When I first started teaching over at Luther thirty years ago and started traveling the church, I often ran into a question that was sometimes asked in an attempt to default the Word and sacrament but was oftentimes asked out of sheer anxiety. What about somebody who has heard the Word and received the sacraments and doesn't believe it? I soon learned to recognize the agony that fielded the question. Because, of course, it's my question too.

All of us have members of our families who have heard the Word as we have heard it, received the sacraments as we have received them, been laid on the belly of their mother, the church, and as soon as they could get legs enough to go, have gotten up and left. So we can speak of sisters, or brothers, or children whom we have brought up in the way they should go and have seen toddle off into some form of emptiness in which, finally, they have found themselves at rest. It's enough to drive you crazy. The people that you love the very most, who are the fruits of the loins that bore you, who are the fruits of your own loins, and there they are, hankering after some stupidity, unable, unwilling, to hear the Word. Of course, the temptation in the face of such frustration is to run to the imperative. You better believe this! That's what my dad told me when I was an atheist in college. You better believe this! And of course, it does about as much good as the amount of air it uses in the declaration. It makes the speaker feel good—"I really told him." There's a little bragging on the pillow at night. "I finally said it." But of course, the emptiness returns. We know this about faith—the law's not going to do the trick. The law's not going to do the trick. So we're going to do two things this morning. First of all, we're going to talk about how faith happens. We've already done that a little bit. We're going to do a little bit more of it, and then we're going to talk strategy. We're going to talk about the fishing.

That's one of the nice things about Oregon—I traded walleyes for steelhead. I served my first parish out there, and I never was quite able to leave, and it was the fish. Of course, the Bush administration flooded the Klamath River with potatoes, so potatoes cost $600 per ton and salmon cost $60,000 per ton, but they figured the spuds were worth the votes. So they've closed the salmon fishing season on the whole coast of Oregon. I mean, I might as well live in St. Paul, for crying out loud! I am a little frustrated, as you can tell.

The good Lord has plans and purposes for everything, so we'll take it from there. So we will talk about how faith happens, and then we'll talk some fishing. We'll talk strategy, the old Lutheran strategy, and some suggestions for a different strategy that we might speak of for giving the gift of faith to those we love.

First of all, God has provided the Word and the sacrament. To obtain such faith—that is, to give the gift, to hand over the goods— God has provided the Word and the sacrament. Now the first and most important thing we have to say about the Word is this. Because Christ Jesus is the Word, it is never merely information. Of course, you can get all kinds of information from the Word. You can learn, for instance, about the miracles that Jesus did, and you can learn about what he expects of you, and you can learn about the gifts he has given to others, and you can learn the Sermon on the Mount, and you can learn about the forgiveness of sins; you can learn all kinds of things. But in the end, in the end, the information is always preparatory. It's on the way to something else, just as your conversations in the family, while they convey information, are on the way to something more decisive—the expression or your love for one another, your joy in one another, your delight. So I suppose marriages and families are made of small talk. There are all kinds of routine information that gets shared.

Carolyn and I are talking on the telephone every day. We've got the same cell phones, so it's free. So it doesn't stop. You know, I keep talking to her all day long, even two thousand miles away, and she tells me about the weather, and she tells me about our dog, and who's sick, and she tells me about her secretary who is visiting and what they've done, and I am very interested in that information. But the magic always happens late in the conversation, and I know enough to wait for it. She expresses herself to me, and I express myself to her.

You see, that's how love works. Love takes possession of the details. Love takes those little clichés, the minutiae of the day, and turns them into gifts. All of a sudden, out of the routine, out of the small stuff, Christ Jesus is breaking loose in the words. So the information, while it is helpful and essential, is really preparatory to this . . . your sin is forgiven. I'm going to raise you from the dead. No power is going to ever hold you. There, Christ Jesus is making love to you. He's speaking His Word to you. He's breaking loose again, you see, He is saying it. And that is what the Word does. The fundamental characteristic of the Word in Christ Jesus is its power.

So I'll bet dollars to donuts that when you start talking about your faith, you will talk about some particular person or some particular relationship, and then you will talk about what they said to you. You will tell of their talents. You will tell about how they encouraged you and how they comforted you, and how they sustained you from difficulty, and how the Word just seemed to be perfectly timed, and how it bore such gifts. That's the Word. That's not an accident. That's not an accident. It's always fun in the gospel—so many people get converted by rumors.

Like that Syrophoenician woman, you know, who showed up. I just love her. But I love Luther's sermon on that text even more. That's one of the greatest sermons ever preached, the sermon on the Syrophoenician woman. You remember. She heard about Jesus. Her daughter was sick, so she showed up at the border. She figured, He's a man of the borders, He'll be there. And so she showed up on the border, and there He came, disciples and the whole business.

She wasn't prepared, though, for the churlish way in which He treated her. Here Luther says that Christ Jesus is pursuing faith like the hunter, driving up a pheasant in the field. He's playing with her but He's playing hardball, and He goes right for her neck. That's just like him. I mean, He is so nasty that way. He should be polite and reduce it to an appeal. He should drop back and honor the free will, right? You know how that would work! If He had relied on appeal, she would have gone home in her unbelief and died. That would have been the end of that.

But what happens? This magnificent woman has been brought to faith on the basis of a rumor. That's all she's got to go on. She has not taken any seminary classes. She has not read any commentaries. She hasn't even gone to church, but she has heard the Word. And what happens? She comes along the border, and she tries to get through to him, and He answers her not a word. As dear Uncle Roy Harrisville used to say, "He who is speaking fills up 66 books and didn't have a word for her." Not one word. Not one word.

So she makes a pest of herself with the disciples. I mean, this woman knows how to get through. I mean, she stood and waited for authorities before. She knows how this works. You get them through the underlings. And so she goes to work on them. And she pesters the disciples until finally they are good and irritated, and they go to Jesus and say, "Why don't you take care of this woman? She's a nuisance. Get rid of her." Jesus says, "That's not right to take what belongs to the children and give it to the dogs." He could get turned in to the state of Minnesota for talking like that. The prophets of political correctness would have him up against the wall in two seconds. I mean, good night! It's a slur. Racism. Right?

Oh, He's on his way to something better. Yes, Lord Jesus. You hear her? She knows who He is. The rumor has brought her. Yes, Lord. Even dogs eat the crumbs that fall from the master's table or from the children's table. There she is. That's faith. That's faith, and Jesus says it now. You know, I love this story. You can imagine Jesus embracing her. You can imagine Jesus taking her in His arms. "Oh woman, great is your faith. Great is your faith." I mean, she stood through His harsh treatment of her and wrestled the blessing out of His hands, and now He rejoices with her. The Word has this power. The Word has this power when it gets loose.

Whenever I think of this text, I think of old Vernon Toso, who was a missionary to Madagascar for all those years. Dear old Vern. He came back and got sick of being home. He was in Wolf Point, Montana, and he wanted to go back to Madagascar. He went and had his physical, and they found a tumor on his liver the size of a lemon. So he resigned his call in Wolf Point and moved into a house they bought south of Manning's Cafe. I know most of you don't know where Manning's is, but you can look it up; it's in the phone book . . . over in southeast Minneapolis. So he moved into that house and he got more and more jaundiced. Duane Olson was his pastor and beloved friend. Duane went and called on him. I went over several times myself.

When it was getting close, I took a pile of Luther books with me. I had marked all these wonderful passages where Luther addresses death directly. It's just fabulous. You know, Luther says things like this: "To be sure, O death, you will have me. But Christ will shove his fingers down your throat and force you to vomit me up." You just gotta love that. So I went over to Vern, who was a man of some considerable color, and his wife took me into the room. I sat down beside him as he was lying in his bed, all yellow. I said, "Vernon, I know who your pastor has been all these years, and how Luther has served you, so I brought him along. And I'm going to read these passages to you. And we'll just let Luther preach to you."

So I read a couple of those passages and then I started into the sermon on the Syrophoenician woman text. Vernon sat straight up in bed and recited the whole thing from memory. It was glorious! Here were a couple sinners right on the edge of death, and there was old Vernon, singing his heart out. He got the whole thing out and then collapsed, and his wife about kicked me out of the house for stirring him up. He told Duane when he died that he wanted to be cremated. And at his funeral, the ashes should be placed in the baptismal font. There you go . . . that's faith.

Well, that's what the Word does, you see. That's what the Word does. It creates faith. It's got such power to create faith that you can be had by a rumor. I mean, you can overhear the gospel and it will take hold of you. I mean, it can be walking by like Jesus along the border and then all of a sudden, bang, you're dead. And being raised to newness of life, that's the Word. That's how it works. That's what it does. It's the power of salvation. It's the power of salvation. Because the gospel literally does what it says. So listen to old Luther. "The law says do this, and it is never done. The gospel says believe in this and it's done already." It's done already.

Now we speak of the power of the Word, and, of course, we speak of the power of the sacraments, baptism, our beginning, our

new birth, the last judgment let out ahead of time and as affirmative—
the Word bearing in on us in some water to give us the new birth—
and the Lord's Supper.

One of the things that has helped me the most this winter
has been the words of institution. "On the night in which He was
betrayed . . ." When I stood up to administer the sacrament the first
time after it was all done, I said it like this: "On the night in which
he was betrayed," because, of course, He entered into the deepest
betrayal. As Steve said last night in that beautiful sermon, they all
showed Him their fannies. In fact, one of them literally did. He was
in such a hurry to get away that he slipped right out of his equip-
ment. Tell that to the people who write *Visions and Expectations*.
Don't you know how to behave? Some pious committee would sum-
mon themselves up to their greatest heights and say that we hear you
were running away naked the other night. Good night. You know,
you're in such a hurry that not even clothes matter.

On the night in which He was betrayed, He took bread and
broke it and gave it to His betrayers and said, "This is my Body, given
for you." On the night in which He was betrayed, He didn't say, "I'm
gonna get you bastards." On the night in which He was betrayed,
He didn't say, "I'm finally gonna catch up with you." On the night in
which He was betrayed, He didn't say, "You'll get yours in the end."
On the night in which He was betrayed, He took bread and He broke
it. He who was broken beyond all measure, He broke it, and breaking
it He said, "This is my body, given for you. Given for you, betrayers,
every last one of you. This is for you." He took the cup and blessed
it and said, "This cup is the New Testament in my blood, shed for you
and for many."

There you go again. You turn Him loose, He can't help it. The
gospel just starts to spill. It just starts to spill. And so, He's expressing himself in the bread, in the wine, breaking loose again to create
faith, to make a believer out of you. To take your sins upon Himself,
joyfully, freely. So that you can't get it back again.

And so too the keys. So too the keys. Remember that story?
We had it again a couple weeks ago. The only way Jesus could get in
the room after the disciples betrayed Him was by absolving them
twice, going through the wall, and absolving them before they had
a chance to fight back. I mean, He knew what would have happened

if He had knocked on the door. "Behold, I stand at the door and knock." Nobody would have answered. I mean, it would have been ten bodies piled against the door, and there would have been a laundry bill. They weren't gonna let Him in. Go ahead and knock. I hear you knockin' but you can't come in. Don't come back! What happens? Oh, it's so beautiful; it's just so great. Just listen to Him. He comes right through the wall because that's the only way He can get in. When He gets in there, the first words out of his mouth are these: "Peace be with you. Peace be with you."

Well, who is He talking to? There are ten there anyway. Judas is dead, and Thomas, who always had, in the end, for unbelief, is off fishin' or something. He's not there. Might as well go to Jerusalem with you. There's no other show in town. Now He has gone to Jerusalem and found out for sure that that's not much of a show either—it's death. So He is gone. So Jesus comes in to those ten. "Peace be with you," he says. "Peace be with you." The betrayers, again, sought out by the risen Lord, breaking out of the spandex, as old Don Juel used to say, tearing it wide open, getting loose. There He is, bearing down on them. Before they've got even a chance to say hello, He has their heads tipped back, is breathing on them and saying, "Receive the Holy Spirit."

This is the church you know. A bunch of betrayers gathered together and Christ Jesus sending His Spirit to break loose on them, tipping their heads back. As Ernst Käsemann liked to say, "The church is always created out of material, which is in and of itself unusable." It always gives evidence of the resurrection of the dead. So that when it looks dead, you know it looks good, because then you know Jesus is likely to show up. That's just how it works. So He breathes on them and gives them the Holy Spirit, and this is what He says: "If you forgive the sins of any, they are forgiven. If you retain the sins of any, they are retained." Right? First thing the resurrected Lord does is turn loose the word of forgiveness so it can be spoken freely and openly and joyfully to any and all. Your sin is forgiven. It's happened. It's happened. So He expresses himself in these powerful ways. Thus faith is always, as the Apostle Paul says, a product of the Word.

But now Article V of the Augustana, having spoken of this, the power of the Word, the Small Catechism spells it out a little bit further. "I believe that I cannot, by my own understanding or effort, believe in Jesus Christ, my Lord, or come to him." These are the most beloved words in the whole catechism. Quoted over and over again by people who have long forgotten the rest of it. But basic to the whole thing, I believe that I can't believe this. Were it left to me, if the gospel were simply an appeal, if that's all it was, was some tickling of my will to enlist me, there'd be nothing but unbelief. That's the natural state. That's the default position of the human self. Flat out wanton unbelief, rejection, betrayal. You hit the button, it just reverses to that position. That's how it goes. It's not that unbelief is an alternative for us. That's who we are. It takes Christ Jesus to flush that confession out of us.

I believe I can't believe this, but what? "The Holy Spirit has called me through the gospel, enlightening me with his gifts, sanctified and kept me in true faith. In the same way, he calls"—and here are the words we want—"gathers." Gathers.

When you tell the story of hearing the Word, you immediately speak of it on the lips of another. The Word never approached you abstractly. The Word came to you embodied in a relationship. The Word came to you embodied on the lips of somebody who loved you. The Word came to you from somebody who cared enough about you to stop and say, "There's something better than this. I've got it for you." The Word came to you in a relationship, so there is no calling without the gathering. And the gatherings exist for the sake of the calling. The Word gets loose, and the Word gets loose on the lips of another, and that other is the beginning of the gathering. So Jesus did not say, "Where there is a minimum of 50 and they follow the model constitution." Jesus did not say, "If the plant isn't producing, close it." Jesus didn't say, "We are looking to locate congregations in growing communities and, therefore, we're not interested in you rejects."

Jesus said, "Where two or three are gathered in my name. I can't help myself. I mean if there are just two or three, I'll be there. Because, if there are two or three, we can start a conversation. I've got another chance to give myself away." That's Him, spilling over with goodness, gracious beyond any measure, giving Himself. "Two or three, that will do. Just give me a couple. I'll take two. If you can get three, so much the better." Of course, you know what would happen if Chicago got a hold of that. Well now, two or three. Let's see. There's the president and there's the vice president, and there's the secretary. And of course the president better be in succession, because, I mean, we don't want the gospel getting loose. Faith might happen. Come on! You have to do all things properly and in order. The anal retentive's view of the Kingdom of God. You just wish somebody would break loose like Jesus did at the Temple and bust something. Just for the joy of a little chaos. It's too much fun.

So there is a gathering. It's a gathering of sinners. It's a gathering of sinners. And that gathering of sinners is critically important, is critically important. My faith is never my work. My faith is the Holy Spirit's work through my neighbors. Jesus knows better than to turn us over to ourselves. He's got enough experience with us to know that's a nonstarter. He knows where that road's going to go. He went there. And He hung there. What we're going to do is decide all over again, and then we're going to congratulate ourselves on how pious we are in the process. "I only did this because I had to. I really liked Him, you know. I could affirm a lot of what He was doing, but in the end, in the end—untrustworthy. You never know when he'll raise the dead. He comes to town and miracles start breaking out. We've got to regulate this a little bit, get it all in a row."

It doesn't work that way. Jesus comes to town, and He is calling Zaccheus out of the tree and looking down on the paralytic who has been lowered to Him through the roof. Can you imagine? What do you think He thought when He was looking at that parade coming down through the roof? Good night. He comes to town, and the blind receive their sight; the lame walk; the deaf hear; the poor have good news preached to them; and He is looking for some more to do the same thing. Faith gathers a community and, through that community, sustains faith in the other.

When I was editing for Augsburg Publishing House, I edited a book written by Richard Koenig, a wonderful friend out east. The book disappeared in about five minutes. I think it is about the finest book I ever edited. It's called *A Creative Minority*. You couldn't even find that book on eBay, but my copy is just about worn out. Koenig argues in this wonderful book that the critical point of faith for children is what he calls secondary reinforcement, or secondary confirmation.

What happens? You bring up a child in the faith. There is the Word; there is the gathering. The critical point comes when the child starts to leave home. In the traditional family, you know who provides the frame of reference. In the traditional family, it's the uncles and aunts—all of the authority and none of the responsibility. The people that teach you to play. When you start having questions about the old man or your mother, you go to your uncle and ask, "What in the world is going on here?" And your uncle tells you that they have been having that problem for a long time. And then quietly reinforces. That's the vocation of an uncle or an aunt: to provide confirmation for what's happening within.

So this was the genius of the early Lutherans in this country. They recognized that being a minority in a new world, there had to be this secondary confirmation. And you know where they provided it? The old Lutherans were really good at three things. They were good at orphanages, better than you can ever imagine. You go along the south shore of the Great Lakes and there is one orphanage after former orphanage after another. Lutherans taking care of the young. At one point, Lutherans owned one-third of all the nursing home beds in the whole country. We're really good at that, taking care of the elderly.

The original Lutherans in this country recognized something else, this secondary confirmation, that the children, in leaving home, needed to have a place in which they could explore their faith and receive it back again. That was the original vocation of the church colleges. Among other things, they were breeding grounds where the Lutheran buffalo went to meet other Lutheran buffalo. That was a wonderful feature of them. They didn't like to advertise that, but everybody knew that was one of the important things they did. Nice girls. Trustworthy boys, at least according to the myths. The church colleges did that for us as a church first, 'til about the 1960s, late '60s, early '70s, when things started to move. The faculties joined the academic unions and told the church to shove off. It's a long time since that happened. There are still some heroes of the faith who had served in those schools, though generally in other departments—political scientists, biology teachers, Greek teachers. They provided this. It is very important.

Now that we have enough on the table here, we can talk about strategy. On the basis of this understanding of how faith happens, the original Lutherans worked out a strategy for handing over the gifts, for passing the faith, that worked superbly and continues to work superbly in traditional cultures. Luther's catechism, the Small Catechism, was commonly called in the sixteenth century "the layman's Bible." Of course, this was a time of limited literacy, so people didn't have scriptures available like we do. They had Luther's catechism; it didn't replace the scripture by any means, of course, but it provided a sum or a key, the commandments, the Creed, the Lord's Prayer, and provided those working elements of the faith with the sacraments in simple explanations that were keyed to the rhythms of everyday life.

So Luther is reading scripture, and he is reading the shape of life out in front of him. And the catechism emerges out of this meeting. And so we've got a document for handing over the faith—the Ten Commandments, the Creed, the Lord's Prayer; the most basic elements of Christian faith are there. And in a form where they can be used.

Elizabeth Eisenstein, who is a historian of print at Columbia University, in a wonderful article on the catechism, points to the second characteristic of this strategy. With the catechism, Eisenstein says, the Lutherans move the altar from the chancel into the kitchen. They moved the altar from the chancel into the kitchen. By providing the basic form of the Word in this simple and expressive way, the Lutherans provided a means of instruction for the parents to use in bringing up their children in the faith. That was the strategy: to have the parents teach the children and to have the parents and the children teach the pastors. So you've got a Small Catechism and a Large Catechism, the strategy being to get these overlapping layers of the Word so that the Word is being spoken to the children at the table in the most intimate and challenging relationships of life. The Word is there, at the table, so the catechism was originally printed on poster board, to be hung in the kitchen. There's the altar. The congregation's table becomes the family table, and the family takes responsibility.

Now one of the most interesting things about this is the way that what Koenig refers to as secondary confirmation of the Word takes place. Lutheranism was born in a situation very much like Iran. I was impressed last night. I sneaked in the back and was listening. I love Harry Wendt, and I love to listen to him. He is one of the great teachers of the church, that guy. I love Stephanie, his daughter, even more. I think she is the greatest announcer I have ever heard on the radio. She was just fabulous, until St. Olaf went and closed WCAL, may they burn forever for having done that. That was a sin against us all. I hope that late president got it just for that. I don't know. At any rate, if you haven't heard Stephanie, you missed a real peach. She can give you an education just like Harry can. Harry will give you the Word, and she will give you the music to go with it. That's just fabulous.

I enjoyed Harry's reference to nine thousand priests. That was the situation in sixteenth-century Germany, too. You couldn't walk across the street without stumbling over a syphilitic monk. You couldn't go downtown to get your groceries without meeting a Franciscan begging on the corner. That's the way it was. The church just permeated; it was pervasive.

So the Lutherans, the original Lutherans, are anti this kind of domination by the church. They're looking for participation. They're not like John Calvin. They're not going to take the world over and transform it. They think of themselves as salt, as light, as leaven. They're going to make sure the Word is there, and they're going to make sure the family is taking care of it, but they're going to rely on the public life to provide this secondary confirmation.

And it worked, basically. It worked. Most of us, I think, came to faith this way. Most of us over fifty-five anyway, or sixty. I think the breakdown took place someplace right between my brother and my youngest sister. It is right in there someplace. It's between fifty-five and fifty. I think that's where the whole traditional structure started to fall apart. And when it started to fall apart, it broke down at every level.

You remember what it was to grow up in a small town. Your faith was everybody's business. Your faith was the business of your congregation. They were watching you, but you couldn't go downtown without having your faith reinforced in one way or the other. The neighbors were all looking after you. There was this secondary confirmation out there. But when it broke down, it all fell apart at once. I'll tell you. When it broke down, it broke down at every level.

Most families no longer eat together. Public life, with all of its attractions, has become so absorbing of time that there is simply not a schedule where families stop. When Mommy and I were raising our three boys, we negotiated with them for some time that would be available to us all. You know when it was? Twenty to seven in the morning. That was the only time of the day we could find to have devotions. Because everybody had some schedule at every other hour of the day. That's the way it works. Most families don't stop to eat, they graze. The microwave goes on and off as various kinds of commercially prepared food are warmed up. So that you can go on to the next thing, your favorite television show, or bowling, or the library, or to rent a flick, or whatever.

So when the family doesn't meet, lots of things start to go wrong. Lots of things start to go wrong, and the first is faith. This morning, I'm staying with Grandpa and Grandma, of course, and this morning we had devotions at the table. When I was listening to Grandpa pray, I thought of all the voices who are praying with me when I pray. I can hear my great-grandpa's voice, and the voices of both my grandparents, my grandfathers and my grandmothers. I can hear my dad's voice, and I can hear my mother's voice, and I can hear my brother's voice. There is a whole community. That community is the gathering in which I was called, and it is the gathering that has sustained me in faith.

Lots of times when I'm lying in bed and can't sleep, I remember my grandma and her prayers. Interminable. But now I can't get enough of them. I tried to rehearse them in my mind because they were so beautiful. That's how most of us were shaped in the faith, us older types, retired types. But for younger people, think of it: they don't even hear the voice of their parents in prayer. So oftentimes, with my advisees over at Luther, I would ask them early, "Have you ever prayed with an adult?" "No." Lots of times the answer was no. "Did your parents pray with you?" "No."

Well, what happens when you take away that embodiment of the Word? Screwy things start to happen. What happens when you take away uncles and aunts? A lot of fun disappears. What else? The secondary confirmation starts to go, you see. What happens—I mean, I was impressed with Harry last night talking about the big picture, the big narrative. What happens when the big narrative is taken over by the advertising companies and the mass media? They don't want to tell you a story that ends on a cross in death. That's a downer. They want to tell you a story where there is no death; it's all resurrection. You just buy their product, and you will be carried beyond the realm of death into the realm of life forever. They tell a different story than we tell. We tell a story of death and resurrection. They tell a story of unlimited resurrection for sale at a price. And they have taken over. They have taken over so that the biblical narrative that, for centuries, has formed the warp and the weft of our public life has disappeared and been replaced by a commercial, an exploitative narrative.

If you think I'm overspeaking, just listen to the radio. Listen to the music your kids hear. That's what's happened. So you take away the family, and you take away the overarching narrative, and you take away the secondary confirmation in our public life so that the Word that you speak to your children is not being reinforced as your children move out into public life. It is being challenged and undermined. It's no wonder, then, that we as Lutherans are commonly described as having lost two generations of our young and being on the way to losing a third. I think probably the third is gone. I went to a Luther League Convention and got adapted to the socially upwardly mobile, which is the primary function of Luther League Conventions. I never got anything reinforced.

How can we talk about another strategy then? I want to talk about just two things. First of all, tending the narrative. I love to tell the story because I know it is true. Tending the narrative means telling the story. Setting out the narrative, the big picture, as Harry called it. Setting out the gifts. Tending the narrative means keeping the story out in front of ourselves and those we love. Keeping the story out there: that means, for instance, Bible study. It means family devotions. It means prayers on arising and sleeping. It means living in the biblical story.

We fell into a tremendous congregation out in Oregon. They have sustained us this year. It's been just fabulous. We go to Bible study every Friday morning with the old saints of the parish. It's just incredible to listen to them, listening to scripture. We have been reading Jeremiah. So we've gotten a good kick in the shins and other parts of the anatomy on a fairly regular basis. And they hang right in there wanting that Word; that's tending the narrative. The Word is there. There's going to be no faith if the Word's not there. There's going to be no faith if the Word's not there. Tending the Word means speaking it. Saying it to your nieces and nephews. Saying it to your children. Saying it to the children of your friends. It means tending the elemental connections with the Word, making sure that it's there. Making sure that it's there. Telling the story.

You know, that reminds me . . . Mike Rogness loves to talk about a convention up at Kabekona Lake, not a convention, but an annual meeting of all the pastors. Old Loyal Tellakson stood up and said, "We will now recite Psalm One." Every pastor in the group stood up and recited it from memory. You know, tending the Word. Tending the Word. That's being in range. Speaking it, hearing it.

Second, it seems to me that our strategy is simply out of whack with what's happened. You know what we do now? Pastors complain that people call them up on Saturday night and want their kid done and then do it anyway. And express their confidence in the future by setting out an imperative that found its way into the green hymnal—"You better take care of these kids!" That's not the job of the pagans who are interested enough to call and ask for baptism. That's our job. And that's our joy. We tend the Word and that means tending the relationships, looking after the relationships.

I remember old Kent Knutson saying this in a class years ago: "If somebody calls you up and asks to have their kid done, say, 'Why sure, bring 'em over.'" But then say this, "You know that child belongs to us now. If you don't place in the child's hands the Holy Scriptures, we will. If you don't bring him to services in God's house, we're going to be dropping by. We've got a couple of frustrated grandparents in our congregation who love nothin' better than lookin' after kids.

They want to tell your kids Bible stories. You go out Saturday night, we'll come by and take care of them."

You see what's happening? We have thought like a privileged majority and we have said faith is a gift, and we have talked about how the wheel doesn't work and so on and so forth, but we haven't taken the next step. We haven't caught on yet. We're a minority. We're not only a minority; we're a minority under siege. As a minority under siege, we don't trust the Word to somebody else; we're going to say that, thank you very much. We're not going to depend on some two-bit television evangelist who is soaking the congregation for money and doesn't have a thing to hand over. We're going to speak the Word. That's our job. We're going to speak the Word. And when we speak the Word, we're not just going to kiss and tell. We're going to stay there and tend the relationships. When we do that, then tending the relationships, we can begin to talk about confirming our witness with our children.

Here's a suggestion. Let the congregation appoint godparents for every child baptized, and let the godparents appointed by the congregation take responsibility for carrying the faith to those kids. They have two responsibilities—to speak the Word to those kids and to show up at their ball games. Right? Two responsibilities. To be there when they are graduating from high school, with the Word again. What's happening there? We're replacing in our congregation the community that's disappeared. You know that could be a lot of fun. That's evangelism. This is not the kiss-and-run kind of evangelism where you challenge somebody and take off. "Nice to talk to you. See you later." This is evangelism that stays. That speaks the Word and stays.

With that, families get far better odds. A couple of kids against two parents is a losing proposition. Grandpa and Grandma have to be there. If they're not, the congregation should provide them. Uncles and aunts have to be there. If they're not, the congregation should provide them. Because bringing up a child in the faith amounts to this: handing over the goods—that is, bestowing the gifts of Christ Jesus and hanging in there to the point of crucifixion and resurrection. You know that could be a lot of fun.

Contributors

Thomas V. Aadland, MDiv, DDiv, theological educator, Lutheran Church–Missouri Synod, and assistant to the Evangelical Lutheran Church in Kenya for the last ten years, training pastors and deaconesses for growing Lutheran churches in East Africa

Michael J. Albrecht, MDiv, PhD, lead pastor at Saint James Lutheran Church, West Saint Paul, Minnesota

Marney A. Fritts, PhD, instructor of systematic theology, Saint Paul Lutheran Seminary, and visitation pastor, Zion Lutheran Church, Kent, Washington

Roy A. Harrisville, BTh, ThD, professor emeritus of the New Testament, Luther Theological Seminary, Minneapolis, Minnesota

Scott L. Keith, PhD, executive director of 1517 The Legacy Project and adjunct professor of theology, Concordia University Irvine, California

Robert Kolb, PhD, professor emeritus of systematic theology, Concordia Seminary, St. Louis, Missouri

Jason D. Lane, ThD, assistant professor of theology, Concordia University Wisconsin, Mequon

Mark Mattes, MDiv, PhD, department chair of philosophy and theology, Grand View University, Des Moines, Iowa

Steven D. Paulson, ThD, chair of Lutheran theology, Luther House of Study

John T. Pless, MDiv, DLitt, assistant professor of pastoral ministry and missions / director of field education, Concordia Theological Seminary, Fort Wayne, Indiana

Rod Rosenbladt, PhD, professor emeritus of theology, philosophy, and apologetics, Concordia University Irvine, California

Ken Sundet Jones, PhD, professor of theology and religion, Grand View University, Des Moines, Iowa

Mark Tranvik, MDiv, PhD, professor of religion at Augsburg University, Minneapolis, Minnesota

Hans Wiersma, PhD, associate professor, Augsburg College, Minneapolis, Minnesota

CPSIA information can be obtained
at www.ICGtesting.com
Printed in the USA
FSHW01n1829021018
52694FS

9 781945 978135